Turntables and Tropes

Turntables and Tropes

A Rhetoric of Remix

Scott Haden Church

MICHIGAN STATE UNIVERSITY PRESS | *East Lansing*

♾ The paper used in this publication meets the minimum requirements of ANSI/NISO Z39.48-1992 (R 1997) (Permanence of Paper).

Michigan State University Press
East Lansing, Michigan 48823-5245

Printed and bound in the United States of America.

LIBRARY OF CONGRESS CATALOGING-IN-PUBLICATION DATA
Names: Church, Scott Haden, author.
Title: Turntables and tropes : a rhetoric of remix / Scott Haden Church.
Description: East Lansing, Michigan : Michigan State University Press, [2021] | Includes bibliographical references and index.
Identifiers: LCCN 2021008673 | ISBN 9781611864083 (paperback) | ISBN 9781609176839 (pdf) | ISBN 9781628954500 (epub) | ISBN 9781628964448 (kindle)
Subjects: LCSH: Appropriation (Arts) | Remixes. | Rhetoric, Ancient. | Mass media.
Classification: LCC NX197 .C48 2021 | DDC 701.1--dc23
LC record available at https://lccn.loc.gov/2021008673

Interior design by Charlie Sharp, Sharp Des!gns, East Lansing, Michigan
Cover design by Erin Kirk
Cover art by thenatchdl

Visit Michigan State University Press at *www.msupress.org*

To Heather, Jane, Lucy, Hazel, Eve, and Violet

Contents

Acknowledgments

There are many people who helped me throughout the process of writing this book. Without the expert help of Damien Smith Pfister, this book would not exist. He provided valuable feedback, encouragement, and wonderful insights. I also thank Ron Lee, Carly Woods, and Glenn Nierman for their feedback and suggestions as they read earlier drafts of this project. Other scholars have been helpful with providing ideas and encouragement along the way, including Phyllis Japp, Gordon Mitchell, Ed Carter, Kerry Soper, Ian Moulton, Joshua Ewalt, Shireen Ghorbani, Miles Coleman, Chris Wilson, Samuel Jay, Michele Kennerly, Brett Lunceford, and Brent Yergensen. I also thank my research assistants, Jesse King and Daniel Montez, for their help. David Kelley, Glenn and Carol Baugh, and Blair and Diana Kent provided further help and support. Catherine Cocks, assistant director and editor in chief at Michigan State University Press, was tremendous throughout the entire process; her clear guidance, enthusiasm for the project, and patience with my delays were instrumental to the successful completion of the manuscript. The anonymous reviewers at Michigan State University Press provided excellent suggestions that helped make the book better. I offer my thanks to the School of Communications at Brigham Young University for providing me with an excellent working environment. I sincerely thank my parents, Steve and Barbara Church, for their encouragement and suggestions. Finally, with love, I thank my wife, Heather, and my five young daughters, Jane, Lucy, Hazel, Eve, and Violet, for their love, support, and patience.

Parts of chapter 2 were first published in *RC to Remix Studies NIP*, Scott Haden Church, Copyright (© 2021). Reproduced by permission of Taylor & Francis Group. Parts of chapter 5 were first published in "Remix, Śūnyatā, and Prosōpopoeia: Projecting Voice in the Digital Age," in *Ancient Rhetorics and Digital Networks*, ed. Michele Kennerly and Damien Smith Pfister (Tuscaloosa: University of Alabama Press, 2018), 229–51.

Prologue

The following prologue is a remix; it is a mosaic composed of sampled quotes from other scholars and remix artists. The text in curly brackets indicate some minor grammatical and stylistic changes that have been made to the sampled material. The source for every quote is provided in the footnote following it. This prologue was inspired by Jonathan Lethem's essay, "The Ecstasy of Influence: A Plagiarism Mosaic" (in Sound Unbound: Sampling Digital Music and Culture*, ed. Paul D. Miller [Cambridge, MA: MIT Press, 2008], 25–51).*

It is self-evident that nothing concerning art is self-evident anymore.[1] In the hothouse atmosphere of the networked age, a myriad of new cultural practices have blossomed and bloomed—practices that have no place in the taxonomy of modernity's prim gardens.[2] Human culture is always derivative, and music perhaps especially so.[3] Gregg Gillis is {. . .} one of the hottest new artists in an emerging genre of music called "mashup" or "remix." Girl Talk is the name of his one-man (and one-machine) band. {. . .} Girl Talk is essentially a mix of many samples drawn from many other artists. Night Ripper, for example, remixes between 200 and 250 samples from 167 artists.[4] Girl Talk songs draw from a relatively small collection of popular songs, which suggests that the goal of this music is not to rediscover obscure tracks but rather to recontextualize famous songs in novel, even awkward surroundings.[5]

Remix is meta—always unoriginal.[6] "Remix" generally refers to the practice of recombining preexisting media content—popular songs, films, television programs, texts, web data—to fabricate a new work.[7] It breaks down, isolates, reorders, decontextualizes {and} recontextualizes sound, playing matchmaker to seemingly incompatible genres.[8] A remix, for example, is not the product of mere promiscuity and simple infidelities. An interesting and compelling remix, for example, does not just fool around with different sounds. It is instead a highly calculated practice that is exceedingly attentive to its source material.[9] The term *scratching* suggests an art of vandalism; like its hip-hop cousin, graffiti writing, it can only be realized by violating its own medium.[10] This sensibility echoes philosopher Jacques Derrida's writings, in which he encouraged readers to play with the text—mocking, deconstructing, and reconstructing it.[11] Remix with "media" is just the same sort of stuff that we've always done with words. { . . . } Remixed media succeed when they show others something new. { . . . } A remix draws upon the work of others in order to do new work. It is great writing without words. It is creativity supported by a new technology.[12]

Remix is more like a virus that has mutated into different forms according to the needs of particular cultures. Remix, itself, has no form, but is quick to take on any shape and medium. It needs cultural value to be at play; in this sense remix is parasitical. { . . . } My goal in this analysis is to evaluate how remix as discourse is at play across art, music, media, and culture.[13] I cannot, however, present them all in complete form, for the time that has been allowed me is too short. But just as is done with fruits, I shall try to produce a sample of each kind.[14] Admittedly, my definition of remix privileges music because it is in music where the term was first used deliberately as an act of autonomy by DJs and producers with the purpose to develop some of the most important popular music movements of the 1970s: disco and hip-hop.[15]

No beings, not even humans, speak on their own, but always through something or someone else.[16] Effective {remix}, according to Dionysius, is not only persuasive but also aesthetically pleasing, as indicated by his emphasis on lifelike, charming composition.[17] The remix when extended as a cultural practice, as a form of discourse, is a second mix of something pre-existent. The material must be recognized, otherwise it could be misunderstood as something new, and it would become plagiarism.[18] Remix { . . . } demands that people recognize some trace of history. Part of the interest in sampling { . . . } is in taking a bit of music that the listener will recognize, who will in turn most likely become excited when she recognizes the sample.[19] And yet, despite all this, the author does not rest in peace. He is continually reanimated and resuscitated.[20] The more perfect the reproduction, the more it becomes virtual. {Who} is the real {speaker}? Who's to say? They've even felt the need to reintroduce {certain mannerisms} to give it a natural effect, or an effect of the hyper-simulacrum of the natural.[21]

Sampling is most fundamentally an art of *transformation*. A sample changes the moment it is relocated.[22] As DJ Adrian explained, "I really appreciate the beauty {...} of maintaining sort of the integrity of the original song and adding something brand new to it, i.e., a brand new vocal [sample], and manipulating it into a completely different song."[23] Why did we have to use the actual original ... the actual thing? Well, it's because the actual thing has a power about it. It has an aura.[24] By "aura" I mean two things: the reverberation that imparts a sense of space, and the slight but constant ambient noise—a patina, perhaps—that is a by-product of imperfect recording fidelity. Digital sampling offers the possibility of what I would call performative quotation. {...} In other words, traditional musical quotations typically cite works; samples cite performances.[25] Sampling practices put the {voice} into conversation with its new {speaker}, creating a synthesis that exceeds the sum of its parts.[26] All men take as much pleasure in listening to this kind of prose as in listening to poetry, and many desire to take lessons in it.[27] And it is also natural for all to delight in works of imitation.[28] We should regard that man as the most accomplished in this field who can collect the greatest number of ideas scattered among the thoughts of all the rest and present them in the best form.[29] The goal is to produce a new, third term that is arguably greater than the sum of its parts.[30] The key aspect of any attributed speech in the ancient world {...} is its appropriateness to both the character to whom it is attributed and the situation in which it is delivered.[31] She or he is always and already responding to the scene or culture in which one already finds oneself and is, for this reason, responsible only for the manner, method, and means of that particular response.[32]

At their best, mashups sound equally right and *wrong*; the fusion can be both seamless, but weird and jarring. Yet again, the original authors no longer have the last word.[33] Mashup culture treats genre in a similar manner as traditional musicians treat instruments, pitch, or timbre, that is, as something that can be modulated, mixed, and made to appear and disappear within a given work {...} Status and reputations within the mashup community hinge upon the capacity to hear affinities between seemingly disparate songs, artists and genres, which requires pluralistic openness to music that has little or no value for professional DJs, music critics, and other individuals who act as intellectuals in popular music cultures.[34] Mashups often blend samples from what might be perceived to be resolute categories, such as high and low, serious and playful, black and white, rock and pop. {...} Cruger argues, "The more disparate the genre-blending is, the better; the best mashups blend punk with funk or Top 40 with heavy metal, boosting the tension between slick and raw."[35] I favor more of a genre clash myself { . . . } This is half the fun for me. Finding combos that shouldn't go together but can.[36]

According to DJ Earworm, the *relationship between source materials* is the primary locus of stylistic originality for mashups.[37] DJ Adrian, a San Francisco DJ and guitarist, argued that { . . . }"Part of the appeal of mashup music is the juxtapositioning." { . . . } You put two things together from two different times that would never, ever go together. That, to me, is talent—hearing that, listening melodically.[38] It's the relationship and recontextualization between the constituent elements that identifies a work and makes it memorable—in other words, the *juxtaposition itself functions as the foreground.* { . . . } Mashups are premised on the notion of *recognizability* and *critique of pop culture*—there's no sense in mashing together samples no one's ever heard before. { . . . } DJ Adrian told me: "A great mash-up . . . makes you realize that all Western music is kind of the same."[39]

The cultural practice of sampling meshes very poorly with copyright, the body of law which turns creative expression into private property.[40] Remix culture, as a movement, is mainly preoccupied with the free exchange of ideas and their manifestation as specific products. { . . . } The principle of sampling at its most basic level had been at play as a cultural activity well before its common use in music during the 1970s.[41] The story of American arts in the 19th century might be told in terms of the mixing, matching, and merging of folk traditions taken from various indigenous and immigrant populations.[42] Matching is the modus operandi for most sampling, remix, and mashup productions.[43] Musical borrowing has a long history within African American culture { . . . } music was treated as communal wealth, not private property. { . . . } African American religious music, from its very beginnings, was based on appropriation. Slaves commonly used African folk melodies with the Christian lyrics forced upon them by their white owners.[44]

Although appropriators of ideas may always have existed, societies have not always recognized a specific concept of intellectual piracy. Far from being timeless, that concept is in fact not even ancient. It arose in the context of Western Europe in the early modern period—the years of religious and political upheaval surrounding the Reformation and the scientific revolution. In particular, it owed its origin to the cultural transformations set in train by Johann Gutenberg's invention of the printing press.[45] The rise of print culture cultivated an "anxiety of influence," where every newly created work has to stand on its own as *wholly original.*[46] Thus were born two enduring ideas that have gained much currency within the modern discursive framework: *talent* and *genius*.[47] This is not the case with oral cultures.[48] If we go all the way back to the ancient world, to the old bardic and prophetic traditions, what we find is that men and women are not thought to be authors so much as vessels through which other forces act and speak. { . . . } Homer is not the "author" of the *Odyssey*; he disappears after the first line: "Sing in me, Muse, and through me tell the story . . ."[49] In African and other oral cultures, this is how culture has traditionally functioned. In the absence of written culture, stories and histories were shared communally between performers and their audiences, giving rise to version after version, each new version surpassing the last as it incorporated the contributions and feedback of the audience, each new version layered with new details and twists as it was inflected through the collective. This was never thought of as copying or stealing.[50] Igor Stravinsky once said, "A good composer does not imitate, he steals." He was one of many European composers who borrowed from folk melodies in composing their own works. { . . . } Creativity is far more collaborative than the myth of the original author lets on.[51]

My point, however, is not to argue the legal issues of sampling—an area I have intentionally avoided, as I believe it overshadows so many more interesting aspects of the practice.[52] Discussions like these are dominated by the music's political consequences and do not leave much room for questions of aesthetics. Mashups are diverse and cannot only be identified as political statements; this probably characterizes the exceptions rather than the dominant form of mashups.[53]

It became evident to me that art is a field in which principles of remix have been at play from the very beginning of mechanical reproduction—hence the prevalence of art aesthetics throughout the chapters.[54] I asked DJ Adrian and Mysterious D { . . . } why artists like Warhol, Duchamp, and the collagists were so often invoked by sample-based musicians. They acknowledged that the comparison is explicitly strategic—in effect, a rhetorical comparison to legitimized art forms of the past as an appeal for artistic legitimacy today.[55] I don't think personally it's fair to not call Warhol an artist because he didn't actually design the soup can. So I don't think it's fair to not think of a remix artist or a remix or a rearrangement of existing source code and not call it art.[56]

The art is to succeed in finding two tracks that fit together musically, resulting in successful songs in their own right.[57] Whatever would be called remix { . . . } is completely contained and exhaustively covered by the existing term "collage." { . . . } Collage is not just an accidental or obvious arrangement of related elements that one might find thrown together in a scrapbook. It is a calculated and deliberately subversive strategy that seeks, by way of the juxtaposition of diverse elements, to produce conceptual frictions and illegitimate fusions that are simultaneously unexpected and insightful.[58] About collage as a technique: the selection, arrangement, and juxtaposition of the found bits of prior culture is the art.[59] The work of composing is not one of invention but one of arrangement. All materials being both unique and fundamentally connected, the strategy and art of connecting forms creative work.[60] The dialectical tension between figure and ground has become an important tool in the arsenal of modern composers. In order to exploit this tension, composers may transpose musical elements from the ground of one work to the figure of another, creating the potential for ambiguous interpretation. { . . . } As Eric Kleptone explained, "with mash-up, what you're actually doing is you're mashing up foregrounds and backgrounds. You're taking a foreground from one piece and you're putting it to a background on another piece."[61] An artist is now much more seen as a connector of things, a person who scans the enormous field of possible places for artistic attention, and says, What I am going to do is draw your attention to *this* sequence of things.[62] Nearly every configurable musician I spoke with rejected the concept of genius, opting instead to discuss "genius moments" or "genius works."[63]

Today's culture hackers meld everything from audio to automobiles, armed with an arsenal of increasingly sophisticated tools that have trickled down from the geek elite into the hands of consumers and triggered a mash-up boom.[64] Sampling is the key element that makes the act of remixing possible.[65] By employing technologically advanced equipment and digital-compression techniques, these hit makers create sounds that are more sonically engaging and powerful than even the most skilled instrumentalists can produce.[66]

Sampling is not just a musical practice; it is a complex cultural practice.[67] Sampling is a new way of doing something that's been with us for a long time: creating with found objects.[68] Every act can be imagined as a process of sampling and mixing that involves the selection, juxtaposition, and manipulation of the world's information as script.[69] In a large sense, one would say there is no pure originality. All minds quote. Old and new make the warp and woof of every moment. There is no thread that is not a twist of these two strands.[70]

Sound is one sense that carries great rhetorical force in and of itself.[71] I confess to being fascinated by many of these sounds on the fringes. I would argue that the strange often affords greater insights into the largest issues I want to examine here. { . . . } But the odd—the marginal—can often tell us more, for the margins often have much to say about the centers that those in the centers might not be aware of.[72] It is changing the very notion of what a "mainstream" is, altering the traditional media interaction habits of individuals as well as the business practices of media organizations, and thereby requiring a considerable renegotiation of the relationships between the two.[73] My reading of remix and its intimate relation to music should be viewed, then, as one way of theorizing about a culture defined by recyclability and appropriation.[74]

The Key

I urge all who intend to acquaint themselves with my speech, first to make allowance, as they listen to it, for the fact that it is a mixed discourse.[75] Such a mosaic image of numerous data and quotations in evidence offers the only practical means of revealing causal operations in history.[76] The notion of a collage text is, of course, not original to me.[77] One of my closest (if most complicated) friends at college was an English major. He was also a brilliant writer. { . . . } Every paragraph was constructed through quotes. { . . . } He built the argument by clipping quotes from the authors he was discussing. { . . . } He succeeded because the salience of the quotes, in context, made a point that his words alone would not. And his selection demonstrated knowledge beyond the message of the text.[78] Method of this project: literary montage. I needn't *say* anything. Merely show.[79]

Introduction

In October 2010, an internet video clip was uploaded to YouTube called "Donald Duck Meets Glenn Beck in Right Wing Radio Duck."[1] In this video—viewed over three million times as of this writing—video clips of Donald Duck are spliced together to reveal Donald as a protagonist who is in the throes of house foreclosure and unemployment, believing himself to be a victim of greedy "fat cats."[2] He finds consolation in the voice of right-wing political pundit Glenn Beck on the radio, which, in the true spirit of demagoguery, exclusively uses pathos to convince Donald that he is oppressed by evil and greedy institutions like Wall Street.[3] Unfortunately, according to Donald's radio, America has lost its way and has been infiltrated by enemies: Marxists, Communists, anti-capitalists, terrorists, and Nazis. This is seamlessly followed by an abbreviated comedic clip from the 1944 Disney film *The Three Caballeros* where Donald is pursued and frightened by a caricatured Latino parrot, presumably representing the Mexican immigrants to whom Beck refers. In order to placate his sense of helplessness, Donald subscribes to Beck's plan to "explain everything that's going on" at "$9.95 a month." After he sends off his money, Donald finds out he has been duped when a cruel anthropomorphic radio is delivered to his house and commences to accuse Donald of being lazy and telling him that he should get a job. Ultimately, the only way Donald can find respite from this barrage of harassments is by destroying his radio.

This clip is an example of a kind of political remix that has become more common with the advent of online streaming video. These videos play with culturally accepted associations by recontextualizing them in shocking or irreverent ways. In this particular case, the creator of the video, Jonathan McIntosh, amplifies Glenn Beck's incendiary political messages by placing them immediately next to each other. The appropriation of visuals from a Disney cartoon articulates the comic framing that underlies the remixed video. The remix presents the audience with an odd juxtaposition: Beck, a self-professed champion of the American cause to achieve greatness, is constructed rather as a bullying fearmonger whose hypocrisy blinds him to his true listeners. He has become worse than the "fat cat" that bullies Donald throughout the clip because there is no transparency in his promises; he is, simply, a hypocrite. This feat is accomplished by juxtaposing the imagery and plights of Donald Duck—a character traditionally empathetic to the plight of the hard-working individual because he is always "down on his luck"—with the ruthless commentary by Glenn Beck.

The lesson for viewing audiences is difficult to miss: Glenn Beck is giving them poor guidance too. The clip's use of the perpetually downtrodden Donald Duck exploits a commonplace of popular culture. Indeed, Donald Duck was created by Disney animators during the Great Depression and was featured in many of the cartoons that were created during World War II. In those cartoons, he was shown as a model citizen by working hard, being thrifty, and paying his income tax to inspire Americans to do likewise.[4] The *remixed* Donald Duck has the same didactic objective as a classic Disney cartoon, but his focus has shifted to warning Americans that they must avoid heeding the scare tactics of political pundits.

Given this ostensibly straightforward lesson, it appears that the clip was created with the objective of persuading audiences. Remix can double as a rhetorical tool because it is a powerful creative technique with a practical purpose to persuade an audience. Insofar as McIntosh's political remix video had an objective to "transform the viewer's state of consciousness from the static here and now to a fluid realm of possibilities," the video demonstrates the rhetorical potentialities of remix.[5]

Classifying the clip as rhetorical, however, raises more questions than it answers, each progressively more comprehensive: What about this artifact makes it persuasive? Does the function of remix make artifacts like "Right Wing Radio Duck" more persuasive than the original sources? If so, what about remix makes it rhetorical? And if remix is rhetorical, what types of rhetorical tropes might it use in the service of persuading an audience? Indeed, the primary purpose of this book is to search for answers to these questions.

Any way one looks at it, "Right Wing Radio Duck" was bound to be controversial, and not only for its ideological orientation regarding (in)famous celebrities. Rather, the fact that McIntosh unapologetically drew on Disney's familiar (and relentlessly protected) brand invites the inevitable legal scrutiny: Isn't this remix video blatantly stealing Disney's intellectual property? Due to these prevailing attitudes regarding the process of sampling, at least among the corporate entities with profits at stake, the word "remix" has become somewhat of a dysphemism in contemporary public discourse. Though some critics argue that remixing vitalizes a cultural commons that thrives on creativity and citizen agency—where McIntosh, for example, could attract attention to an issue he believed was important—others see it instead as a criminal practice tantamount to piracy.[6]

In the first several seconds of the video clip, there is a telling message on the title screen that attempts to navigate around potential copyright infringement. First, after classifying it as a "Cartoon Remix Video," McIntosh includes a disclaimer for his sampling of the Donald Duck cartoon clips: "This work constitutes a fair use of Walt Disney's Doanld [*sic*] Duck—Some rights reserved," followed by the icons for Creative Commons and Fair Use.[7] Fair use limits the reach of copyright protection, often cited by documentarians and political activists to justify their use of copyrighted material without permission. McIntosh appears to be claiming that a transformation of the original context and intent of these clips to a significant degree should inoculate him from Disney's prosecution. But fair use remains a murky legal doctrine because, though its criteria have crystallized in past digital-sampling lawsuits, some courts still question fair use's applicability. As Harvard law professor Terry Fisher states, "Some courts have gone very far in rejecting the defenses . . . Others are significantly more generous. So the bottom line is the law is unstable in this area."[8] Despite several precedents, the legal doctrine of fair use as a defense for remix still remains somewhat nebulous.

Though the definition of remix can be unclear, there are several important components that make a remix classified as such: It is the appropriation of individual or cultural ideas and their subsequent reassembly generally through the aid of technology. Or, as stated by Harvard law professor Lawrence Lessig, "Remix is collage . . . it succeeds by leveraging the meaning created by the reference to build something new."[9] Remix happens when people use technology to enter into closed systems of intellectual property in order to reopen them so that they can borrow, add to, or alter the existing content.[10] The user may choose to appropriate—or *sample*—portions of that material with other materials and often layer them on top of each other to create a *mashup*.[11] According to the perspective of those who participate in the practice of sampling and repurposing, a "new" composition is subsequently born. Thus, remix fructifies digital technology's artful sensibilities by creating an art form where cultural artifacts are digitally appropriated, manipulated, and transferred into new digital forms.

There are recurring terms anchored to the practice of sampling: invariably, questions of legality, property, and piracy appear. Indeed, one of the comments immediately below a political remix video on its YouTube page forum—a place usually reserved for ad hominem attacks, euphemisms, and profanity—exclaims, "I'm seeing some serious copyright violations here!"[12] The fact that these terms frequently cluster around remixed texts illustrates a tension between ideas inherited from the liberal tradition and the more democratic leanings of a participatory, digitally mediated culture. Remix challenges time-honored Western traditions like authorship, property, and originality, and therein lies much of the controversy regarding intellectual property and its digital sampling. Though current copyright laws were initially created to protect the creativity of the artist, those same laws are increasingly being viewed as outdated or unreasonable in an age where much creative output is originating from the manipulation of previous works.[13] Indeed, precisely because remix culture is stimulating creative output from citizens across the world, it is often lauded as a mechanism of participatory engagement. Gregg Gillis, a Pittsburgh disc jockey (DJ) who calls himself Girl Talk, argues, "[with remix,] music is becoming a lot more democratic."[14] Remix may be understood in this way because it is often seen as a changing of authorship from the producer to the user, "shift[ing] the locus of musical expertise, creativity, and skill to listeners of pop music."[15] Remix, in other words, is a gauge for measuring how the digital era has gradually shifted cultural opinions about the concept of authorship. For example, should the aforementioned remix video be considered the work of Disney artists, Glenn Beck, or Jonathan McIntosh? What is the definitive point where a remix is sufficiently transformed from its source material that it assumes a new authorship by the remixer? This notion of authorship has a place within the controversies surrounding remix culture as well.[16] There are other questions crucial to examining "Right Wing Radio Duck": Is it a persuasive artifact? If so, what are its rhetorical properties? Is there a rhetorical logic that characterizes remixed artifacts? If so, which tropes make up that rhetorical logic? These questions are an impetus for this book.

Getting at the rhetorical properties of remix is a complicated process. Part of that process involves looking at how remix is being deployed in contemporary culture. Consider three recent online examples of remix, each more rhetorical than the last: In late 2017, acclaimed YouTube remix artist Swedemason uploaded the video "Trump vs Talking Heads—Swedemason."[17] In this video, the classic new wave hit "Once in a Lifetime" is imagined through the voice of former U.S. president Donald Trump. Trump's head is cut-and-pasted on top of Talking Heads' composer and singer David Byrne. Once the verse begins, snippets of Trump's speeches are sampled and recontextualized to match the words of the song. In this video, Swedemason uses a remix tactic called *pwning*, a "cut-and-paste [technique] to make a public figure say or do something different from what he or she originally intended."[18] Although this tactic is deployed by remix artists in order to challenge hierarchies of power, that objective is not immediately clear when one watches the video.[19] But the meaning of the lyrics becomes more poignant once they are uttered in the voice of Trump, rather than through Byrne's pseudo-preacher intonations. If, indeed, the song is about an artifice that lurks behind the goals of obtaining wealth and prestige, that message becomes more trenchant when Trump is the mouthpiece. That message becomes even more powerful because of the obstinate and goofy faces of Trump that were selected to match Byrne's jerky motions. Then, in the coda of the video—as he repeats the refrain about things always staying the same—the voice of Trump is paired with video of him infamously mocking a disabled reporter.[20] The message that appears from the remix is that Trump as a politician is forever destined to be a fraudulent leader and a tone-deaf buffoon.

In late 2019, another remix artist performed a *pwning* of Trump. This one, "Queen—Bohemian Rhapsody (Donald Trump Cover)" by user Maestro Ziikos, is an even more sophisticated remix, because it not only appropriates Trump's words, it auto-tunes them (by shifting the pitch and drawing out the length of his syllables) to make it sound as if Trump is actually singing the iconic Queen song.[21] The song gains new meaning, however, once the political battles and controversies surrounding Trump become injected into the song. For example, the person playing the piano appears to be Russian president Vladimir Putin—a humorous choice by the remixer, given the frequent allegations that Trump and Putin colluded for political purposes. The political pseudo-narrative continues when Trump "sings," asking to be let go, and he is met by a chorus of Democratic leaders, Nancy Pelosi,

Bernie Sanders, and Hillary Clinton, responding that they will not let him go. The operatic back-and-forth continues as a political volley when Melania Trump and Vice President Mike Pence respond, "Let him go!" Given the partisan, charged political atmosphere of 2019 and 2020 marked by impeachment proceedings, the reimagining of the epic and iconic tune is apropos; it demonstrates how remixing public figures by repositioning them in the context of a song narrative can shed light on a contemporary controversy through its use of rhetoric.

The final example demonstrates the rhetorical potential of remix in a different way. In this Twitter account, called "President Supervillain" (@PresVillain), Trump's words—particularly the ones that sound the most diabolical—are injected into comic-strip panels. The apparent congruity between the words and new contexts that results is shocking. In this case, Trump's tweets are presented as comic-book dialogue in the voice of supervillain Red Skull. In one example, Red Skull is plotting some poor victim's demise while declaring, "I would bring back waterboarding and I'd bring back a hell of a lot worse than waterboarding!! I don't think we go far enough!!!" In another, the supervillain says "Just to reiterate, if Turkey does anything that I, in my great and unmatched wisdom, consider to be off-limits . . . I will totally destroy and obliterate the economy of Turkey!!! I've done it before—!!!"[22] Although this example is still a *pwning* of President Trump, it adjusts the formula: rather than making a public figure say the words of another, it takes the actual utterances of that figure and presents them using the voice of someone else. The takeaway of these rhetorical messages is clear—Trump is as guilty of villainy as the evilest villains in the comic books.

As evidenced by these examples, remix clearly can be employed in the service of rhetoric. The rhetorical power of remix also can be observed beyond political messages. Remix has tremendous cultural salience as a manifestation of the networked logic that permeates contemporary society, effectively becoming a glimpse into an interconnected system of cultural practices caught in transition.[23] Remix culture, initiated and sustained by new technologies, privileges the amateur over the professional and collaboration over individualism.[24] It has instigated a shifting of authorship from the producer to the user/consumer, where the onus of creativity is centered on the audience.[25] The very idea of a network entails a hybridization between an individual node and a traditional community. This overall destabilization of heretofore taken-for-granted cultural assumptions is one reason why remix culture has become so controversial.

At the same time, remix represents a new understanding that creative and artistic products exist in an open-source culture, an era where digital technologies have extended the traditional space- and time-bound restrictions of information, and where information has become essentially available to the use and benefit of the public.[26] Because these rapid technological innovations always outpace the vocabulary of media theory, one of my objectives is to develop a critical vocabulary needed to address those media innovations in a culture permeated by technological change. Since that vocabulary is derived from the language of rhetorical studies, I aim in this book to isolate the rhetorical tropes embedded in the practice of remix.

In discovering this tropological vocabulary, I am inspired by the rich panoply of twentieth-century avant-garde art that presaged the contemporary move to remix culture. Rhetorical theorist Richard Lanham argues that in an age oversaturated by information, the most rhetorical artifacts are the ones that can attract the most attention. He considers avant-garde artists as rhetoricians par excellence, individuals who are in the business of grabbing people's attention.[27] Following his lead, I pave the way to developing a critical vocabulary of understanding remix with an appreciation for the artists of the vanguard, whom I consider to be proto-remixers. Because the tenor of their work is so radical, and yet so often revered in contemporary culture, I believe that injecting their art into the following discussion will help us understand how remix has moved from the margins into the mainstream.

In order to develop this vocabulary, however, remix needs to be discussed across modes and platforms. This is not just a book about remix in music; it's a book about remix in culture and across history. Nor is it a book exclusively about the aesthetics of the practice or about the philosophical dimensions of the ongoing discussions about the practice of remix. *Turntables and Tropes* is about the rhetorical dimensions of the creative practice of remix.

The Significance of Remix

The concept of remix is complicated and wide-reaching. In some ways, all thought—and thus all cultural artifacts—could be considered remixed, for symbols themselves always preexist their deployment in some way. In order to articulate the parameters of this analysis, I will address some perplexing questions that remix culture poses to scholars of rhetoric and media studies. Among these are (1) what is remix?, (2) why is it significant?, (3) where does it come from?, and (4) how does it work? Considered holistically, the book will explore different dimensions of the phenomenon of remix with the objective of better understanding how to answer the first question.

This section will offer some thoughts toward an understanding of the second question: Why is remix significant? There are several reasons for its cultural salience: (1) The cheap production and circulation of remix software and music distribution technologies have enabled many people to participate in the practice; (2) remix exploits an ostensibly grassroots ethos that also encourages the public to engage with information in new ways; (3) these remix technologies have become firmly embedded within the ebbs and flows of youth culture, which have an outsized influence on cultural shifts over time; (4) remix often manipulates popular cultural artifacts like pop music stars and politicians, which generates greater publicity; (5) remix also draws attention to videos and songs concerned with everyday life, thus connecting to audiences less concerned with pop culture or political artifacts; and (6) remix has become a driving factor behind the spread of online memetic culture. Though there are undoubtedly other reasons why remix has moved from the margins to the center of current public discourse, the following discussion is intended to provide a starting place for understanding its significance.

First, in today's networked culture, remix has become an incredibly popular global practice because of the widespread circulation of remix software.[28] As music began to evolve beyond the analog technologies of the seventies and eighties and into the cheaper and more accessible digital technologies of the nineties, the practice of remixing music became more common. The equipment that the DJs of the eighties used to remix music often would run to thousands of dollars, but as the personal computer became more popular, and as software for those computers became easily available, people gained easier access to remixing. In the second decade of the new millennium, remixable music can be accessed from a cloud.[29] The launching of YouTube in 2005 was another harbinger of the increasingly frequent appearance of (and easy access to) remix, one that pushed the practice far beyond any previously imaginable thresholds of popularity.

Consequently, this increased access to relevant software leads to another likely appeal of remix—its association with grassroots applications of new communication technologies. Remix as a cultural practice is often assumed to be a part of a more egalitarian, open-source culture enabled by digital technologies that make information more available for the creative use and benefit of the public.[30]

Curiously, though, the everyday revolutionaries who oppose corporate rock are not the only individuals who facilitate this grassroots culture. High-profile artists like Radiohead and Nine Inch Nails have also participated in the democratic production process of open-source remix culture by releasing basic tracks from songs to the public.[31] This is in stark contrast to earlier in the twenty-first century, when the band Metallica was at the center of an effort to stop users from participating in peer-to-peer music services like Napster.[32] Some contemporary artists have taken the grassroots ethos one step further; since 2007, both Radiohead and Girl Talk have made their music available for digital download to the public free of charge, or on a "pay-what-you-can basis."[33]

But remix refers to much more than just music. In the case of this book, at least, remix is an all-encompassing term that refers to the digital manipulation and recombination of mediated texts, whether they be aural or visual.[34] What ties each of these different media for remix together is that they can be considered as unauthorized remixes, or reconfigured materials for which the remix artists did not seek out permission from the original authors.[35] In some cases, though, remixes can also be authorized; I will also address remixes from institutions like Nike, NBC, and Netflix. Trying to define remix, in other words, is a practice that is bound to be controversial. Rather than focusing on delineating the elements of that definition, I will focus on vocabulary that may be applied across the definitional divide. I take the perspective of remix studies scholar Eduardo Navas, who argues that remix is a form of discourse. He explained,

> As a form of discourse Remix affects culture in ways that go beyond the basic understanding of recombining material to create something different. For this reason, my concern is with Remix as a *cultural variable* that is able to move and inform art, music, and media in ways not always obvious as discussed in remix culture.[36]

Echoing the multimodal perspective articulated by Navas, the rhetorical tropes discussed in this book can be applied to both music and other digitally remixed texts.

Next, remix is embedded in youth culture (and vice versa). The relatively inexpensive software that aids remixing music has worked in tandem with the increasing popularity of pop and dance music to create ideal conditions for its circulation within that culture.[37] For instance, youth are heavily invested in technologies that facilitate communication and entertainment. The tools for remix are available and popular on computers on college campuses and in dorm rooms worldwide. In addition to their fondness for and proficiency with new technologies, young people tend to exploit a general distrust of authority (hence the popularity of rock 'n' roll music with youth since the 1950s). Remix allows youth to subvert the status quo, whether it is their parents (who taught them to never steal) or the recording industry (which traditionally has appeared greedy and detached). By being engaged in the seemingly subversive practice of sampling, they enact this disregard for authority when they use these digital technologies. As such, when music playback changed from analog to digital devices (from record players and cassette tapes to compact discs and MP3 players), the production of remixes percolated somewhat from the realm of professional DJs to amateur mashup artists. This change of technology, coupled with the subversive qualities of rock 'n' roll and its related appeal to tech-savvy youth, created ideal conditions for remix culture. In dozens of interviews that media scholar Aram Sinnreich conducted with remix artists (among others), a recurrent mythic theme emerged of the remixer: a young amateur with a laptop, or "some kid in his bedroom."[38] This characterization of the individuals who remix music is not far off when we look at remix in the digital age.[39]

The increased cultural disposition toward remix in the last decade has intersected with developments in internetworked technology, specifically online video. Often popular videos on YouTube will be centered on some aspect of celebrity culture or famous political figures, or, not surprisingly, both. For example, one remixed clip that gained rapid viral traction in early 2012 is "Barack Obama Singing Born This Way by Lady Gaga."[40] Like the Trump clip mentioned earlier, in this clip, the former U.S. president Obama is shown "singing" the song through creative editing of words that he had spoken at various formal speech events to match the lyrics of the song. This video received over two million views within a week of being posted in part because articles about the video infiltrated popular news sites on Yahoo and Mashable. Even just a few years before this video was posted, it would have been implausible that so much attention would be affixed to any remixed artifact. Yet, the accessibility of online video creates an appropriate vehicle for the distribution of these artifacts.

Remix is not only popular because of pop culture or political artifacts online. In the early years of YouTube, some of the most popular clips on the website were amateur clips of children simply acting cute, which were subsequently remixed. For example, the videos "Charlie Bit My Finger" and "David After Dentist" have together earned billions of views on the website. These nonscripted, cinéma vérité videos are essentially windows into the lives of regular people who film their children. And the formula works: at one point, "Charlie Bit My Finger"—a short clip of two British children, one of which bites the other's finger—was the most popular clip of all time on YouTube.[41] The relevance of these videos to remix, however, comes from the *responses* to these videos. When a video truly achieves a heavy circulation throughout the internet, there is usually a spate of remixes of that video that often become very popular in their own right. For example, "Charlie Bit My Finger" spawned an auto-tune remix that became very popular, earning over 13 million views. This response video was created and uploaded by Schmoyoho (the username for the Brooklyn-based auto-tune pioneers the Gregory Brothers), remixing the video via auto-tune technology to make the brothers appear as if they were singing a song.

Another popular clip, "David After Dentist," is a video of a boy who has just left the dentist from a routine operation. The sedatives used during the procedure have left David in a hilarious haze, from which he makes a series of nonsensical statements like "is this real life?" while his father, the cameraman, kindly responds. This popular video inspired the mashup video "Christian Bale Takes David to the Dentist," which has earned millions of views on its own. In this response video, the original footage of David is layered on top of the audio track of actor Christian Bale giving a profane rant on the set of *Terminator Salvation*. In this disturbing mashup, then, it appears as if Christian Bale is the father of David, responding crudely and harshly to David's innocent inquiries. Another video, "Chad After Dentist," parodies the original by placing the character Chad Vader—himself a parody of the *Star Wars* character Darth Vader—in the back seat of an SUV and making similar statements as David. Finally, in what is truly the pinnacle of postmodern pastiche, a video called "Chad Meets Christian While He Does David After Dentist" combines the audio track for Christian Bale and the video of the character of Chad Vader, the parody of Darth Vader, parodying the video for "David After Dentist." This video is notable for several reasons. First, as a parody that lampoons a mashup of a video of a real-life event, it suggests that digital technology offers the hyperreal potential of merging life with art.[42] Second, the popularity of remixes on YouTube has become so pronounced that many videos on the website are simply referring to past remixes, thus evincing the intertextuality of the practice. Therefore, remixes and *remixes of remixes* have become the norm on YouTube to the point that the source material has become a barely visible palimpsest. In fact, remixing has become so normalized on YouTube that it is no longer even recognized as such.

Speaking of popularity, remix is also one of the reasons for the spread of online meme culture. Memes, or "aggregate texts, collectively created, circulated, and transformed by countless cultural participants," are ubiquitous in the current media environment.[43] These user-generated texts, whether they be image macro memes or YouTube video memes, depend on remix as a tool for their transformation. Memes are classified as such because they exist in groups—or "families"—of similar content that are held together by shared characteristics called *quiddities*.[44] They are collectively created templates that allow for individuals to express themselves in unique ways, as long as they adhere to the structures (and, therefore, constraints) of the templates.[45] Memes that are remixed are digitally manipulated in some way.[46] In other words, in order to create a meme, a user must first pick another meme, acknowledge the template that exists, then follow it while altering the content in novel ways. Remix, then, is the guiding force and the creative logic behind contemporary memes.

Remix is significant because it is a creative mechanism for much of the content in the media environment. But remix is also interesting because it contains a tremendous potential for persuasiveness. This potential is facilitated by its effective use of rhetorical tropes—like *asyndeton*, *oscillatio*, and *mimesis*—in tandem with aesthetic norms. Indeed, this assumption will form the backbone of this book.

Rhetorical Tropes

A key argument of this book is that remixed music and videos are persuasive because, as a creative practice, remix uses certain rhetorical tropes to achieve its purposes. Tropes are an essential component of rhetorical messages. Ancient Roman rhetorician Quintilian defined a trope as "a shift of a word or phrase from its proper meaning to another."[47] Contemporary American rhetorician Kenneth Burke called tropes ways for discovering and describing "the truth."[48] A trope is a rhetorical shortcut used to embellish and transform texts. However, tropes are more than merely figures of speech—they are tools.[49] As a former *Newsweek* editor once said about Burke, "Who else but Burke has taken literature so seriously that it could become the ground which underlies all human activity?"[50] Essentially, tropes can provide meaning to what is not stated directly or literally and perhaps in some cases draw attention to an important idea.[51]

Just as rhetoric is a tool for accomplishing a strategic purpose, remix is a tool for accomplishing a creative purpose—though these purposes can be easily conflated. Remix itself is not a rhetorical trope, however, it is a cultural practice and a creative method that uses rhetorical tropes.[52] In the context of viewing remix as a cultural practice, I will demonstrate how rhetorical tropes can be used to tease out the polysemic meanings of remixed texts. The rhetorical tropes that I will consider are *kairos*, *imitatio*, perspective by congruity, possession by misnomer, *oscillatio*, *asyndeton*, *mimesis*, *śūnyatā*, *prosōpopoeia*, *enthymeme*, *eudaimonia*, and *suasoria*. But before discussing how these rhetorical tropes function persuasively, I will first consider some of their historical antecedents.

Developing a Critical Vocabulary of Remix

Many of the critiques of remix, from legal and aesthetic perspectives, draw from perspectives that do not use the same language as that used by artists who actively participate in remix culture. These approaches are predictable, even necessary, in considering the role of remix in contemporary communication. These critiques, though, need to be supplemented by a theoretical explanation of remix that goes beyond the staid questions of copyright law and originality. There have been notable theoretical approaches to remix that focus primarily on the cultural logic of mashups and mashup communities, the metaphysical properties of sound recording and mashups, and the implications of copying and imitation in remixing.[53] While these approaches address important theoretical questions about the phenomenon, I will concentrate instead on understanding the rhetorical tropes and aesthetic dimensions of remix.

Instead of focusing on "the *rhetoric of* remix," or how remix is framed in broader public discourse, this book investigates the *rhetorical properties* of remix. My objective is to address the rhetoricity of the practice itself, focusing primarily on how remix overlaps with rhetoric via its use of rhetorical tropes. In addition to being a rhetorical account of remix, this book doubles as an intellectual history of the *idea* of remix, examining the artistic margins of modern- and networked-era culture and how they have, in some ways, reverted back to classical norms. As such, I redeploy traditional rhetorical concepts in order to understand the contemporary practice of remix; indeed, I will in a few cases integrate my object of study into my method by remixing parts of the rhetorical tradition.

Theorizing about remix from a communicative perspective helps develop a critical vocabulary through which we can critique this new digital species of discourse. Several questions, then, guide this analysis. First, are there unique rhetorical dimensions to remix? Second, how can rhetorical tropes elucidate features of remix and its broader cultural significance? Third, what would a critical vocabulary to address the rhetorical features of remix look like? Finally, as a follow-up question, how could a critical vocabulary to address remix be crafted from one of the oldest arts, rhetoric—and is it appropriate for the rhetorical tropes to be repurposed in this way? These questions guide my approach to remix.

CHAPTER 1

The Gutenberg Parenthesis

Remix throughout History

Before exploring the rhetorical tropes that proliferate in remixed texts (and, indeed, make them possible), it is important to first establish a historical context for remix. Remix has received considerable popular and scholarly analysis. This book diverges from these extant approaches in two ways. First, remix is usually conceived as primarily a technological or musical phenomenon. Literature regarding remix, for example, gravitates to a description of digital sampling and analog antecedents like dance club DJs. I make the case in this book that remix is also a *communicative* practice, a frame that illuminates the rhetorical dimensions, persuasive possibilities, and cultural implications of remixed artifacts. Second, remix is usually thought of as a new phenomenon because it is performed through the relatively new medium of the internet.[1] Seeing remix as a function of the recombinatory capacities of digital media elides an appreciation of historical antecedents to remix. I argue, alternatively, that historical antecedents to remix can be located in the rhetorical tradition. This communicative dimension is not limited to audio media or visual media—remix is a communicative practice that takes place across all media, including the spoken word.[2] Situating remix within that history provides a different angle of vision by which to consider the import of remix culture. In order to gain some critical purchase on the implications of communication in digital times, we must appreciate prior communicative formations.

Locating remix in a broader historical trajectory provides a richer sense of the phenomenon's parallels with communicative practices. By providing an intellectual history of the idea of remix and examining classical rhetorical norms as antecedents to contemporary remix culture, I will examine twentieth-century avant-garde art, arguing that it has the same function as antecedent to remix. In doing so, classical figures like Isocrates and modern figures like John Cage become recast as proto-remix artists. By looking at the twentieth-century margins, it will become more apparent how contemporary remix practice is not "new," but rather a logical evolution of a long-extant philosophy that has evolved into its current digitally networked incarnation.

Thinking Outside of the Parenthesis

In order to grasp the communicative dimensions of remix, it will be important to situate remix within a larger history of the interaction between technology and society. Media theorist Marshall McLuhan argued, "Technology means constant social revolution."[3] McLuhan was primarily interested in how technologies modify human perception and experience, arguing that human history could be divided into three epochs defined by their technological innovations: the typographic era (initiated by the invention of the alphabet and the practice of writing), the mechanical era (initiated by the invention of the printing press), and the electronic age, within which we now live.[4] Each of these eras consisted of progressively literate cultures that greatly advanced human thought and knowledge. Though he neglected to name the era that existed prior to the invention of typography, broadly calling it "primitive . . . society," it became the focus of much scholarly interest to McLuhan and subsequent related scholarship.[5] Relevant discussions in media ecology literature have coined these communicative cultures as oral and literate cultures. Roughly, oral culture existed before literacy and thus used verbal narratives and auditory acuity to communicate identity and tradition, while literate culture's reliance on writing and eventually print secured advances from sharing information.

To media scholars, the preliterate culture of orality is defined by the oral histories it maintained.[6] Its cultural narratives and texts were created in a spirit of collective remembrance. This age was dominated by a collective interactivity because of the important mandate to keep cultural records alive. After all, in an oral culture, "when the talking stops the culture vanishes."[7] Thus, a collective culture of creation was central to nonliterate cultures, long before the concept of the individual as creator came to fruition.

This collective remembrance was also inherently fluid. Stories could change and be re-created in structure and tone as they were passed down through generations. These narratives were collective histories of their people and they were created in the spirit of an ongoing collaboration with progenitors and progeny. Because of the orality of these stories, they were also highly contextual, dependent upon their oral delivery for their rhetorical efficacy. Their performance, then, was as important as their content. The quintessential oral cultures were classified as such because their cultural performances were executed through speech, contextualized within a particular situation, and reliant on a series of traditional commonplaces.

Once writing was invented, the means of creating cultural texts shifted from oral culture to scribal culture.[8] Though some fundamental changes took place during the time of writing, they were even more drastic in the print era that followed. The era of typography was ushered in by the invention of the printing press by Johannes Gutenberg in the mid-fifteenth century. Though cultural change did not noticeably take place until a full century after Gutenberg's invention, the press became monumental in shaping technology and human perception.[9]

Thomas Pettitt's figure of the Gutenberg Parenthesis, adapted from a concept by Lars Ole Sauerberg, concisely captures how the era of the printing press generated communicative norms that departed from oral culture regarding the creation of cultural texts.[10] Whereas on the printed page, "a parenthesis [syntactically] interrupts a line of thought which resumes when the parenthesis closes," the Gutenberg Parenthesis serves the same function, positioning the digital era to share more similarities to the cultural milieu of the classical age than the modern age of typological innovation.[11] Inside the parenthesis, however, shifts occurred that markedly separated the modern age from its preceding era. As can be seen in figure 1, the nature of textual production changed with the advent of the printing press. Whereas cultural narratives were created collectively in an oral culture, printing culture allowed for individuals to assume authorship for texts. Narratives in oral culture had been contextual: dependent on verbal delivery, performance, and context. Within the parenthesis, however, the importance of performance waned. In its place, the notion of composition came into being.

PRE-PARENTHETICAL	GUTENBERG PARENTHESIS	POST-PARENTHETICAL
Re-creative	Original	Sampling
Collective	Individual	Remixing
Con-textual	Autonomous	Borrowing
Unstable	Stable	Reshaping
Traditional	Canonical	Appropriating
PERFORMANCE	**COMPOSITION**	**RECONTEXTUALIZING**

FIGURE 1. The Gutenberg Parenthesis, a term coined by Lars Ole Sauerberg and developed by Thomas Pettitt, charts how cultural production has changed over historical eras.

Composition of a text became associated with individual achievement. In the perception of this era, texts were no longer drawn from a creative collective, but rather from the genius of the individual who conceived them. According to Elizabeth Eisenstein, in print culture, "the storyteller was replaced by the exceptional literate villager."[12] Collective authority became undermined by these new concepts of individual rights, property, and the solitary author. Even now, the collective creation of texts feels somewhat foreign—this is surely a testament to the permanence of the cultural effects of the printing press. When text became linked to an individual, as demonstrated in figure 1, it also became autonomous, original, and stable. Text is autonomous because it can be read and understood in a space that is different from the one in which it was written. Text is original because it is the product of a mind that has produced novel thought and recorded it on pages. For instance, when one reads the words of Enlightenment philosophers like Descartes or Hume, he or she is partaking of the culmination of their work and genius. Because of this genius, then, their words become canonized texts for future generations. During the heyday of the printing press, even the ancient sages, who were actually drawing on a wellspring of collective wisdom, were recast as individual authors in order to valorize the then-nascent concept of individual authorship.[13] Composition also superseded performance inside the parenthesis, though the place of performance within it remains ambivalent. To be sure, there existed a hearing public alongside the reading public, and people would read aloud to others. Performance, then, still existed in some capacity after the shift began. However, many salons and coffeehouses were eventually afflicted by a "sullen silence" as the transition to silent reading began.[14] With the influx of new visual symbols came an increase in scientific and mathematical thought in the scribal age and a decrease in the emotional mysticism of the previous age.

Incidentally, a similar shift was taking place in the realm of musical composition as well. The invention of movable type, for example, led the way to the creation and mass distribution of music notation.[15] This also had the effect of preserving music for future generations, which allowed more of the public to participate in the creation of music. Thus, the creation of a "musical public" took place. Likewise, the preservation and notation of music also iterated that composers were owners of their craft, capable of creating the new concept of the masterpiece.[16] Composers were able to master the skill of making music and therefore acquired respectable social status while their works were subsequently published and copyrighted. This legal precedent essentially reified the concept of a musical genius, as well as creating a paradox of sorts: just as musical publics were being created—meaning that compositional power was moving increasingly away from the margins and into the centers—it was also consolidating power into the hands of those who did compose due to their genius status. Additionally, they were rewarded for their expertise as they sold their published work. As Jacques Attali, an important theorist in music and sound studies, wrote, "the artist was born, at the same time his work went on sale."[17] The composer received much adulation, due, in part, to technology and its requisite shifts in the paradigm of music. In short, this advancement in technology corresponded with a transformation of musical norms, changing them from an era where performance was integral to keeping music available for public consumption to an era where the publication of music and its subsequent mass distribution became more common.

Technology is responsible for the gradual shift from producers into consumers in the field of traditional music.[18] This further transformation of musical norms was due, in part, to advancements in technology, namely, the invention of the player piano and its sister products the gramophone and the phonograph. These contraptions served to further usher in an age of consumption in music. It was no longer as common for buyers to acquire notated music to create it themselves on their pianos, because suddenly they were able to buy and reproduce it with little to no effort on their part.[19] The oral and performed nature of music had shifted yet again, away from the silent notation of the works into their aural reproduction.

Given these seismic shifts, how do we make sense of how digital mediation shapes communicative norms? As the transition commenced from printed word to digitized text, nonlinear logics shifted to the cultural forefront.[20] The post-parenthetical era's technological affordances have enabled remixing to become a key mode of cultural production, and sampling to become a defining practice. Much like the pluralism that defines postmodernity, an amalgamation of many different voices becomes the essential trait in the construction of a cultural text.[21] Digital technology speeds along the collapse of the authoritative text because the possibility of creative appropriation suggests that texts should no longer be considered finished—bringing us again back to the collectivity of the oral tradition.[22] If the notion prevails that songs or other texts should be considered as "raw data" to be repurposed later, appropriation is not just an aesthetic sensibility (akin to the collages of modern art), but also a structural necessity for remix to even be classified as such. Further, context becomes crucial again, but only insofar as it is different from the source context. Though performance still exists in contemporary public culture, it is a different variety than that of the bards in the pre-parenthetical era. In contemporary remix culture, performance has become indistinguishable from composition. The phenomenon of a DJ performing/creating a remix in a dance club is an example of the blurring of performance and composition. When a DJ uses a laptop to create a mashup of two or three samples spontaneously at a show, he or she is both composing and performing simultaneously. Further, the DJ's artistic expression is doubly communicated by the source material recordings as well as the choices of which samples to layer on top of each other.

Our video example from "Right-Wing Radio Duck" looks a little different with this background on remix and the Gutenberg Parenthesis.[23] Using Pettitt's vocabulary, we can understand better how the video is an illustration of how culture is now squarely situated within the post-parenthetical era. According to the new cultural means of invention, the video illustrates the practice of "appropriation": it "borrows" animated clips of Donald Duck from Disney and audio clips from Glenn Beck's radio program.[24] It then "reshapes" both visual and audio texts, cutting them up and changing the order from that in which they were originally made available for consumption. In this way, both visual and audio clips are "recontextualized," in that they are all removed from their original sources and sequences. The clips have been chosen for rhetorical efficiency by the remixer; thus they are "sampled" like the best food at a buffet. The samples are then "remixed," mashed together in a way that they are able to circulate new meanings through digitally connected communication networks. In other words, the collection and stitching together of these disparate media have transformed them from something previously released (and thus "old") to something novel (and thus "new"). Further, issues once relevant to these clips are no longer seen as such. For instance, "borrowing" either shifts to a more ambivalent meaning or no longer becomes relevant in this context. Whereas the Donald Duck clips had teams of animators, musicians, and actors working to create the original clips, and the audio clips had Beck as responsible, no longer does this seem to be the case. There is suddenly an omnipotent hand operating above the creation, and no, it's not Walt Disney from beyond the grave! Instead, it is video remixer Jonathan McIntosh. His intent is now imposed over the original intents of the Disney crews and Glenn Beck. But does this ambiguity of authorial intent now mean that those original authors are now divorced from their work? Because McIntosh found the clips and remixed them together in a novel way, does that make him the new author? Because those clips were likely found online, does that mean that they are commodities available for the manipulation of any internet user? These questions illustrate the complexity of the post-parenthetical age.

The Gutenberg Parenthesis cleverly organizes and concisely surveys much of the literature in media studies, particularly in the field of media ecology. There are more connections that are not articulated in the Parenthesis, however. In the era that followed the invention of the printing press, certain schools of thought developed that would dominate the intellectual landscape for centuries. The Enlightenment, the precursor to modern Western liberalism, was one. The ideology of the Enlightenment contained, in part, a strong emphasis (sometimes paradoxically) on absolutism, rationality, rights, ethics, empiricism, equality, and individualism.[25] Three philosophers of the time cogently exemplify the Enlightenment in terms of their own theories: Descartes, Hume, and Kant. Their accumulated and representative thought would continue to inspire contemporary Western liberalism. I discuss the Enlightenment here because it offers a direct contrast to the post-parenthetical era that would follow.

The Enlightenment and the Western Liberal Tradition

Seventeenth-century French philosopher Rene Descartes perhaps most famously articulated the philosophy of the Enlightenment by declaring, "*cogito ergo sum*," theorizing that inquisition and rationality calls one into existence.[26] Descartes advocated a brand of scientific rationalism in his thought that embodied absolute standards of truth. This absolutist perspective, called a philosophy of self-evidence and modeled upon the mathematical certainties of geometry, posited that all phenomena were determined though universal laws.[27] By considering the world in these terms, Descartes theorized in ways where logic was of utmost importance. Descartes also marginalized emotion because of its deviance from scientific certainty, contemptuously calling it "passions" and relegating its status to merely something originating from the pineal gland.[28] Thus, for our purposes, a theory of absolutism and individualism originates in Cartesian thought. This perspective continued to hold throughout the modern era. Eighteenth-century Scottish philosopher David Hume contributed to the ideology of the Enlightenment as well, being influenced by the inductive empiricism of another contemporary, Sir Francis Bacon. More than a rationalist, Hume was an extreme empiricist, deriving ideas from "purely sensory impressions."[29] He believed that only phenomena that could be observed through the human senses had scientific validity. Auguste Comte, a philosopher from later that century, upped the ante by considering science to be a kind of religion.[30] In so doing, Comte believed that all phenomena, especially the social sciences, could be studied like the physical sciences where absolute truths would emerge through their investigation.[31] This variation of Hume's skepticism led to an important hermeneutic he called positivism, which continued mostly unhindered throughout modernism.

Immanuel Kant also labored largely within the philosophical confines of the Parenthesis, though his philosophy is a bit more complicated than simply an extension of Cartesian and Humean thought. For example, Kant did not argue that philosophy needed to be purely objective like Descartes, but rather made a space for subjectivity in his philosophy.[32] However, the intellectual commitment of absolutism is demonstrated clearly in Kant's theorizing about what has become known as the categorical imperative. In this important component of his ethical philosophy, Kant posits that a general understanding of morals should be applicable to the human race *in toto*. This universal moral obligation is agnostic to individual intent or motivation and is the basis for Kant's influential discourse on rights.

Political theorist Ronald Beiner argues that the moral vocabularies articulated in Kant's concept of the categorical imperative helped shape contemporary Western liberalism.[33] Though liberalism is a notoriously "slippery" political term, my definition of it remains narrow here for my purpose of illustrating it as a foil to remix culture.[34]

Similar to the intellectual commitments of the Enlightenment, then, liberalism places a primacy on that era's ideals, which include notions of authority, Kantian notions of rights, Cartesian notions of individuality, and Lockean notions of property. Liberalism's emphasis on absolutism is similar to Plato's Theory of Forms more than the pluralism that postmodernism advocates. In this theory, Plato considers ideals of Truth, Beauty, and Reality as existing in absolute forms independent of the terrestrial perspective. Only through its efforts to reach those ideals can humankind improve itself and advance. Like this Platonic philosophy, liberalism and modernity see the concepts of Genius, Creator, Author, and Original each as foundational master narratives. Liberalism holds that absolute standards should govern our conceptions of authorship and originality. This belief clearly contrasts with the cultural production potential of digital media, and thus the moral language of liberalism and the perspective fostered by centuries of existing inside of the Parenthesis is largely incompatible with describing the post-parenthetical era broadly and remix specifically. In other words, remix clearly challenges values rooted in Platonism.[35] We will revisit the dissonance between classical, modern, and postmodern values in more detail in the next chapter.

Examining Remix from within the Parenthesis

Remix questions the modern notion of the individual genius, considering the genius to be one who can utilize technology to create something appealing from past cultural texts.[36] Property acquires a new meaning altogether, irrespective of traditional definitions. Each of these preconceived liberal notions that constitute the legal and intellectual heritage of Western liberalism are challenged by remix culture.

However, the classical rhetorical tradition offers a more compatible pairing with remix culture. The Aristotelian notion of prudence, for example, invites orators of political discourse to speak to the events in the current context rather than relating to external events. Ronald Beiner believes that the language of morals should shift from Kantian universalist morals back to a more Aristotelian language of morals and character.[37] His exhortation becomes even more relevant in the case of sampling and remix. One way for prudence to take place would be to use the "practical judgment" cultivated from one's character in assessing a situation. This is the role of a moral agent to make the correct decision rather than to fall back on the language of preconceived judgments. While the Aristotelian perspective sounds suspiciously like the situational ethics that occur when the individual considers nothing above and beyond the current context, it appears to take on a more moderate function than relativism. In short, it takes into consideration special circumstances, thus circumscribing the rigid absolutism of Kantian ethics.

In the contemporary copyright debate, I agree that the language of morality is stifled today because of vestiges of Enlightenment thought. The Kantian notion of ethics that should be generalizable to an entire society has been codified into law—still remnants of the ideological clusters that originated during the modern era. This modern perspective on rights is evidenced by the names appended to the practice of sampling: "piracy" and "theft," for example. Because the legal system is standardized to the point that sampling has traditionally been considered theft, legal decisions are not always contingent upon changing technologies and their corresponding cultures.[38] With relatively new forms of cultural production proliferating and technology evolving day by day, the relationship between legislation and remix is becoming increasingly complex. The language of the debate does not reflect that complexity.

The tensions on both sides of the debate have been derived from—and codified into—legal procedure. The vitriol on both sides also reflects the ambiguity and "murkiness" of the legal perspective on the debate, because, frankly, the terms "remix" and "sampling" are far from being uncontested. According to media studies scholar Aram Sinnreich, the very ambiguity (and legally unprecedented nature) of the idea of sampling is what may be causing these discursive and ideological clashes:

> Questions of ethics, legality, and aesthetics aside, even the material and physical metaphors we use when describing the subject [of sampling] seem to miss the mark. Sampling isn't "taking," because the source material is still available... It's not "borrowing," because the sampler doesn't ever return the work... It's not "quoting" ... How can we accuse or defend someone from a charge of theft, if we don't know whether they've taken something? How can we make a claim to originality when

> we don't really know what constitutes copying? How can we understand what a DJ is saying if he or she is using someone else's voice?[39]

Indeed, the language of the intellectual property debate is dependent upon a new technological grammar, wherewith the stewards of that grammar must *relearn* how to use even ostensibly self-evident concepts like "property" and "ownership."

Both sides use the same language but use the words in different contexts. The notion of property, for example, is a word rooted deeply in the Western liberal tradition. Enlightenment-era philosopher John Locke celebrated humankind's natural right to property as the fruit of its labor, and this right was reified in the Manifest Destiny period of American expansionism.[40] Key to these understandings of property is a teleological envisioning of labor, one that yields ownership. This is a similar philosophy that undergirds the tenets of copyright law: if artists are to be granted copyright protection for their work, it is because they labored to create that work and thus are entitled to have ownership over it. However, it is that ownership that causes advocates to fight for more flexible copyright laws. Once ownership is granted, the art becomes exclusively fenced off from creative appropriation. The lingering milieu of modern ideology, then, necessarily clashes with a contemporary culture that is increasingly infiltrated by a perspective rooted in the invention of open-source technologies.

This ideological clash between modern and open-source culture has colored the debate between those who support traditional copyright (the "Copy-Right") and those who advocate copyright reform ("the Copy-Left").[41] This shift may also be due, in part, to the drastic clash that open-source culture provides when paired up against modern ideology. Modern culture's embrace of individualism away from collectivism evolved as Cartesian thought flourished during the typological era. As Marshall McLuhan noted, "Print is the technology of individualism."[42] Whereas the age of orality consisted of shared verbal narratives with no name of origin attached, the nascent scribal age allowed authors to attach their names to works, and the printing press allowed them to circulate those works widely.[43] The printing press created the cult of the Genius, the idea that works could be disseminated to others to partake of that author's insights, which had now become his or her property.[44] Legal discourse eventually codified this notion of authorship as law in order to preserve it. Indeed, in this tradition, "property" becomes the natural designation for the composition of an autonomous individual.

Contemporary remix culture is analogous to an ideology spawned by the open-source movement of collaborative computer software production in the seventies. Essentially, the ideology is based upon the concept that individuals working together can do a better job than the corporation. Whereas corporations will traditionally use copyright as a means to restrict intrusion on their intellectual property, musicians inspired by open-source ideology want to share their music in order to improve it.[45] These ideas naturally violate the modern metanarrative of the Genius, and the corollary concept of the Masterpiece. For if a genius creates a work of art, who would challenge that singular achievement or assume that it could be improved? After all, open-source ideology suggests that artifacts are considered perpetually unfinished, waiting to evolve through the intervention of other remixers.[46]

Open source is also situated within a discourse that demonstrates the superiority of production over content.[47] Illustrating this primacy, the DJ Danger Mouse once revealed his motivations for creating his famous mashup album *The Grey Album* in this way: "I thought it would be more challenging and more fun and more of a statement on what you could do with sampling alone . . . It is an art form."[48] Danger Mouse's quote suggests that the production process constitutes the art, and the actual content or final output is less important.

Extending this thread, I argue that most mashups and other remix aesthetics are rhetorically appealing because of their production values. Technology allows for an easy yet sophisticated integration of musical beats and melodies. However, the pleasure of consuming a mashup is not contingent only on its aesthetic value; the pleasure is derived from the fact, colloquially, that there are people out there who can *do that*. There is a frequent sense of marveling that comes from hearing a musical mashup between two seemingly incongruous forms of music from artists with reputations and styles as varied as the Beatles and Jay-Z, or Christina Aguilera and the Strokes. Indeed, the appeal of mashups appears to be the fact that someone actually made the mashup in the first place, whether as an ideological affront to the original song or artist, or as an aesthetic affront to a song's original generic style.[49] The song itself is immaterial; what remains in the consciousness of the listener is the practice that yielded the song.

The ideology undergirding the early open-source theories of software holds that a product is never actually finished because it is perpetually changing, inviting others to contribute their own resources to better the product. This same mandate composes the Copy-Left's proposed solution to the intellectual property debate:

there needs to be a legally sanctioned means of sharing ideas freely in order to create conditions for artistic works to build on each other.[50] A digital repository called the Creative Commons is a step toward this ideal. This website allows the user to search for material, whether it be text, video, or audio, that can be shared without fear of legal recourse. In fact, this content is available because its respective creators allowed it to bypass the strictures of current copyright law. Importantly for their cause, because the length of the copyright term is too long, the Creative Commons allows for much of this content to be "changed, customized, remixed" and thus become part of the cache of cultural output available to be used again and again.[51] In sum, the advocacy for a creative commons is a formal codification of the open-source culture into an attempt at social change.

Still, these cultural logics of remix directly challenge modern notions of individuality and genius. Because contemporary law is structured around the modern concept of the genius, a new legal vernacular is needed to discuss the place of a practice so entrenched in the open-source ideology.

The Gutenberg Parenthesis directly provides a starting frame from which remix can be discussed. A knowledge of the distinctions between these eras and their corollary literature is important to my framework for understanding remix culture. This culture is characterized by components that are distinctly post-parenthetical: an increased interaction between the text, producers, and consumers, and a clear fragmentation of once-unified cultural texts.

Participation and Fragmentation in the Digital Age

The Gutenberg Parenthesis schema claims that the post-parenthetical era shares more similarities to its classical antecedent than the era couched within the parentheses. This idea can be extended by appreciating how both eras privilege participation. For example, in oral cultures, a group of people would collectively collaborate on creating its narratives; in the culture of digitality, people likewise collaborate on creating narratives through internet-enabled participation. However, because a clear linkage between the pre- and post-parenthetical eras is not so seamless, comparisons should not be made indiscriminately. For example, while oral narratives were largely unified in form, post-parenthetical narratives are unmistakably fragmented. In other words, the classical era and remix culture overlap in their shared emphasis on participation, and yet depart from each other once remix culture unabashedly embraces fragmentation. Despite this formal discrepancy, cultural artifacts from both eras were/are still considered fluid and open to additions.

Participation

Marshall McLuhan made bold claims about the connection between pre- and post-parenthetical eras long before Pettitt made the same claims. In his own parlance, McLuhan argues that the contemporary historical epoch is a time of return to many of the characteristics of the age of orality. Because of the new global dependence on electronic technologies, for example, the world had returned once again back to its former state as a village, but with technology had become a global village.[52] Speaking as a beneficiary of thirty years of the existence of the browsable internet, McLuhan's innovative speculations seem prescient indeed.

Using his observations about anthropology as support, McLuhan argues that the electronic age instills within us many of the same mental processes as those that originated in primitive society. He illustrates this controversial claim by citing an example of preliterate African natives. Research suggested to McLuhan that the people of these cultures had a difficult time accepting the passive role that audiences are expected to assume when they listen to or watch media. They could not "accept [their] passive consumer role in the presence of film . . . they like[d] to participate."[53] McLuhan argues that these preliterate peoples exemplified a culture that retained a semblance of epistemological purity from the oral era, a culture that insisted wholly on participation and complete narratives.[54] As these examples suggest, the electronic era had shifted human consciousness and thought patterns closer to the premodern oral era than to the modern typographic and mechanical eras. I wish to take McLuhan's formulations about the electronic age one step further (given that they were published in 1962) and apply them to the post-parenthetical era, a time in contemporary culture defined by networked interactions and the digital production and replication of cultural texts. Participation as a characteristic provides inroads into making this application.

Participation is especially apparent in online culture, where remix is a metaphor for the shift in how we engage with information.[55] Participation is both a guiding force and a symptom of the internet's shift from Web 1.0 to Web 2.0. When the internet was initially launched, it was largely a purveyor of information to the consuming public, consisting of static web pages created by companies with corporate interests. In traditional mass media, corporations essentially filtered and then pushed bits of information at the users. News broadcasts would give "top stories," while publishing houses would offer "best sellers." Even in the heyday of Web 1.0, however, Nicholas Negroponte anticipated a dialectical change in information distribution from "push" to "pull."[56] The digital age would enable users to customize and filter the information they received. Though in the early days of the internet, users could choose where they wanted to search for information, they were still limited largely to monolithic websites like AOL or Yahoo to feed them the bits of recent happenings. Because of its potential for customization, Web 2.0 offered an even greater opportunity for "pulling" information.

Web 2.0 is shorthand for a suite of digital media that eases the process of publishing content on the web. As a corollary to its content-publishing capacity, Web 2.0 also demonstrates the tremendous role that participation plays in the contemporary incarnation of the internet. Having been coined in 2004, the term indicates a sea change in the structure of the internet because of its shift in focus from *pages* to *people*.[57] According to this model, the people shape the content of the internet rather than corporate entities. This bottom-up distribution comes from the fact that content has become increasingly user-generated. As evidenced by the enormous popularity of Facebook, Twitter, Reddit, and YouTube, much information is generated by a culture of participation. Accordingly, expertise on the internet is shifting from the voices of a consolidated minority who "earned" it through their own education and training to the hands of the many. Consider Wikipedia. The popular online encyclopedia is an example of what Damien Smith Pfister considers "networked expertise," an emerging phenomenon where a large group of individuals collaboratively create an online entry and thus aggregate multiple perspectives from the periphery into a central node of information.[58] This networked expertise is emblematic of a new shift from older modes of communication. Whereas with traditional mass media, information would be distributed via the "one-to-many" model, Wikipedia illustrates how the participatory culture of the internet offers a "many-to-many" model of communication.[59] Within this new system of expertise, the amateurs are valorized, not the professionals. These amateurs are not the "credentialed" experts, but rather "ordinary people" who write about politics and cultivate cultural controversy by their access to the frontlines of newsworthy events. They "provide a wider range of perspectives and a deeper communal memory that can be brought to bear to analyze, evaluate, and comment on current affairs."[60] Networked expertise is a necessary evolution because the abundance of information in a wired globe far surpasses the abilities of traditional experts to report from the scene as the event is unfolding.[61] These citizen journalists are the "army of Davids," using technology to overpower the Goliath institutions that once governed the internet.[62]

Critics, however, might consider this new communicative model of "many-to-many" to be more an issue of "many-*too*-many." For example, former NBC news anchor Brian Williams argues that the abundance of celebratory voices might drown out more important (and helpfully diverse) voices and ideas.[63] While this critique could be read as a nostalgic pining for older models of expertise, the cultural politics of the medium do demand some skepticism. First, despite the celebrated participatory culture of the internet, there still remains a participation gap separating those who use the internet. Despite the grassroots ethos of YouTube, for instance, certain demographics prevail on the site. The site favors English-speaking populations, as well as those who are technologically competent, let alone those who can afford access to the computers.[64] Thus, Web 2.0 may not be as democratic as it may appear. These "grassroots" sites are still held in check by corporate gatekeepers. YouTube content is owned by Google, Facebook and Instagram content is owned by Facebook, Inc., and these conglomerates have much say in what content is posted and what content is removed.[65] Further, much of the user-generated content is commodified, with an increasing number of ads not only supplementing videos and content, but also becoming the content itself. Large advertising companies have Facebook pages and their ads often earn millions of views on YouTube. If content interferes with the intellectual property of larger corporations, for example, it will almost certainly be removed once it is discovered on these sites. Further, it is theorized that those who actually post content are still a small minority of those who frequent these sites. Jakob Nielsen gauged online participation by his 90-9-1 rule, which posits that in online communities, only one percent of users actually account for most of the contributions. Nine percent of the users contribute from time to time, but a full 90 percent of users are considered "lurkers," those who read or observe but do not contribute.[66] In this way, though participation is at the forefront of contemporary internet culture, it does not guarantee that all who partake of these websites actually contribute and shape their interests.

Despite these criticisms, remix in the digital age can be considered part of an emergent participatory culture. Remix *requires* the participation of the user to alter the original cultural artifact. Though remix has existed for many years, the participatory culture of the internet has facilitated the spread of remix beyond musical boundaries. Web 2.0 encourages an active engagement with cultural texts.

It also amplifies the once-rare possibility for independent fans and artists to place their work alongside other (more officially sanctioned) works.[67] This aggregation afforded by Web 2.0 provides potent opportunities for remix culture—even, perhaps, establishing a tipping point for the role of remixes in public culture.

Remix also highlights a discrepancy between the digital age of creative production and the modern era: the nebulous relationship between producer and consumer. When a mashup is created, the notion of authorship becomes muddled. Whereas inside the parenthesis, creative works were clearly assigned to the "genius" who created them, mashups encourage collective creation and thus no longer bifurcate the producer and consumer. Some have argued that new technologies undermine the producer/consumer dichotomy entirely.[68] With these new practices fostered by recent technologies also comes a need for new terminologies to explain them. Axel Bruns has satisfied this need by coining the compelling term "produsage" to describe the producer/user phenomenon.[69] Within the digital age's participatory culture, users may come to collaborative spaces initially as conventional "users," but then participate in content creation. Thus, the consumer of the content becomes a hybridized producer and user: a "produser."[70] YouTube, as well as remixing software more generally, clearly encourages produsage. It is within the parameters of produsage that we see a clear illustration of Pettitt's post-parenthetical age: a culture that considers property to be shared and yet individual achievement in creation to be recognized.[71] This apparent paradox presents one of the distinctions between the pre-parenthetical age and the post-parenthetical age. Although individualism exists most visibly inside the parenthesis, there are still vestiges of it in the post-parenthesis. Anybody can contribute a mashup in its technological utopia, and yet within online mashup communities there are still "star remixers."[72] Therefore, for all of the democratic potential of the participatory culture of mashups, the specter of genius still haunts the practice.

Fragmentation

The ascendance of remix as a cultural practice reflects a postmodern culture that values fragments and pastiche. Fredric Jameson, perhaps the most prominent theorist of postmodernism and late capitalism, considers pastiche closely related to parody. However, in postmodern cultural production, pastiche has slowly surpassed parody as a dominant productive trope. Pastiche is a representation of the superficiality of postmodern culture, a "blank parody, a statue with blind eyeballs," devoid of the substance, satire, or the humor of traditional parodies.[73]

It is this hollow spirit of pastiche that often characterizes the digital age, an age that is changing so rapidly that it must, by necessity, lack permanence. Part of this perfunctory bias stems from its fragmented nature. The pastiche that characterizes the digital age is a necessary consequence of the internet. While older traditional media like the television, the newspaper, and the radio placed information in a more or less conveniently cogent narrative, the internet's vast repository of information defies unity of narrative.[74] Remix culture privileges associative logics, linkages by congruities, and the showcasing of disparate bits of cultural texts.

This perceived fragmented condition of the internet is perpetuated by the "bits" from digital texts that the audience consumes. Henry Jenkins argues that "Each of us constructs our own personal mythology from bits and fragments of information extracted from the media flow and transformed into resources through which we make sense of our everyday lives."[75] Those bits and fragments of information are gleaned in innocuous ways, from mundane activities like watching television, looking at posters, overhearing comments, and reading the back of cereal boxes.[76] From these "bits," people draw conclusions and create their own personalized meanings. In other words, people try to make "chaos meaningful" by ordering together these bits provided them by the fragmented texts in the media. Therefore, media consumers are essentially remixing the bits of information available to them at any point throughout their lives. This process—facilitated by an internal remix within the boundaries of the mind and influenced by mediated rhetorical information—would seem to suggest that remixing is a natural process: "We cannot help but make meaning by ordering as we scoop up bits, make them cohere, and then move on to the next coherence."[77] Barry Brummett suggests that rhetorical *homologies* are the formal glue that holds these "bits" together in an epistemic mosaic. These homologies are parallels between the content of popular media and the lived experiences of the media consumer. Though the experiences portrayed in popular media and those experienced by the consumer may appear to differ, the consumer may draw linkages between both and thus use that cultural text to make better sense of their real-life problems.[78]

Remix attempts to alleviate the inherent emptiness of pastiche through its use of rhetorical homologies. Not only does remix create transitions linking fragments, it exploits the personal meanings embedded in those fragments. Though it samples only portions of certain songs or videos, it is able to leverage the meanings from the source material that still resonates with the audience. Popular music has a tremendous ability to produce a pleasure of identification within the audience.

This may indicate that music allows the listeners to identify with the artists, with certain social groups, or with their own selves at an earlier time.[79] Certainly because of this potential, songs carry within them intimate meanings that vary depending on the listener. Those meanings are inextricably linked with the songs, and as long as the essence of the original is maintained, those meanings remain even in remixes. Remix's reliance on homology thus reveals one of its rhetorical dimensions.

Similar to the homology, the personal salience of the discourse facilitates the responses to discursive milieus. If they are memorable, discourses can affect our attitudes and become retroactively fitted into our lived experiences.[80] Shortly before Brummett proposed his mosaic model in rhetorical criticism, Michael Calvin McGee pondered the role of fragmentation and rhetorical texts in a mediated society. In that essay, McGee discusses the "fragmentation of culture," a condition that has resulted in the atomization of texts that were once considered discrete "totalizations." A cultural heterogeneity has permeated the formerly homogenous audience of these texts, however, and discourses have grown increasingly interconnected. Thus, the texts have become fragmented and can no longer be considered holistic, harmonious, or finished. In fact, McGee argues that texts can no longer even be considered as such, only "discursive fragments of context"; discourses are synecdoches of the larger texts and contexts within which they are situated.[81] They are reconstructed by audiences that join together fragments of extant discourses. Considering discourses as fragments, then, emphasizes the importance of context: "Discourse ceases to be what it is whenever parts of it are taken 'out of context.'"[82] Discourses gain their unique identities from the contexts within which they were created. Texts are referents for their contexts. For example, Martin Luther King's "I Have a Dream" speech is a discursive fragment formulated in response to the particular context of civil rights and racial inequalities.

Because of these cultural and discursive fragmentations, according to McGee, orators no longer construct the discourses that are subsequently consumed and interpreted by the people. Rather, these roles have switched: Now, "*interpretation* [is] the primary task of speakers and writers and *text construction* [is] the primary task of audiences, readers, and critics."[83] Because of the fragmented discourses that circulate throughout culture, the critic needs to be able to reconstruct the discourses by observing the rhetorical artifacts that are left over. In this way, rhetorical critics are cultural critics; whereas the cultural critic examines artifacts in order to better understand the culture that produced them, rhetorical critics look at fragmented discourses, situate them in their respective contexts, and then isolate the insights that are learned in order to reconstruct the texts that produced them.[84] The tasks of these critics parallel those of the professional DJ; they will become responsible as interpreters of the fragments for providing other missing fragments to formally connect them together.

McGee's claim that the consumers of discourse are now more responsible for its construction than its producers is remarkably prescient. His claim, in fact, has been echoed decades later by scholars of remix culture. Indeed, remix is characterized by its fragmentation and its blurring of the line between producer and consumer. Remixed artifacts are also never considered finished or a "totalization" by any means. Still, despite their ostensible fragmentation, these remixed texts may be considered more holistic than how McGee views discursive fragments. The very fragmentation of the texts allows remix to recombine them into holistic end products. Though this paradoxical notion of "holistic fragmentation" appears to be a postmodern phenomenon, it in fact eschews some of postmodernism's key characteristics. Rather than offering the equivalent of fragmented and free-floating signifiers vis-à-vis the postmodern orientation, remix offers a means of assembling contingently structured texts. In this way, the uniquely recombinatory nature of digital media allows remix to hybridize a postmodern perspective on fragmentation with a modern perspective on holistic narratives.

Influential cultural critic Theodor W. Adorno also provides an important perspective on fragmentation. In his prolific and intimidating corpus of work, it's not only the *content* of his argument that deserves discussion. Rather, his honorary status as academic remix artist comes from his innovative choice of method for making his arguments. His preference for using fragmented discursive form puts him in a crucial place intellectually for framing our discussion on contemporary networked culture.

Adorno's corpus of work demonstrates his rare ability to cognitively remix the thoughts from many different disciplines and then effectively mash them up to become a novel form of theorizing. Adorno's extensive repertoire of knowledge prompted Susan Sontag to famously say, "A volume of Adorno's essays is equivalent to a whole shelf of books on literature."[85] The point to be made here is *how* he synthesizes and presents those insights in new and meaningful ways. In other words, Adorno remixes extant theories and presents them in different contexts. Adorno chronicler Ross Wilson argued that Adorno "was especially attentive to the ways in which . . . literature might be philosophical [and] philosophy might be literary."[86] I would add that he used musical issues to frame most of his views on society.

Adorno and Remix

Adorno condemned pop music as being aesthetically and ideologically sterile. According to the critique, because a pop song is necessarily commercial, it must be standardized in its form to an obscene degree to ensure its fetishization and consumption.[87] However, in a rhetorical sense, this is pop music's greatest asset for DJs. Pop music has a two-pronged utility: its standard form allows for it to be spliced easily into samples and reinserted into other pop songs to create novel mashups. Adorno, in his condemnation of popular music, argued that pop music is victim to a cookie-cutter mentality inherent in its makeup: "It would not affect the musical sense if any detail were taken out of the context . . . The beginning of the chorus is replaceable by the beginning of innumerable other choruses . . . Every detail is substitutable; it serves its function only as a cog in the machine."[88] Adorno, instead, celebrated "serious music," nuanced and lengthy suites of classical music that exhibit notes that are completely interdependent with the piece as a whole. This substitutability of pop music, however, enables its rhetorical function as fodder to be easily sampled. As Kembrew McLeod argues,

> Mash-ups pretty much demonstrate that Theodor Adorno, the notoriously cranky Frankfurt School critic of pop culture, was right about one key point. In arguing for the superiority of European art music, Adorno claimed that pop songs were simplistic and merely made from easily interchangeable, modular components. Yes, Adorno was a snob; but after hearing a half-dozen mash-ups, it is hard to deny that he is right about that particular point.[89]

To illustrate this point, one needs to look no further than a mashup of two popular songs from a decade ago: Justin Bieber's "Baby" and Rebecca Black's "Friday." A YouTube video presents a mashup of both songs layered on top of each other, and the similarities between both are striking.[90] Both songs appear to confirm Adorno's critique of popular music in that each are structurally identical. Both songs even contain a hip-hop interjection in the final third of the song where an obligatory rap break is inserted. This mashup illustrates more than the similarities between both songs, however. It reveals a more sinister dimension of pop music, the tyranny of standardized form. Often, according to Adorno, a song becomes popular, thereby establishing a formula that becomes crystallized over time. Therefore, subsequent songs, if they desire to become popular and, importantly, fetishized by the masses, must follow that formula. It is as Daphne Keller states: "Human culture is always derivative, and music perhaps especially so. New art builds on old art."[91]

Though Adorno's critique of pop music has often been the subject of ridicule, it becomes amplified when applied to the practice of digital remix. In mashup communities, the ability to find two songs that can sound "right" together is important to remix culture, especially in live situations where a DJ more immediately adapts to an audience.[92] Though DJs are lauded for their creativity in finding disparate samples—often from completely incongruous genres—and then mashing them up in novel ways, they are still governed by three important rules for making effective mashups. These entail that (1) the samples must be bound by a unifying beat; (2) the samples should be familiar to the audience (thus emphasizing their allegorical potential and ability to function as a commonplace between the DJ and the audience); and (3) the samples should ideally be drawn from opposing musical genres to enhance the novelty of the remix. David Gunkel proposes a similar assessment of mashups:

> The mash-up constitutes an extreme form of this mechanical substitutability and replication that Adorno attributes to all popular forms of music. In fact, mash-up artists seem to repurpose Adorno's indictment as if it were an instruction manual, deliberately substituting one chorus for another and rearranging details without regard for the original integrity of the whole.[93]

Following Adorno's critique of pop music, remix celebrates that pop music is low culture and that its components are entirely substitutable. However, remix simultaneously confirms Adorno's critique on its own by functioning as "a cog in the machine" of the culture industry via its dependence on the unifying function of the beat to impose order over the chaos of fragmentation in remix.

Remix Both Subverts and Confirms Adorno's Claims

As in pop music, the tyrannical expectations of form can be oppressive, but so can the compositional voice of the DJ. Part of the subversive function of remix is derived from the fact that remix artists may use mashups to playfully make the standardized form of popular music explicit. True as this may be, remixes are still not somehow exempt from the grip of the monolithic culture industry that produced the offending pop music in the first place. The compositional voice of the DJ can become oppressive as well, due to the tyrannical expectations of form. Adorno ably addressed this issue in his study of Richard Wagner. The composer and the conductor (in Wagner's music, at least) function as "the striker of blows," changing the supposedly democratic practice of composition into a form of terrorism: "Democratic considerateness towards the listener is transformed into connivance with the powers of discipline: in the name of the listener, anyone whose feelings accord with any yardstick other than the beat of the music is silenced."[94] Despite the ostensibly democratic practice of digital remix, where anyone with the requisite software is empowered to sample and recontextualize any piece of music he or she wishes, a tyranny of composition still abounds in several ways: the logic of the unifying beat still exerts its power over the production process, the need to sample songs familiar to the audience still governs the selection process, and the need to draw samples from opposing genres governs and restricts the compositional process. As Adorno stated in his original critique, the composer exerts an oppressive viewpoint every time he or she silences that which does not conform to the beat, and this can serve as the impetus for the composition: "The whole of [Wagner's] music seems to have been worked out first in terms of the beat, and then filled in."[95] Despite the ballyhoo that remix is a collaborative enterprise that circumvents the oppression of authorial intent, the logic of the unifying beat still exerts its power over the compositional process, even in remix.

Discursive Dissonance

Though some critics feel otherwise, Adorno is prescriptive as well as descriptive about the ills of aesthetic standardization. As a student of Arnold Schoenberg's twelve-tone technique, Adorno argued that musical dissonance is an antidote of sorts to the listener's quiescence and submission to the culture industry. By listening to art that confronts (rather than evades) dissonance and "terror," the listener can become emancipated from the culture industry by being wrenched from his or her stupor into using active, reasoned contemplation.

Crucially, Adorno not only theorized about musical dissonance, he also performed discursive dissonance in his writing. J. M. Bernstein explains that Adorno believed that the influence of the culture industry was so pervasive that it precluded any useful critique using standard linguistic conventions.[96] Like remix artists,

Adorno used fragmentation in his craft as a form of resistance. Keith Tester has argued that Adorno's objective was more than just to simply obfuscate: "Certainly, Adorno's prose is not easy (but he did not want it to be; if we want easy things we can watch the television), and his answers are difficult to accept. He offers no happy endings (because, for Adorno, if we want happy endings we can go to the movies)."[97] In Adorno's embrace of fragmentation in his arguments and word choice, he is using an innovative method of argument calculated to open up new ways of thinking in his readers.

Adorno's performed fragmentation demonstrates his prescient method of making argument into the networked era. Because of his discursive dissonance, his work need not be read as a linear narrative. In a documentary on Adorno's thought, media scholar Dennis Richmond offered a challenge for approaching Adorno's work:

> Don't pick any place in the text. Just open it up at random . . . find something, read a paragraph, stop. Flip to another page, entirely at random, open it and read that. As strange as it sounds, you will find connections. Adorno wrote it that way. He was thinking about forms, and how, okay, there are these fragments, and they can give us a little chunk of the truth. But then what is that network of fragments? So he's thinking about a counter-systemic totality, as it were. And in a strange kind of way, there's something [in his thought that is] very suggestive about the digital commons.[98]

Adorno's rigorous theories and innovative methods position him as an influential voice of scholarship in remix culture. In fact, this method was influential even during Adorno's lifetime; his Frankfurt School colleague Walter Benjamin used the same mosaic approach in his book *Arcades Project*, which was further emulated in the most notable books by Marshall McLuhan several decades later.

Rhetoric in the Digital Age

Remix is appealing in a clandestine way; it uses the same tools of persuasion that rhetoric has used for centuries. Because the digital age shares so much in common with the pre-parenthetical age—an age when rhetoric was first theorized in earnest—the distance between remix and rhetoric is perhaps not as far as one might imagine. In fact, remix shares a common purpose with rhetoric, which is to attract, focus, and sustain the audience's attention. As such, a rhetorical perspective on remix serves as a valuable complement to other interpretations of the practice.

Rhetoric is an especially useful method for examining issues of the digital age when one considers the overabundance of information created by networked environments. Richard Lanham has argued that living in the information age is akin to drinking from a fire hose: the production of information has completely overwhelmed any feasible attempts of paying attention to it all.[99] In 2002, researchers at Berkeley calculated the total amount of electronic flows of attention to be 17,905,340 terabytes of data.[100] To put a number that staggeringly large into perspective, we might consider that it is the equivalent of all of the information contained in 1.8 million Libraries of Congress. The number has doubtlessly grown exponentially in the decade since the research was conducted; Cisco estimates that 44 zettabytes of data will exist in the world in 2020—a tremendous jump from the 8 zettabytes of data that existed in 2015.[101]

The digital age also amplifies a fundamental shift in the way we interpret and live within the world around us. This information-saturated era could be called the age of "fluff," as Lanham affectionately termed it. This classification is notable for the era it contrasts with, the age of "stuff." In that era, which maps onto the interval represented by Pettitt's parenthesis, "stuff" essentially referred to the physical world surrounding humankind. These tangible things—"the world we stub our foot on"—received the lion's share of human attention.[102] Disciplines like engineering and physical science emerged with the sole purpose of studying "stuff." Anything that was not "stuff" was considered "fluff," which was seen as a sort of ornamentation, devoid of any real importance. *Substance* (stuff), then, was always considered superior to *style* (fluff). This perspective was a product of the modern era; because of the primacy of Humean empiricism as opposed to, say, Ciceronian ideas of style, "stuff" was assigned a prime place in human culture.

This hierarchy was not always firmly in place, however. In the pre-parenthetical era of classical Greece, style was considered to be highly essential for persuading audiences.[103] This high regard was cemented by style's designation as one of the five canons of rhetoric. The canon of style (along with invention, disposition, memory, and delivery) formed the basis of rhetorical pedagogy in classical times. Style was considered essential to speaking effectively in public. However, Plato's Socrates would tarnish this reputation, viewing rhetoric pejoratively as a "knack," much like cooking.[104] In that way, rhetoric was seen as "irrational verbal excess," concerning itself only with appearance rather than deep philosophical questions like the nature of truth, beauty, and justice.[105] What is often forgotten, however, is that rhetoric and dialectic (antecedents of the modern style vs. substance debate) were not discrete and opposing fields. Aristotle bridged the gap through his investigations into the sciences, and even famous sophists like Prodicus, Thrasymachus, Hippius, and Protagoras split their academic allegiances between rhetoric and science.[106] As Cicero would later write, they all "spoke and wrote a great deal at that time about the nature of the physical world."[107] In targeting rhetoric and the sophists of the day that taught it, Socrates (via Plato) initiated a stigma that became unfairly attached to style and rhetoric that would become repeated often.

Though style was rehabilitated somewhat in later years in the works of Roman rhetoricians like Cicero and Quintilian, the stigma was attached anew by Renaissance philosopher Peter Ramus. Ramus stripped the invention and disposition components from the rhetorical canon while he derisively amplified its more ornate components like style and delivery. Ramus's marginalization of rhetoric reified the substance-over-style hierarchy that came to dominate the modern era. Through the nineteenth century, Aristotelian rhetoricians aimed to reintegrate logic into more contemporary definitions of rhetoric. However, a group of scholars called the Elocutionists did not help their cause. These people were dedicated to the task of essentially beautifying speech and were thus lampooned by other academics as belonging to no more than a pseudo-discipline.[108] Despite this, in the early years of the twentieth century, the discipline of rhetoric began a slow rehabilitation due to the work of the Cornell School, a group of humanist scholars determined to carve out a space for rhetoric apart from other disciplines.[109]

Yet, despite the dawning of a new era for the study of rhetoric, the relationship between rhetoric and style remained tenuous throughout the twentieth century. A new perspective on style coalesced with the advent of the digital age, when the age of "stuff" started shifting slowly into the age of "fluff"; stuff suddenly became less important than *information about* stuff.[110] Much as the information contained within books had long been superior to the physical dimensions of books, information in the digital age became more important than the stuff that contained it. And yet, paradoxically, the medium of the internet also became more important than the content as well; Marshall McLuhan's axiom "the medium is the message" is a fitting descriptor of the information age. Though information is increasingly disembodied and therefore renders previous physical containers of information less relevant, the fact that it is disembodied allows that data to be transmitted and archived easily. Thus, the medium becomes the message.[111]

Indeed, information today has become "disembodied," existing in *terra nullius*, a site separated from time and space. Gordon Hull considers this a postmodern algorithmic space where information is only visited by computers and never seen by humans.[112] Thus, representations become more important than actual incarnations. An illustration of this hierarchy of representation over physical object is the increasingly ubiquitous and miraculous world of online banking. In the age of mediated information, we rarely ever see (or hold) any of our income, we only know of its numerical representation. When we are paid, our employer's accounting department directly deposits our money into our online account, thus augmenting the number there. When we pay our bills, we diminish that number by moving it from one online locale to another. Thus, numerical representations surpass the hierarchy over actual physical objects—quite a difference from the time not terribly long ago when citizens were dedicated to stuffing dollar bills into their mattresses. Likewise, symbolic representations become more important (or at least more noticed) than physical objects.[113] Online personas on sites like Facebook illustrate this point, where accurate (or, as the case may be, exaggerated) profiles often receive more attention than the individual in the flesh.

As a consequence of this influx of digital content, the human attention required to notice pertinent information hidden within the deluge of inconsequential information is becoming increasingly scarce. Hull argues that "the growth of disembodied information places an enormous weight on our selection criteria for sorting that information."[114] Lanham tackles the issue this way: "We're drowning in [information]. What we lack is the human attention needed to make sense of it all . . . Attention is the commodity in short supply."[115] In fact, Lanham considers information "raw data" until human attention actually turns it into useful information. Therefore, the digital age has become an economy of attention, where there is a greater need than ever to create cultural products that attract and sustain the precious attention of humans.[116]

In a highly mediated public culture, then, style moves from the margins to the center. The popular site Pinterest illustrates this reemergence of style and aesthetics. The basic premise of the site is to find information online that is interesting to the user, who then "pins" that information to her or his own news feed. Friends of that user then are able to access that pinned information in their own news feeds, and they, in turn, can re-pin it for other friends. Websites like Facebook and iTunes have used similar strategies for garnering attention for years. What makes Pinterest unique is its clear emphasis on aesthetics. The website only allows users to pin images to their pages. Even when users wish to pin inspirational or humorous quotes, they must find an image that contains a visual representation of that quote. Given the surge in popularity of the website (and Facebook's tendency to mimic other successful websites), social network leader Facebook has changed its interface to value images more by minimizing the size of text and enlarging images. This emphasis on images in contemporary internet culture suggests that aesthetics and style are shifting to the forefront of strategies to attract the attention of the public.

In the age of fluff, rhetoric has a renewed centrality. While rhetoric has traditionally been called the art of persuasion, it might now be considered as "the economics of attention." Rhetoricians have implicitly assumed that attention was a scarce resource all along, and therefore rhetorical theory teaches us how to "skillfully allocate" that resource.[117] In Herbert Wichelns's essay "The Literary Criticism of Oratory," the objective of the orator is to move the audience to action (or at least assent).[118] In order to persuade the audience, it must be given options and then be directed to focus its attention on certain choices. Rhetoric has been defined as the "art of using language to help people narrow their choices among specifiable, if not specified, policy options."[119] It invites "people to attend to what we would like them to attend to."[120] It is incumbent upon the orator to harness and direct his or her audience's attention.

This same notion of gathering people's attention is prevalent in cyber-activism. In March of 2012, a wildly popular (and controversial) video went viral on YouTube called "Kony 2012," receiving 84 million views in two weeks. Posted by the group Invisible Children, the video was created in order to draw attention to Ugandan warlord Joseph Kony, who had been abducting children for decades. In the video, the filmmakers exhort the audience to make Kony's name "famous" in the year 2012, so that "American advisers" can help the Ugandan military capture Kony. Incidentally, in the video, the filmmakers interview street artist Shepard Fairey, a man who had become famous for using repetition and ubiquity of street art and stickers to gather attention. In the documentary *Exit through the Gift Shop*, Fairey discusses how "the more stickers that are out there, the more important it seems, [and] the more important it seems, the more people want to know what it is, the more they ask each other, and it gains real power from perceived power."[121] In both instances, repetition and ubiquity allow cultural texts to receive attention exponentially; in Fairey's case, he posted stickers and street art to so many locations that its ubiquity bestowed a perceived power upon it. In the case of the Kony film, social media allows that ubiquity on a global scale and performs the legwork for the filmmakers.

The task of rhetoric parallels the cultural logic of remix: it aims at getting people's attention. In the age of orality, the orator would get people's attention through his or her exquisite vocal delivery and memory. So, how does one acquire people's attention in the digital age? One way might be though style and aesthetics (and often through remix). When DJs choose one sample of music over another, for example, they make a rhetorical choice because they deem one sample to be more appropriate than another. One task of rhetoric is to choose certain linkages between disparate things that the audience had not before considered. The DJ participates in a similar practice, creating linkages between samples, exploiting and leveraging the audience's understanding of the samples in their original contexts in order to create persuasive mashups. Thus, at its core, the practice of remix is extremely rhetorical. Like rhetoric, remix also transmits a certain perspective via the choice of samples (or, in rhetoric, arguments). Though I will provide further evidence of this assertion in the next chapter, it is sufficient at this point for me to say that rhetoric is not only a useful hermeneutic for remix, but for many types of digital texts.

CHAPTER 2

Isocrates and Kairos

Remix in Ancient Greece

The popularity of remix is partially due to the digital technologies of music editing software and video websites like YouTube. Remix, however, is not new, nor is its production exclusive to technology. Contrary to common perception, remix existed long before digital media. As suggested by the figure of the Gutenberg Parenthesis, the notion of remix harkens back to the classical culture of collectivism, re-creation, and performance in cultural production.[1] I argue that the rhetorical theories fostered by that classical era can shed light on contemporary practices of remix. To advance this claim, this chapter crafts a genealogy of remix through the history of classical rhetoric. In earlier chapters, I suggested that there are many similarities between remix and rhetoric; here, I wish to make my earlier argument more robust. Remix *is* rhetoric. As I examine the classical antecedents to remix, it will become more evident that the rhetorical education provided by the sophists thousands of years ago is a useful method for exploring remix today. I will also outline the rhetorical tropes of *kairos* and *imitatio* as tools for understanding remix.

Classical rhetoric and today's digital culture share some surprising similarities. Some of these were discussed in the previous chapter, namely, that rhetoric and contemporary digital media are both concerned with attracting and sustaining the attention of audiences, primarily by using style and aesthetics as vehicles for persuasion. Further, the inventional strategies fostered by remix echo the rhetorical theories of invention from the classical era. Because of these similarities, the rhetorical tradition is useful for examining and understanding digital artifacts. Admittedly, this argument might sound a bit bewildering, for remix and rhetoric appear to be an odd couple. After all, rhetoric is thought of as the art of persuasion. What's more, rhetoric has been traditionally defined as "the art of speaking well," concerned primarily with speech.[2] Remix, in contrast, is considered to be a technological phenomenon involving at least two texts and some sort of technology to blend them together. I argue, however, that rhetoric is not only an appropriate lens for understanding remix, it is particularly useful in isolating both (1) how it can be persuasive as a form of speech and (2) how its aesthetic form (its strategic use of repetition and transitions, for example) can be persuasive as well.

Inserting aesthetics into the mix complicates matters further. How has the relationship between rhetoric and aesthetics traditionally been understood? In the colloquial phrasing of Facebook: "It's complicated." Rhetoric and aesthetics are usually intellectually, and institutionally, separate. Anyone who self-identifies as a rhetorician has traditionally needed to parse out (and perhaps even repudiate) the role of style in rhetoric. Rhetoric, for those in other disciplines, still carries all of the connotations of merely prettifying speech. In outlining the objectives of one such book, a psychologist author reveals that tension in an almost defensive manner: "The present intention is to promote an *argumentative* rhetoric, rather than a rhetoric of adornment."[3] This parsing is not limited to external readings of rhetoric; even the most influential perspectives of the latter half of the twentieth century, from within the discipline, focus primarily on rhetoric's argumentation and role in public address rather than its inherent aesthetic properties. Chaïm Perelman and Lucie Olbrechts-Tyteca coined "the new rhetoric" as an argumentation-centric model. Stephen E. Toulmin, a philosopher and not a rhetorician per se, created a model of argumentation that became highly influential in rhetorical circles.[4] Similarly, Wayne Brockriede wrote that rhetorical critics should structurally emphasize arguments in crafting their critiques.[5] Rhetoric is still highly lauded as a pedagogy of argumentation, but rather downplayed as an art capable of transmitting beauty.

The placing of rhetoric and aesthetics as oppositional poles is, in part, a product of the modern era's framing of rhetoric.

Because of the above factors, speech is often regarded as rhetorical (and not aesthetic). Remix, on the other hand, is rarely (if ever) seen as rhetorical; most of the attention it receives is related to its aesthetic form. However, there are aesthetic and rhetorical dimensions operating in both modes of communication. In this particular case, recognizing the twinned forces of rhetoric and aesthetics—the pragmatic and the beautiful—helps identify how the hypernetworked practice of remix is, in fact, linked to the classical era. Doing so also sheds light on how remix culture can function as a site of persuasion. Here, then, I address the rhetorical dimensions of remix, interspersed with remix's aesthetic properties. I will address the aesthetics of remix in more depth in subsequent chapters. Outlining the rhetorical antecedents of remix sets the stage for the ways that remix parallels rhetoric, thus setting a theoretical frame for the analysis.

Rhetorical Antecedents to Remix

The work of classical rhetoricians overlaps many of the issues of contemporary remix culture, especially how remix can be persuasive. In this way, we can cautiously consider classical philosophers of rhetoric to be proto-remixers, or DJs of the classical age. To make this case, I isolate several parallels between classical rhetoric and remix, many of which can be found in the rich writings of Isocrates. To a lesser extent, Aristotle also contributes some important parallels.

Introducing Isocrates

Isocrates is one of the most important philosophers of rhetoric in the classical era. He lived in Greece from 435 to 338 B.C.E. and was tremendously influential in his day, having established a school for training citizens in the practical art of speaking persuasively.[6] Still, Isocrates has sadly been relegated to a somewhat marginal status in the history books while the work of his contemporaries Plato and Aristotle continues to be valorized. There have been some speculations as to why this is the case. Patricia Bizzell and Bruce Herzberg assert that Isocrates has not attained the same status as other ancient philosophers because he rejected the

Platonic objective of searching for absolute truth. Instead, he was fiercely practical in his pedagogy, emphasizing how his students could address problems relating to government and the physical world (as opposed to Plato's ideal world). This fact is coupled with another that was likely more damning for Isocrates: he is often associated with the sophists.[7]

Because of his choice of career in speech pedagogy, Isocrates was indeed linked to the sophists, and yet he sharply set himself apart from them.[8] His *Against the Sophists*, in fact, attacks sophists as charlatans who speak only to entertain or to flaunt their abilities. He believed that their pursuits of sensationalist effects and feigned morality brought the name of sophist into ill repute: "Who can fail to abhor, yes to contemn, those teachers . . . who devote themselves to disputation, since they pretend to search for truth, but straightway . . . attempt to deceive us with lies?"[9] Further, because they were continually showing off their skills at oratory, they were "damaging their own cause and giving license to their auditors, not to ridicule what they say."[10] To distance himself from the sophists, Isocrates contended that he directed his pedagogy at inspiring others to imitate the examples of other admirable orators and leaders. Incidentally, this distinction for creative imitation is not only crucial for his pedagogy, it illustrates why he might be considered as an exemplar for contemporary remix. He felt so strongly that his legacy would align him with this goal rather than the ignoble pursuits of other sophists that he crafted a defense of himself near the end of his life, *Antidosis*.[11] In it, he boldly argued that he was innocent of any charges that he was "corrupt[ing] young men by teaching them to speak and gain their own advantage in the courts contrary to justice." Rather, he felt that his character should be commended for "inspir[ing youth] to a life of valour and of dangers endured for their country."[12]

Despite his frequently misunderstood affiliations, Isocrates is more important today, as an intellectual progenitor, than ever before. Remix is surely one reason for this. In a McLuhanesque manner, Isocrates anticipated later technologies by being one of the first to use the new technology of writing to publicize his ideas. Indeed, he "never delivered a speech, and few of his discourses were written for delivery . . . [he] has been called the first great publicist of all time."[13] Classical theorist George Norlin notes that Isocrates chose not to address assemblies as an orator, nor to hold public office. Instead, he chose to direct political affairs by writing pamphlets and distributing them to the people. For this reason, Isocrates has even been called the world's first blogger.[14] Perhaps not coincidentally, he has also been associated with being one of the first to use the technique of sampling frequently in his discourses.[15] In light of that link between Isocrates and early technologies of communication, Kathleen Welch argues that we need to understand Isocrates first to better understand writing and digital culture: "We do not now know Isocrates' rhetorical theories well enough, because we have not understood classical Greek rhetoric and writing practices for our electrified time."[16] I respond to that call here by discussing the rhetorical antecedents to remix culture. They are illustrated through the *philosophia* of Isocrates and his practices as they relate to kairos, imitation, and sampling.

Kairos

Isocrates performed and seemingly adumbrated the future practice of remix. In his *Antidosis*, he stated that his text would be composed of his present discussion, but that he'd also insert writings from "the past" because they were pertinent to his discourse.[17] More recently, Girl Talk describes this same process as it relates to DJs: "I have many folders detailing the music [samples], whether it's a melody or a beat or percussion. I kind of have a running list of things where they fit in by tempo, so if I have that bit of Drake or that bit of Willow Smith vocals, and it's at a particular tempo, I can go into this text document and look at it and say, 'Oh, here's the list of melodies that go well here.'"[18] He, like Isocrates, explains the process of taking existing texts and applying them to new texts based on their "appropriateness to the subject at hand."[19]

There is evidence in the trends of Isocratic discourse that it parallels some of the defining philosophies of today's postmodernism.[20] Isocrates favored *kairos*, or good timing, proclaiming "oratory is good only if it has the qualities of fitness for the occasion, propriety of style, and originality of treatment."[21] This validation of particulars challenges Enlightenment beliefs in universal truth, veering instead toward the pluralism of the post-parenthetical era. Rather than subscribing to an all-encompassing Platonic absolutism, which was later characterized by Ronald Arnett as "modernist bravado," Isocrates opted in his oratory to let the context determine the response.[22] Considered many centuries later, Isocratic thought relates to postmodern concepts of situatedness where each situation dictates an appropriate response, thus challenging master narratives that had hitherto been unchallenged.

Kairos is neatly related to the practice of sampling. The Isocratic belief in "fitness for the occasion," for example, permeates contemporary remixes, especially when a DJ searches for an appropriate sample to use in a song. This ability to find two songs that can sound "right" together is important to remix culture, especially in live situations where a DJ more immediately adapts to an audience.[23] Maggi Payne, a composer of electronic music, describes the process this way:

> In terms of recording new works it's so great to work on a project where you build tracks over time, and finally it just builds and builds and builds into this wonderful entity. Then in the process of mixing, everything gets revealed. It's just such an amazing thing to do, to put all these sounds together and work out their juxtapositions and layering.[24]

Sampling, for a DJ, entails that songs become affixed with varying degrees of use-value. Isocrates exemplified the same *kairotic* tendency in his use of discrete and sometimes incongruous discourses to fashion his own. Preferring to label himself a philosopher rather than a sophist, Isocrates explicitly called his brand of prose *philosophia.*[25] Considered atomistically, this *philosophia* was the actualization of many discrete processes and vast in breadth.[26] By compiling the many contexts in which Isocrates used the stems of the word, David Timmerman and Edward Schiappa found that it encompassed rhetoric, philosophy, culture, "training in discourse," and "the art of political discourse." It included the cultivation of the mind, the development of practical wisdom, and the production of civic discourse through ethical means.[27] This description highlights the eclectic pastiche of interdisciplinary commitments Isocrates demonstrated in his writings. In addition to those listed previously, Isocrates's discourses frequently and adeptly combined *encomia*, art, politics, fiction, and history.[28] His disparate interests and ability to interweave them suggests that Isocrates engendered a philosophy of fragmentation and reassembly. In a different context and era, DJs exemplify this ability through their remixing. In describing the remix of Justin Bieber's "Baby" and Slipknot's "Psychosocial," Brøvig-Hanssen described one aspect of kairos:

> [Through] the cultural, ideological, and music-stylistic incongruity of its two contributing tracks, the resulting mashup also reveals a sense of congruity or

> resolution in its experience. Despite their very different stylistic musical languages, the tracks are made to share the same pitch material and tempo, which makes the mashup function harmonically and rhythmically.[29]

The fitting together of these disparate songs exemplifies the ability of a remixer to recognize the kairos of each sample.

The marked contrast between Isocratic kairos and Platonic absolutism illustrates a principal tension that exists between Platonic and Isocratic thought; the kairos embedded in Isocrates's discourses must be viewed as subversive to the influential writings of Plato. More importantly, his pedagogical strategy of focusing on kairos as opposed to universalism predicted some of the debates surrounding remix that would come millennia later. I address the polarity of their positions here because it yields some insight on the contemporary moralizing of remix and its logic of contextual appropriateness.

Isocrates deliberately eschewed the primary philosophical objective of Plato, perhaps because he considered the Platonic search for transcendent truth "almost . . . immoral."[30] If this were the case, it was surely because this transcendental search was not as practical to Isocrates as other endeavors. It may have also been considered immoral because Isocrates and the sophists had entirely different understandings of philosophy from Plato. The Platonic perception of philosophy was that one could correlate logic and moral reasoning, where moral principles needed to be articulated and gleaned from rational dialectics before one acted.[31] In this process, Plato argued, reason needed to be interrogated so that a universal Truth could emerge through that dialectic. In contrast, Isocrates argued that morality was generated in one's conduct and actions rather than from a pursuit of truth. His work "proceeded on the thesis that *doing* right is imperative, regardless of what you think."[32] It was through this argumentation that citizenship—or "honesty of character"—could be taught to the people.[33]

Some theorists attribute other motives to Isocrates for his rejection of Plato's absolutist objectives. Bizzell and Herzberg, for example, argue that Isocrates believed this search for Truth was immoral because such a search would bring social isolation, whereas "the community has an undeniable claim on the philosopher-rhetor."[34] This investment in community is more aligned with the pre- and post- phases of the Gutenberg Parenthesis than the ethos of individualism that permeated modernism. That primacy of community is also important to remix artists, who not only believe in the collective creation inherent in the practice but are also often active in online communities.[35]

Though Isocrates prided himself on the moral influence of his actions, he focused on pragmatism rather than the explicit objective to teach ethics, virtue, and justice.[36] Indeed, this constituted one of his criticisms of sophist orators, because it was a claim that he believed they simply could not fulfill. Isocrates, instead, focused more on strength of character, believing discourse to include external manifestations of internal thought processes; roughly, some things needed to come from within. As such, there were certain issues that could not be learned from masters. Oratory, for instance, was considered a creative art, not something learned through rote instructive techniques.[37] Isocrates considered natural ability to be the primary requisite of a good orator, followed (in order of importance) by practical experience, and, only then, formal training.[38] His understatement of the role of virtue in his teaching anticipates the suppression of modern notions of ethics in contemporary remix culture. As I suggested earlier, mashup logic is more *kairotic* than ethical; the fragment of music that sounds the best with another is the one that gets sampled, irrespective of ownership or ethical issues with its appropriation. Additionally, Isocrates's hierarchy of learning oratory is also echoed in today's remix culture: In mashup communities, good remix artists are judged as such because of their "capacity to hear affinities between seemingly disparate songs, artists, and genres, which requires pluralistic openness to music that has little or no value for professional DJs, music critics, and other individuals who act as intellectuals in popular music cultures."[39] In other words, remix artists are valorized because of their innate abilities to make connections between disparate songs. These abilities are not taught by masters (intellectuals), nor are they learned by practice (professional DJs).

Isocrates has been criticized for other values that we now consider to be postmodern, including relativism. However, his use of relativism differs from much postmodern theorizing about the concept. He did not advocate relativism with the objective of devaluing universal principles; instead, the Isocratic *philosophia* strongly emphasized context. For example, while Platonic thought would contend that one regime of governance would unequivocally be the best for the polis, Isocrates would propose a caveat: whether a regime is good or bad depends on the individuals in power, and how they exercise that power.[40] In that way, Isocrates believed that the context wherein the individual finds him- or herself located would allow the character of that individual to emerge.

Many of the same values that undergird the post-parenthetical era were anticipated by the teachings of Isocrates. No doubt these sophistic values evoked the discomfort and condemnation by Plato, much like the values that were repudiated in the absolutist milieu of the modernists. It should also be stated that, though these values anticipated several of those of postmodernism, Isocratic teachings on kairos, particulars, and situatedness had different objectives and flavors. Whereas postmodernism is largely considered a challenge to modern values, Isocratic teachings were instituted not (explicitly) as ideological statements, but rather as tools in a pedagogy of civic behavior.

Imitation

In order to teach his students what he considered to be their civic duties, Isocrates relied on strategies similar to what we now identify as logics of remix. Imitation was key to this pedagogy. Imitation is often considered to be an aesthetic concept, being associated with art and appearance.[41] The classification of imitation differs by discipline: in Platonic philosophy, imitation is concerned with the actual world striving to imitate the ideal world; in aesthetic philosophy, imitation is used to interpret and portray the actual world by the poet; and in classical rhetoric, imitation guides the student to emulate the skilled orator.[42] Isocrates proposed, "You should listen to the poets and learn from the sages and so equip your mind to judge those who are inferior and to emulate those who are superior to yourself."[43] Like the art of poetics, imitation can be examined using a rhetorical approach to form. Aristotle noted that form is essential in creating aesthetic experiences, both for their beauty and subsequent imitation. Form also extends to the rhythm and meter of language or dance, which can be rhetorical: "for even [the orator or dancer] by the rhythms of his attitudes, may represent men's characters, as well as what they do and suffer."[44] Imitation is natural because, as Aristotle notes, the human is "the most imitative creature in the world, *and learns at first by imitation.* And it is also natural for all to delight in works of imitation."[45] Lloyd Dunn, a member of the mashup artists The Tape-beatles, for instance, appropriated, or imitated, other works in their music in reverence to other artists: "What we want[ed] to do was . . . pay homage to the Beatles and their studio recording experiments in the 1960s."[46] The beholder of the mashup aesthetic draws pleasure not only from its power to imitate but also through its power to teach new perspectives.

Perhaps predictably, the rhetorical doctrine of imitation was shunned during the Romantic era and is still misunderstood as the act of merely repeating or copying existing texts. This misconception stems from the modern ideologies discussed in a previous chapter: If indeed the artist is considered to be a solitary genius, then certainly any form of imitation must be considered a grievous form of theft that turns one's masterpiece into the derivative work of a petty criminal. Because this Romantic perception of imitation necessarily expunges any element of creativity out of the practice, rhetoricians have recently attempted to correct this perception by publishing work that clarifies the dimensions of imitation in its original classical context. Rhetorical theorist Michael Leff distinguishes it, for example, as the product of the intersection between rhetorical production and interpretation. In the classical era of Cicero, the practice of imitation was exemplified through the notion of *imitatio*, the process of reading historical texts and then mining them for insights into inventing persuasive arguments.[47] Because of the preeminence of imitation as a classical pedagogical tool, John Muckelbauer hastens to remind readers that "imitation was the single most common instructional method in the West for well over two millennia." Muckelbauer goes so far as to suggest, in a statement that surely must appear as heretical to some, "Western thought itself might be an imitation."[48] Incidentally, this same thought may be amplified by remix. As mashup artist DJ Adrian explains, the objective of some mashup artists is to make "you realize that all Western music is kind of the same."[49]

From an Isocratic perspective, imitation should be classified as a mechanism of rhetorical invention: "the classical imitative system . . . was perfectly capable of accounting for and even encouraging invention."[50] Classical imitation spurs rhetorical invention primarily in four ways: interpretation, variation, creativity, and novelty.

Interpretation is one key component in distinguishing imitatio from pejorative perceptions of the term. Recall that the *philosophia* of Isocrates could be translated as a form of practical judgment. Judgment is essential to the role of imitation in rhetorical invention: like Aristotelian prudence (and Isocratic kairos), the creative imitation of other orators allowed neophytes to gain experience by isolating what was appropriate for what situation and then using it accordingly: "Rules were general, but rhetorical cases were particular and could not be resolved by theoretical knowledge per se . . . it could show by example what the rules could not tell."[51] Further, the student needed to exercise prudence in selecting the right model to imitate. One of the objectives of imitation is to try to create an exact replica of the model. However, if the model was flawed in some way, the student should have been sufficiently conscientious to avoid imitating the weaknesses, interpreting instead the strengths upon which he or she should focus. Because the particular was far more important than the general to Isocrates, interpretation was a natural element in his pedagogy of imitation.

Imitation is also an inventive practice because it yields variation rather than exact reproduction.[52] This variation is closely related to the students' mandate to conduct research before imitation. Roman rhetorician Quintilian, channeling Isocrates's strategies of imitation, invited students of rhetoric to perform "an investigation of [an author's] good qualities" before imitating them.[53] Because those good qualities could certainly be amplified by the addition of the good qualities of other orators, the student was encouraged to imitate a number of models. In effect, this would create a mashup of the numerous good qualities of multiple model orators. Adaptation by the students also allowed for variation. Because students in the Isocratic school knew the shortcomings of their respective abilities, they were encouraged to select as models those qualities of orators that would best complement their own "natural genius."[54] The variation that emerged from the selective imitation of multiple models allowed for classical imitation to produce inventive discourse in that way.

Creativity also permeated classical imitative practices. In fact, Isocrates viewed imitation as a "creative and productive process," determined by the inventiveness of the speaker.[55] For Isocrates, "The key to developing skilled speakers and sophisticated audiences is to traffic in representative examples of democratic speech and action, and to learn how to use those models adaptively, flexibly, creatively."[56] When taking the variation of differing models into account, the students were able to creatively manipulate the speech to tailor it to their own ends. Knowing which portions of which speeches to imitate required a great amount of knowledge on the part of the students, but knowing how to reassemble those examples together into one unified product required a high level of creativity. Imitating the model became a challenge not to reproduce it identically, but somehow do so differently.[57] In Aristotle's *Poetics*, he argued that a poet must not merely imitate the world around him, but actually make a contribution to that description, concerned with the probability of those events.[58] This same mandate would force the student orators to think in creative ways while assembling their imitations. In the school of Isocrates, "students [had] to not only acquire expertise but also learn to use it according to standards of opportunity, propriety, and originality."[59] This creative component of imitation was so pronounced in Isocrates's teachings that he perceived literal imitations to be the product of a lower-level training—indeed, training from the sophists whom Isocrates despised.[60]

Because of the different levels of skill among the students and the various sources from which they drew their imitative inspiration, a certain level of novelty would inevitably emerge in their final discourses.[61] Ultimately, the success of those imitations would be gauged by their collective novelty, "by the inventiveness of the speaker and the sophistication of the public audience, not by fidelity to the original form."[62] The sophistication of the audience is also important to contemporary remix because DJs need to create commonplaces with the audience. As explained by Adam J. Banks:

> The role of the DJ is richly rhetorical because playing records or reciting rhymes or mastering technologies alone is never enough. The DJ has to know his or her audience enough to know what to say and what to play at all times in real time: what to play to get people to stop standing on the walls and get out on the dance floor, to get them from just dancing and posing on the floor to really enjoying themselves, to break the ice between people who might be glancing at each other, to take the crowd "there" to that ecstatic place where even people who are not on the floor tap into memories, playing in the tensions between familiar associations and new connections, new contexts, and experience the kind of release that sends them home drenched in sweat and the sensory.[63]

Due to that level of novelty and the commonplaces created with the audience, classical imitation did not resemble the Romantic construction of the term that is invoked today.

Because classical imitatio encompasses both traditional notions of imitation and rhetorical invention, it parallels the role of imitation in today's remix culture. Remix is predicated upon imitation; in order to use a song to create a new mashup, the DJ will certainly imitate the artist of the original song. And yet, as in the time of Isocrates, the DJ is not merely repeating the original song, but rather manipulating it sufficiently in order to use it in a new context. Some DJs remix songs sufficiently that they are completely altered into unrecognizable samples. For example, the DJ EL-P confesses, "If you can catch me [using familiar samples] then I haven't done my job. Straight up, it's my fault."[64] When students of rhetoric would imitate multiple orators and converge those examples into their own tailored oratory, "the whole [was] necessarily different from its parts."[65] Likewise, a good mashup will be carefully crafted with many of the same factors in mind as the classical practice of imitation. It will likely contain the DJ's unique voice, despite the fact that the mashup is composed of other songs entirely.[66] It will certainly be novel; after all, novelty is so crucial to mashups that one could not be classified as such unless it was sufficiently novel. Also, when DJs imitate artists by sampling their songs, they often do so to pay homage to that artist.[67] They acknowledge that the sampled artist has created a fantastic original piece, worthy of being used as a sample.[68] This imitation-as-homage model is a contemporary manifestation of Isocratic practices of imitation.

Sampling

Sampling as a musical practice rejects linear order and focuses instead on aesthetic appropriateness. This eschewal is similar to Aristotle's emphasis on fit rather than chronology as outlined in his *Poetics*. Referring to different genres, Aristotle wrote about the primacy of arrangement in the plots of tragedies, stating that the order of a plot should be carefully constructed. Notably, however, he never argued that this art of imitation needed to (or did, by any means) follow a linear or chronological order. Probability became more important in art than chronology. Classical scholar Takis Poulakos explains:

> To be artistic, a sequence of events must be governed by probability: one episode must follow *because* of another, not merely *after* another. Without probability, art loses its essential quality, since it is clear that "a poet's object is not to tell what actually happened but what could and would happen either probably or inevitably."[69]

In line with the Isocratic belief that kairos (not chronology) should dictate how discourse is crafted, probability is essential to musical sampling as well. In remixes, the DJ chooses samples that will fit together naturally in a way that, hopefully, encourages the listener to recognize their congruity. In other words, once a good mashup is created, the listener will appreciate the mashup, in part, because the smooth layering and musical similarities of the source samples emphasize their fit for the mashup. As Joanna Demers writes, "Materials that might have different tempi, rhythms, or keys are mixed in such a way as to make their combination seem necessary, almost inevitable."[70] The Aristotelian objective of probability over chronology, then, offers classical parallels with mashup logic. This same concept is reflected in remix artist Osymyso's claim that "talent is the ability to know what [sample]'s going to work with what."[71]

Isocrates participated in sampling as well, usually in two different ways: through *kairotic* production and amplified aesthetic form. Regarding the former, he considered sampling to be a productive concept, linking it to rhetorical invention: "We should regard that man as the most accomplished in this field who can collect the greatest number of ideas scattered among the thoughts of all the rest and present them in the best form."[72] This quotation validates Welch's claim that Isocrates used an associative (rather than linear) logic in his discourses.[73]

Similar to the practice of sampling in remix, Isocrates suppressed chronological and linear linkages in his discourses. Likewise, musical sampling is usually decided by the use-value of the samples, without regard to copyright violation or other factors. DJs factor in the diversity and sheer volume of samples as they make mashups. Isocrates appears to have brought in samples of other speeches in his own, using what helped him make his particular points. He considered his work to be "mixed discourses," composed of samplings of his own words from previous works as well as the words from others.[74] In *Antidosis*, for example, Isocrates sampled not only his own writings (like his *Hymn to Logos*) but also those of Homer, Thucydides, and Socrates; in fact, it is considered to be essentially a remix of Plato's *Apology*.[75] His rationale for sampling revolved around the appropriateness for the setting. This most important of Isocrates's works was a fictional trial in which he was charged to defend himself. In doing so, he argued that sampling allowed him the easiest route for building his case for himself:

> I am charged with offending by my words, I think that I shall be in a better position to make you see the truth; for I shall present in evidence the actual words which I have spoken and written, so that you will vote upon my discourses, not from conjecture, but with clear knowledge of their nature. I cannot, however, present them all in complete form; for the time which has been allowed me is too short. But just as is done with fruits, I shall try to produce a sample of each kind. For when you have heard a small portion of them you will easily recognize my true character and appreciate the force of all my speeches.[76]

Isocrates's justification is ostensibly utilitarian, yet it presents something more valuable for my purposes: by demonstrating how sampling can be used persuasively, he outlines a template for thinking about the rhetorical dimensions of remix.

In the above explanation of his discourse, Isocrates used samples so that the audience could be aware of only his best and most representative work. In the musical context, this could be considered a contemporary explanation of mashup culture. A song may be sampled because it is representative of an entire genre of music or perhaps a musical movement.[77] Music has a powerful ability to represent emotions and it is perhaps even more effective than language at this purpose. Thus, for a DJ to sample a particular song allows him or her the unique ability to economically cull certain emotions from its audience. Or, the associations may be more than emotional and perhaps are gleaned from the "shared cultural resonance" of certain recordings.[78]

Critical theorists have long condemned pop music as being strictly commercialized, both aesthetically and ideologically.[79] However, because music has such a powerful link to the listener's emotions and memories, a fraction of a song—indeed, sometimes only a few words—is usually sufficient to register those emotions within the listener. Thus, pop music's form allows the DJ to easily evoke the emotions of the audience by simply choosing samples of iconic songs, then mashing them up with other representative samples. In an Isocratic sense, then, the practice of sampling is rhetorical in that the orator pays tribute to other orators by using portions of their original works. Even "a small portion of them," in Isocrates's words, is sufficient to do the trick—as long as they are appropriate for the new context.

The discourse of Isocrates also parallels today's sampling in its amplified aesthetic form, especially its focus on repetition and transitions. First, Isocrates used repetition in his speaking and writing.[80] In several of his discourses he used both verbal and thematic repetition, unapologetically repeating past statements he had used previously (sometimes verbatim).[81] As a rationale, Isocrates explained in *To Philip*:

> And let no one suppose that I desire to conceal the fact that I have in some instances expressed myself in the same manner as upon a former occasion . . . I have preferred not to go through the effort of striving to phrase differently what has already been well expressed.[82]

Repetition in oratory functions rhetorically; it breeds a sense of familiarity in the audience with the ideas being expressed, thus "disarm[ing] readers and render[ing] them receptive."[83] Repetition also functions pedagogically; the orator can employ it with the objective of helping the audience remember and ultimately learn through its recall.[84]

Isocrates's use of verbal repetition demonstrates a range of his rhetorical strategies that mirror current sampling. In a musical context, repetition is key for upholding the structure of the song; through recurring motifs, themes, and lyrics in songs, the song is communicated to the listener as bona fide, complete with beginning, middle, and end. Because repetition is foundational to the genre of pop music, DJs strategically employ it in remixing as well. In the case of samples, DJs often choose to flip the "figure/ground" distinction of a song.[85] In this context, the "figure" refers to the melody of a song, the noticeable (and hummable) tune of the song, while the "ground" refers to the accompaniment to the melody. This might entail the drumbeat used in the background, a looping bass line, or a guitar solo. DJs can strategically isolate parts of the ground of a song and graft them on top of another song's melodies. The point here is that this entails important aesthetic choices for the sample to work. If the DJ wants to make the mashup sound palatable, he or she will use repetition to mimic the structure of pop music.[86] If a figure is to be "demoted" to the ground of another song, it must be looped continually throughout the song in order for it to achieve a semblance of the traditionally steady and constant ground. Thus, the listener can be reminded that the remix is a holistic musical statement like a pop song. The use of repetition in the discourse of Isocrates was surely innovative. Kathleen Welch claims his use of sampling is evidence of Isocrates's germinal role in the rhetoric of the electric age: "Isocrates' ability to write with this kind of abstraction . . . and to incorporate that ability into his theory of rhetoric puts him in a crucial place intellectually."[87]

Second, Isocrates used smoothing transitions in his discourse. As mentioned earlier, his intellectual commitments were in some ways a mashup of the extant knowledge of his day. At times, these fragmented discourses were quite disparate and required a fluency with transitioning in order to make them sound unified. His ease with language betrayed an aptitude for creating beautiful prose and yet still distinguished him from other sophists. Isocrates philosophically distanced himself from the "common herd" of sophists, but he also separated himself stylistically.[88] While the discourses of Gorgias were characterized by stylish manipulation of words and phrases, Isocrates used his discourse in a more holistic manner, subordinating words to a larger unifying force. George Norlin explains that "[Isocrates] is an architect, looking to the effect of the whole edifice, not to that of single bricks or stones."

In employing this holistic perspective, Isocrates paid particular notice to crafting syntactic connections, taking "infinite pains with composition—the smooth joining of part to part," thus creating a pleasurable final discursive product.[89] Though both Gorgian and Isocratic rhetoric used style, Isocrates approximated the patterns of common speech more than Gorgias, who tended to emphasize the poetic in speech.

Holism guided Isocrates's effort throughout. One of his major contributions was considered to be the periodic sentence, a linking of multiple words and phrases that, in lesser hands, would appear to be an ugly conglomeration that disrupted the flow of his arguments. However, these long periodic sentences—often comprising half of a written page—were crafted to a degree that suppressed its fragmentation and amplified its unity: "All the parts of the discourse are rigorously subordinated to the design of an organic whole."[90] Isocrates had the vision to inject artistry into his speech, which was executed through his ability to transition effectively.

The holistic discourses of Isocrates antecede the architecture of remix. A DJ needs to make aesthetic choices in order to aggregate many disparate samples and craft a unified final product larger than the samples contained therein. In this way, the rhetoric of Isocrates had aesthetic similarities to music. In *Evagoras*, he created a genre of discourse called an encomium, which effectively was a hybrid of music and rhetoric, considered the discursive equivalents of hymns.[91] His corpus of work demonstrates that Isocrates was mindful of the rhythms innate in speech, and he produced discourses that were both "imaginative" and "ornate," "giving [to oratory] the same degree of pleasure as is afforded by poetry."[92] Despite this appended aesthetic dimension to his rhetoric, however, this approach detracted somewhat from his overall objective of clarity. The symmetrical "padding" of his periodic sentences, for instance, has been criticized for making his writings unnecessarily prolix.[93] This same problem afflicts remix, exemplifying open-source culture's emphasis on production over content.[94] Though DJs may strive to create smooth transitions between disparate samples, the practice may still detract from the overall content that they produce.

CHAPTER 3

Give Me a Beat

Girl Talk, Kenneth Burke, and Remix Aesthetics

The ominous metal strains of guitars and Ozzy Osbourne's unmistakable vocals greet the ears of the listener. However, this isn't really Black Sabbath. True, it's their song "War Pigs," but it also features the drumbeats, rapping, and vocal refrains of 2-Pac, Jay-Z, JC, and Ludacris—in the first 30 seconds of the song.[1] These snippets of music, taken together, constitute the opening track "Oh No" of Girl Talk's 2010 mashup album *All Day*. The song, like the album, is a conglomeration of disparate samples of music. The majority of these samples are derived from hip hop, with the vocal tracks layered over backing tracks provided from funk, punk, classic rock, and alternative rock. At one point in the song, at about 2:10 in, there are six different samples layered on top of each other and played simultaneously. The curator and mixer of these songs is Gregg Gillis, AKA Girl Talk, who had just turned twenty-nine years old when he released this, his fifth studio album. To be sure, much of what Girl Talk releases contains extremely intriguing musical material. However, his work has traditionally attracted attention primarily because he never asks permission from the artists who write and record the samples he uses.

In this chapter, I continue to examine the idea of remix situated within a network of historical norms. So far I have addressed classical antecedents to remix, as well as modern attitudes regarding the concepts of imitation, property, and the genius. I now move to examining the musical remix and the open-source culture that spawned it. I do so because an examination of how the margins of music are moving to the mainstream reveals how the post-parenthetical era is reverting in some ways back to pre-parenthetical norms.

Remix and Copyright Law

In 2003, a disc jockey named Danger Mouse independently released a collection of songs he called *The Grey Album*; this album proved to be controversial when it gained broader public attention the following year because it employed his deft mixing skills to create a mashup of the rapping of Jay-Z and the music of the Beatles.[2] Throughout the album the listener is treated to Jay-Z's rapping style from his *The Black Album*, laid over a track of fragmented and repeating loops from the Beatles' "The White Album." This album also created a public stir because of the copyright issues that inevitably arose: EMI, the record company that owned the rights to the Beatles' music, quickly demanded that the distribution be stopped.[3] Digital sampling is often viewed as a commercial practice, where the sampling of a short musical phrase may increase the commercial appeal of the song to the public. However, in the case of Danger Mouse, "*The Grey Album* is not a minimalist piece of sampling; on the contrary, it is a maximalist appropriation of the work of the Beatles and Jay-Z."[4] The practice of sampling that entered the mainstream with the creation of this album remains controversial because of its legal implications.

Copyright and Music before Digitality

Remix is based on the belief that songs are always incomplete, thus inspiring the practice of manipulating songs by someone other than the original artist to change, modify, and perhaps improve the original. This perception of music never being complete is historically responsible for generating an early form of remix; some historians of the remix movement place its contemporary genesis in Jamaica with the creation of "dub" in the seventies—long before digital sampling became the choice of remix artists.[5] Dub was created when studio engineer "King Tubby" Ruddock used his Kingston studio equipment to strip the vocals out of a reggae recording and then manipulate the backing track arrangement. Dub could be used to loop parts of the recording to extend the length of the song, or it could be used to equalize the recording levels to different settings, thus changing the sonic qualities of the song. Most importantly, dub anticipated remix culture by enacting the philosophy that music could be considered as "modeling clay rather than copyright property."[6] In using studio equipment to alter the recording of a song into something else, Ruddock had unwittingly started a movement.

In subsequent years, the dub aesthetic migrated stateside to evolve into an early version of hip hop. Remix became an important part of the African American narrative tradition.[7] Musical remixes started garnering attention as they were created by DJs, professional entertainers who would play vinyl records on turntables at dance clubs. This practice of using turntables and mixing the audio together from two different vinyl records was very popular in the dance scene. In seventies-era New York, DJ Kool Herc, a Jamaican expatriate, started creating extended "breaks"—isolated rhythmic instrumental sections of songs—by using two copies of the same vinyl and alternating (or cross-fading) between them in order to draw out these breaks.[8] These breakbeats were essential to early remix culture. As Kool Herc explains, "As long as I kept the beat going with the best parts of those records, everybody would keep dancing. And the culture just evolved from that."[9] Afrika Bambaataa translated this practice into the 1982 recording "Planet Rock," which liberally sampled Kraftwerk. This track and his 1981 release "Jazzy Sensation" have been called the first commercial hip-hop recordings.[10] Remixing and sampling continued in early hip hop, most notably in the works of Public Enemy, De La Soul, and Beastie Boys, artists who all took advantage of an unprecedented "golden age" of hip-hop sampling.

This golden age of sampling was unprecedented because sampling had been legally prosecuted as early as 1956. Songwriters Bill Buchanan and Dickie Goodman released a novelty record that year called "The Flying Saucer," a humorous pastiche of many of the popular recording clips of the day.[11] The record turned out to be tremendously popular and spawned another similarly themed single that same year called "Buchanan and Goodman on Trial," which humorously chronicled some song publishers' objections to the copyright infringement in "The Flying Saucer." This second recording was met with more legal action, though the case was ultimately ruled in the favor of Buchanan and Goodman. In the rationale for the ruling, the judge argued that they had created a parody of the hits and thus had "created a new work."[12] This case anticipated what would later become known in digital sampling litigation as the fair use defense.

Because of the fair use doctrine, Buchanan and Goodman were largely able to escape legal prosecution for their records because the judge ruled that the samples on the record were parodies and thus the creation of new work. The same defense was echoed more than fifty years later by musicians as a justification for their sampling; the fair use doctrine in copyright law is commonly invoked by sampling artists, most notably by Gregg Gillis. Broadly, fair use allows people to use portions of others' copyrighted material in certain circumstances. As an example of fair use, news broadcasts can play brief snippets of copyrighted shows or songs on the basis that those clips are there for educational purposes, for example.[13] Fair use can also be invoked if the work is deemed satirical, educational, or transformative.

Buchanan and Goodman's fair use case preceded what has since been called the "golden age of sampling" of hip-hop music by thirty years, or roughly between 1987 and 1992.[14] This five-year span was labeled as such because hip-hop albums during that time liberally sampled popular music while being largely exempt from legal action. Rappers KRS-ONE, Public Enemy, and Beastie Boys all released albums and songs that heavily sampled others, and yet they were able to fly under the juridical radar because the nascent hip-hop scene was not yet widely regarded as commercially viable. However, as hip-hop albums exploded in popularity in the early nineties, the record labels' response to the practice of sampling became unavoidable.[15] As musicians began to notice that their music was being sampled and making money for other artists, they began enforcing copyright law with a new intensity. Lawsuits against sampling artists De La Soul and Biz Markie, for instance, sent the message that the practice of sampling needed to change: either the (offending) sampling artists could ask permission of the original artist and pay a fee to license the sample, or they could stop sampling altogether.

Creative Responses to Copyright Law

So sampling did change, at least for a time. As remix artists became increasingly savvy about the intricacies of copyright law, their method of extracting and deploying samples would often change to circumvent the law. Their adjustments were surely due to financial necessity, as licensing samples could be extraordinarily expensive. An explanation first requires some legal background: there is some degree of slippage between terms in U.S. copyright code, like "musical works" and "sound recordings."[16] This also means that if artists wish to legally sample other songs that are covered by copyright law, they need to obtain licenses for both the musical composition and the sound recording.[17] The musical composition copyright covers the mechanics of the song—meaning the chords, lyrics, and the melodies—while the sound-recording copyright relates to the actual performance of that song by the artists that was recorded and captured.[18] Because copyright law entails that each song be protected twice, an artist or label can request a substantial amount of money for an artist to sample a particular song. Further, the process for securing a license to sample a song can be lengthy.

As a response to the recording industry's sample clearance system, rather than surrender the option to create samples (and thus compromise their hip-hop ethos and brand of creativity), some sampling artists found ways to resist the system. For instance, some started using a strategy called "replays," where artists would find a sample they liked, record a new version of the sample in the studio, and then incorporate that sample into their music. In this way, they would only need to obtain the musical composition (master use) license to use the sample.[19]

Another way remix artists would try to resist the sample clearance system would be through a type of pseudo-sampling—samples that would try to obtain the aesthetic effect of sampling without actually sampling any other recordings. One group called Portishead recorded themselves onto a vinyl record and then had their DJ play that sample off records and scratch it on their recording.[20] In this way, they were able to provide a mimic of a sample and all without actually violating any copyright laws.[21] These practices demonstrate that their resistance to the regulation of the musical industry spawned some of their aesthetic innovations.[22] Indeed, remix artists often use this practice, but not always as a self-preservation strategy against copyright violations; often, the sampling artist will use technology to change the pitch, tempo, or playback of the original piece of music in order to make it nearly unrecognizable.

These creative responses to possible copyright litigation reflected a larger change in sampling. No one has resurrected the "Wild West" ethos of digital sampling better than Gregg Gillis. In 2001—nine years after the alleged golden age of hip-hop sampling ended—twenty-one-year-old Gillis released his first album, *Secret Diary*, under the stage name Girl Talk. Girl Talk's mashups used songs that used samples of music often for only seconds before a new one would appear, culminating in a mashup album of hundreds of samples. Since his first release, Girl Talk has released five more "official" albums, garnered a firestorm of critical attention and academic articles, and even incited one film director's call for a more robust open-source culture, which is "a visible example of a type of creativity, of innovation, which has been around for a very long time, but which has reached new salience on the Internet."[23] Perhaps surprisingly, the legal response to Girl Talk's mashups has mirrored the legal permissiveness of the golden age of sampling; none of Gillis's releases have incurred any lawsuits. Instead, his albums have been "allowed to float along in a lawsuit-free zone, a tacit endorsement of sorts from the major labels."[24] And with each release his popularity has continued to grow; after he released his album *All Day* as a free download online in November 2010, the servers on the hosting website crashed from the sheer amount of downloads.[25] A city councilman in Gillis's hometown of Pittsburgh even declared December 7, 2010, "Gregg Gillis Day."[26] This amount of attention and acclaim for one who remixes samples from songs without the artists' consent is shocking, given the monikers that hip-hop artists Biz Markie and De La Soul received after they had lost their cases just two decades earlier: thieves.

Despite the ongoing debate over copyright and intellectual property, I now move beyond the questions regarding copyright to understand the persuasive capabilities of remix. To evince remix's shrouded rhetoricity, we have to recognize that remix is more complicated than the sum of ethical assessments about the practice. Gillis's music provides a representative anecdote of the rhetorical potential of mashup aesthetics. In the analysis of some of Girl Talk's mashups that follows, then, I will identify rhetorical and aesthetic components of each. Considering remix as profoundly rhetorical (rather than in exclusively legal terms) changes how we see the copyright debate.

Girl Talk

For good or ill, Gregg Gillis's musical alter ego Girl Talk seems to be mentioned by everybody. Because Gillis does not seek or receive permission for the music he samples, he is often treated in copyright discourse as a synecdoche of the more widespread epidemic of unauthorized musical sampling. Conversely, copy-right-reform activists celebrate Gillis for his bold approach to creating music.

Kembrew McLeod and Peter DiCola, clearly fans of Gillis's work, choose to open their book *Creative License* by discussing his 2008 album *Feed the Animals*, which they herald as "part parlor game, part dance party soundtrack, and part love letter to four decades of popular music."[27] Released in 2010, Girl Talk's *All Day* continues the dance-fueled mayhem that propelled the success of his previous releases. As representative of remix culture, his mashups are, by their very nature, incongruous with copyright culture: "The cultural practice of sampling meshes very poorly with copyright."[28] None of the Girl Talk releases have acquired permission to use the sampled material because Gillis has not sought to do so. Because it appears his goal is to "recontextualize famous songs," his works are a work of arrangement rather than invention.[29] Thus, Gillis walks "the boundary between copyright theft and fair use," in part because legally sanctioned samples—those borrowed with the consent of the copyright owner—can cost a lot of money. Because Girl Talk's releases generally use three to four hundred samples, obtaining the rights for each of those could potentially cost him tens of millions of dollars.[30] In fact, if the most groundbreaking sampling albums of the nineties—Public Enemy's *Fear of a Black Planet* and Beastie Boys' *Paul's Boutique*—were to have acquired the rights to all of the samples they used, they would have had $6.7 million and $19.8 million in losses respectively.[31] With Girl Talk, then, the aesthetics of the mashup albums become paramount to legal considerations.

I turn now toward the aesthetic dimensions of Girl Talk's releases and their corollary rhetorical potential. The (remixed) words and theories of Kenneth Burke provide a framework for addressing these dimensions, effectively reconceptualizing them for their use in a digital context.

Digital Invention and Form

Despite Kenneth Burke's uneasiness with technology, there is a common thread between his intellectual passions and remix: aesthetics. Burke was a musician and, in fact, worked as a music critic for a time in his youth.[32] He also wrote extensively about art and form, particularly in his early work. Burke's unique appreciation of aesthetics, rhetoric, and culture makes him an appealing, if unlikely, muse. Indeed, the Burkean predisposition to see the interconnectedness of aesthetics, rhetoric, and culture provides a readily remixable template for analysis. His work on form is indicative here.

Form was crucial to Burke in his writings. In *Permanence and Change* and in *Attitudes toward History*, he argues that form is as important in uncovering human motives as it is to art. As an example, Burke uses poetic devices—like the literary genres of comedy, mystery, and tragedy—to explain the psychology of the brain and how it "equips itself to name and confront its situation."[33] In *Counter-Statement*, Burke essentially equates an aesthetic experience to a rhetorical experience: it is immediate, individual, and emotional.[34] Form is considered profoundly psychological in that it can affect the mindset of the audience. Form, then, is one of the bridges connecting rhetoric and aesthetics in Burke's writings. Form also provides inroads in this analysis, for the rhetorical critic must be "grounded in an awareness of form and pattern."[35]

Form is particularly important to the mashups of Girl Talk. The congruity of musical form in Girl Talk's mashups brings his use of digital invention to the fore. Two important elements of digital invention underscore the rhetorical properties of mashup aesthetics: novelty and surprise.

Novelty

Historically, novelty has functioned as a key component of rhetorical and aesthetic invention.[36] In the rhetorical context, orators aim at surprising the audience through the novelty of their arguments. By using these innovative strategies, the orator can more easily traverse the ultimate objectives of speech: "to enlighten the understanding, to please the imagination, to move the passions, [and] or to influence the will" of the audience.[37] Enlightenment-era philosopher George Campbell equated novelty and surprise with an orator's wit, writing that a speech done properly will "excite in the mind an agreeable surprise, and that arising, not from any thing marvelous in the subject, but solely from the imagery she employs, or *the strange assemblage of related ideas* presented to the mind."[38] Still, paradoxically, the orator's wit appeals to bodily instincts as well—the faculties for humor and emotion. Hardwired into the ideas of the novelty and surprise of rhetorical invention is the potential for intellectual satisfaction it offers the audience. Sometimes, the wit of the orator may even provoke a spontaneous exhibition of laughter. While Campbell downplays humor as necessarily inferior to true wit, it is certainly linked to moving the passions of an audience.

Also notable in Campbell's envisioning of effective rhetoric is his statement that the audience will be delighted by the "strange assemblage of related ideas" presented by the orator. Certainly this statement can find purchase in the practice of remix. Though Campbell was outlining the place of novelty in effective speech in this statement, the literal application of these words to remix showcases how the practice sees novelty as essential to its persuasive ends. What is a mashup other than a "strange assemblage of related ideas"? It is incumbent upon a remix artist to find a surprising cache of samples to mash up in a novel way. Though the attached samples may indeed sound strange, they were initially congruous enough to be mashed up together. In fact, if the congruity of the ostensibly disparate samples is sufficiently amplified by the mashup, the passions of the audience may be revealed in the form of laughter, much like the witty orator of Campbell's theorizing. The "contextual incongruity" of samples often seems humorous because they seem to fit together despite their clashing origins.[39] The [in]congruous mashups of Girl Talk, linked together by a relentless beat, certainly display a level of playfulness. It is in Girl Talk's "strange assemblage of ideas" that his mashups demonstrate his effective use of novelty.

Girl Talk's mashups also demonstrate a craft refined vis-à-vis a continued interaction with his audience from live shows. The Renaissance philosopher of rhetoric Giambattista Vico offered a perspective on invention similar to this interaction, focusing specifically on the process of creating a *sensus communis* (common ground) with the audience. Like George Campbell, Vico also associated rhetorical invention with wit, called *acutezze*. In the Baroque tradition, from which Vico based his concept of wit, *acutezze* meant "combining two apparently dissimilar things into a metaphor that highlighted a heretofore unnoticed similarity."[40] This dissonance is based upon Aristotle's concept of a proportional metaphor, a variety of *gnomai* ("witty sayings") used by the orator to make difficult concepts easier to understand. For our purposes, the most germane aspect of this instructional technique of the proportional metaphor is its embrace of disparate ideas and its ability to reconcile them. The proportional metaphor, as a display of the orator's wit, functioned to smooth out the jagged edges of contrasting terms. Moreover, the technique "became more highly prized as the terms of the proportion were more seemingly discordant."[41] The Baroque tradition dictated that this Aristotelian idea should be used in order to demonstrate a novelty of argument, as well as impress the audience: "The beholder or reader considered first how anyone could have thought of such a comparison, and then (if it were a successful conceit) how he could have missed it. This experience, said the poets and the critics, constituted aesthetic truth."[42] In short, Vico's use of *acutezze* culled ostensibly incongruous fragments (seeing these, Aristotle's proportional metaphor would cry out "the more different the better!") and then stitched them together. Using this rhetorical orientation as an analytic lens, Girl Talk demonstrates his "wit" and effective use of rhetorical invention every time he performs a mashup that uses seemingly incompatible samples. But his aesthetic deployment of novel connections as a commonplace with his audience is not the only component that reveals the underlying rhetoric of his mashups; Girl Talk effectively harnesses the element of surprise in his work as well.

Surprise

In a musical context, remix leverages the meaning of old songs to create new songs. Thus, sampled songs function persuasively because of their explicit use of the enthymeme. Remix acts as a bridge between the *old* and the *new*, referencing something old and re-dressing it as something new. Its success in bridging the old and new together, however, is contingent on the remix artist's ability to capitalize on the familiarity of the songs being sampled. As Kembrew McLeod argues, this need for referentiality limits the creative scope of mashups: "Because they depend on the recognizability of the original, mash-ups are circumscribed to a relatively narrow repertoire of Top 40 pop songs."[43] To avoid an inevitable trap of overfamiliarity, the best DJs deploy the element of surprise when mashing up those recognizable samples. This entails that he or she strive to defy the expectations of the listener. When done effectively, the DJ's performance can have a visceral impact on the audience. Bill Brewster and Frank Broughton describe such a performance in this way: "What would be served up on a particular night depended on any number of variants. He could shock you. He could thrill you. He could amaze you. He could even appall you. The only certainty was that he would surprise you."[44]

As a component of rhetorical invention, surprise evokes emotions within its audience. Surprise, as a corollary to suspense, appends a psychological dimension to aesthetic form. When the artist creates a work, according to Burke, the audience's emotions may become connected to that work: "[The artist] is the manipulator of blood, brains, heart, and bowels which, while we sleep, dictate the mould of our desires." Artistic form is the vehicle for that artist to dictate the audience's desires, usually by exploiting the audience's "ignorance of the outcome."[45] Leonard Meyer, writing about the emotional potential of music, likewise argues that music invokes emotion when a portion of the composition diverges from, or defies, the listener's expectations.[46] Girl Talk's mashups certainly defy expectations. Whether one is listening to a live performance or "studio" album, it is virtually impossible to predict which songs Gillis will sample. His mashups employ the element of surprise by using an array of samples in no particular or logical order, which subsequently elicits an emotional response from the audience. This response is brought forth by a layering of samples that pair up familiar songs, which function rhetorically via their allegorical nature. Girl Talk uses invention in his mashups, then, for both cerebral and emotional ends, using its potential for surprise and novelty to create a pleasurable text.

Remixing Rhetoric

Rhetorical theorist Kenneth Burke once wrote that "all living things are critics." He was arguing that all living organisms constantly interpret the signs and symbols that surround them and then subsequently formulate judgments. To illustrate, Burke gave an example of how a freshwater trout, snipping at a hook and yet having the "good luck to escape with a rip in his jaw, may even show by his wiliness thereafter that he can revise his critical appraisals."[47] Over time, that trout becomes more educated at reading the signs and making informed judgments. This same capacity to judge, however, can reap negative consequences as well. Chickens, for example, can be educated to eat from the hand of their owner every time a bell rings. But when the owner uses that same bell to recruit chickens to chop off their heads, they come just as eagerly. Humans, too, have a great ability to reason and make critical judgments. But with their larger capacity to find solutions comes a larger range of problems. For instance, Burke argued, they might mistake their power of abstraction for reality and consequently instigate wars. Still, the ability to interpret and judge (that is, to be a critic) is as ubiquitous as humanity.

The context of the digital age gives critics an opportunity to reconsider Burke's statement that "all living things are critics." It is my contention that there is a parallel between Burke's point about criticism and the practice of remix. The ubiquity of new, internetworked digital technologies allows remixing to take place on an unprecedented scale. In fact, it is progressively easier to remix now, given that some internet applications allow users to remix for free simply by clicking and dragging their mouse.[48]

However, remixing is not simply a technological process; it's a human one. Even scholarship, to a degree, is remix. Like Newton's dictum states, we learn by standing on the shoulders of giants. We take their thoughts and arguments, mash them up in novel ways, and then use them as a foundation for our own scholarly creations. And yet, there also needs to be a caution in asserting "everything is remix." Like Burke's chicken that runs to both the dinner bell and the slaughter bell, our abilities to reason dictate our reactions to remix, often in misleading or harmful ways. Rather than "standing on the shoulders of giants," critics often frame remix as "stepping on the toes of giants." Copyright law and the intellectual property debate weigh heavily on this perspective. Many advocates of remix, on the other hand, extol the virtues of the practice and paint it with the broad strokes colored by cyber-utopianism. This latter contingent believes that remix is the only way to liberate youth culture from enslavement by oppressive copyright law.[49] My intent is neither to glorify nor vilify the practice of remix—at least in the same way it is usually addressed in scholarship. Rather, my purpose is to explicate it. Our understandings of remix benefit not from considering it as ethically right or wrong, but from seeing it as a nuanced and evolving phenomenon that is not likely to go away anytime soon. In the following section, Kenneth Burke's provocative writings on rhetoric will be helpful for the purpose of explicating remix.

For those who are familiar with Burke, the very idea of using his theories to examine digital media would likely be viewed as a sort of comical mistake. During his life, Burke was notoriously opposed to the relentless march of technology and called himself an "anti-technologist."[50] When he was first married in his early twenties, he abandoned living in New York City in favor of living out in the country in New Jersey. For the next four decades, he lived with his family in a house with no running water (and, in fact, no electricity for three of those decades).[51] Despite his knowledge of a dazzling number of things, his oeuvre was not always abreast of the latest innovations in technology. Indeed, his works were fraught with anxiety over technology.[52] He considered technology mainly a vice, a "counter-nature" to humankind.[53] Technology, to Burke, needed capable hands to control it and curb its destructive potential (or at least to rally an "organized distrust" of it).[54] In short, his writings on the topic are generally antagonistic.[55] For this reason, conventional wisdom suggests that Burke's theories would not be the best framework to use in discussing the complexities of remix. However, by remixing Burkean theory, I intend to dynamically update his work and make it flexible enough to interpret digital artifacts. By utilizing his theoretical ideas as guides into the rhetorical nature of remix, I aim to present his work in a more contemporary light. In other words, I wish to decontextualize Burke but reserve the essence of some of his theories, and then redeploy him in a manner more suitable to the digital age.

Perspective by Incongruity

Girl Talk's albums exhibit the strategic mashing up of incongruous musical genres in order to create a congruous mashup.[56] This logic of digital conversion is rooted in a rhetorical process, described in depth by Burke, called "perspective by incongruity."[57] However, there are notable differences in Burke's theoretical orientation and its application to the context of remix. Therefore, I alter "perspective by incongruity" to become "perspective by *congruity*" when applied to remix. I later remix "exorcism by misnomer" into its digital counterpart "*possession* by misnomer." The following discussion of Burkean resonances of perspective by incongruity in the mashups of Girl Talk is particularly useful because of the radical context: "One sees perspectives beyond the structure of a given vocabulary when that structure is no longer firm."[58] The true heuristic value of this Burkean concept becomes apparent when it is applied to the mashup. As mashups collapse the distinctions between traditional music and sampling, they also offer a broader perspective of the structure of remix culture.

Perspective by incongruity performs a variety of rhetorical defamiliarization. Rhetoric and language can sometimes shock individuals out of their routines and into thinking about certain issues in new ways. This is important because humans often fall into a "trained incapacity," where they become accustomed to specific ways of seeing the world. These worldviews can be detrimental in that they cause people "to misjudge their present situation."[59] This incapacity can be directly related to the vocabulary that one uses; humans will typically identify with groups, and the vocabulary indigenous to that group will articulate the understandings of their motives: "[A motive] is a term of interpretation, and being such it will naturally take its place within the framework of our *Weltanschauung* [worldview] as a whole." In order to be freed from that singular worldview, the speaker needs to be linguistically innovative: "different frameworks of interpretation will lead to different conclusions as to what reality is."[60] To achieve that level of novelty, the speaker will either invent new terms or use old ones in new ways. Perspective by incongruity entails that texts be repurposed to match other contexts and thus defamiliarize the intended audience into perhaps adopting new perspectives. This move toward defamiliarization is analogous to Girl Talk's task to create mashups that surprise because of their novel connections.

Though rhetoric and poetry have marked contrasts, the primacy of paradox provides a bridge between both.[61] It is paradox in language that provides novelty of argument as well, by surprising the listener through the use of strategic incongruity. In the understanding of digital invention that I have been advancing in this chapter, novelty and surprise are exhibited through the DJ's use of planned incongruities. However, these incongruities are only part of the rhetorical potential of mashups; *congruities* also foster the rhetorical process.[62]

Perspective by Congruity

Writing about perspective taking, Burke argued that each time humans adopt a way of seeing, they are also adapting to a way of *not* seeing: "A focus upon object A involves a neglect of object B."[63] Similarly, in *A Rhetoric of Motives*, Burke speaks of identification as a dialectical phenomenon. An act of inclusion can simultaneously be an act of division. When one group uses language to define the parameters of inclusion in that group, that same language necessarily excludes those who do not meet those parameters.[64] However, the ordering of the Burkean binary of *inclusion/exclusion* flips once it is applied to remix culture—instead of inclusion being the positively valenced side with exclusion as an unfortunate consequence, exclusion takes precedence. When remix artists sample musical excerpts, the more clash in the genres from which the samples originate, the better the mashup. Rather than the deconstructive "atom cracking" that incongruous perspectives offer toward analyzing human motives, remix becomes a means of "atom fusion," or the transformation of incongruous elements into a congruous whole.[65]

Rhetorically, while perspective by incongruity entails wrenching individuals out of old perspectives by emphasizing ostensibly incompatible terms, the remix-activated *perspective by congruity* allows potential dissonance or clash to exist in the source material, but it attempts to supersede these incongruities through its consonant framing of samples. Indeed, perspective by congruity actually redefines dissonance as something no longer painful, but rather considered pleasurable instead. Paradoxically, for perspective by congruity to function effectively, it needs to exploit the former clashing status of the sampled materials and yet explicitly demonstrate their new status as matching. Thus, the remix artist displays the true transformation of the samples through their consonant interaction with each other when layered together. In other words, with perspective by congruity, the creative process continues to be essential, but the consonant layering of the samples in the final product—the content of the remix—overshadows the production process.

Perspective by congruity can also be appreciated as an aesthetic strategy. Remix artist DJ Earworm illustrates in his description of originality in remix: "[Stylistic originality can reside] in the way that [DJs] think about words, or maybe the interplay of the words. You might recognize it in the song choices. The relationships between the songs. Some people prefer ironic relationships. Some people like puns, you know. Some people just want to have genre clash."[66] Pithily summarizing DJ Earworm's insights, Aram Sinnreich wrote, "the *relationship between source materials* is the primary locus of stylistic originality for mash-ups."[67] Thus it is for perspective by congruity. By using clashing genres as source material and implementing transitions and layering as smoothing techniques between those contrasting generic samples, remix artists demonstrate digital invention at work when they illustrate just how similar opposites can be. Therefore, the aesthetics of the remix play a part in its rhetorical potency.

Girl Talk's mashup "In Step," from his 2008 album *Feed the Animals*, is an example of perspective by congruity. In this mashup, Girl Talk deftly creates a mélange of congruous samples from a diverse group of incongruous musical genres. At the beginning of the mashup, Roy Orbison's classic rock song "You Got It" is overlaid with rapper Drama's "Left Right Left." One of Girl Talk's most effective samples begins shortly thereafter when Salt-N-Pepa's hip-hop hit "Push It" is sampled over the top of Nirvana's grunge anthem "Lithium" right after the iconic break in Deee-Lite's pop "Groove Is in the Heart." Ludacris raps during Fergie's "Glamorous," while Earth, Wind & Fire's "September" provides the instrumental backing, and INXS's "Need You Tonight" and Kraftwerk's "Tour de France" provide the rhythm—all at the same time. The song concludes with one of the most critically revered rock songs of all time, the Beach Boys' "God Only Knows," while one of the rap fragments from Ludacris's "Glamorous" plays over the top.[68] This massive pastiche of samples takes place in a little less than three and a half minutes. This mashup is a master class in perspective by congruity, illustrating how these clashing songs can be made to not only sound structurally congruent, but harmonious as well.

Another Girl Talk mashup that illustrates perspective by congruity is track 5 from *All Day*, "This Is the Remix."[69] The mashup begins with the iconic record-scratching effect from Herbie Hancock's "Rockit," while Mr. Cheeks raps "this is the remix." However, the perspective by congruity begins to take place shortly afterward, when Bananarama's eighties hit "Cruel Summer" is featured prominently along with Justin

Timberlake, Lady Gaga, and Diddy-Dirty Money on top. Certainly, the incongruities of the songs stem from the decades in which they were released, but each is tied together by their shared embrace of the genre of pop. Appropriately, an interlude from Genesis's eighties smash "Tonight, Tonight, Tonight" follows, then Lil' Kim and Snoop Dogg's drum beats (featured in different songs) are sampled over the top of The Jackson 5's bass-driven "I Want You Back." And yet, surprisingly, the seventies R&B standard transitions (with the help of Beastie Boys and a few others) into the Toadies' nineties grunge rocker "Possum Kingdom." After a full minute and a half of Toadies (a veritable lifetime in the frenetic sampling world of Girl Talk), the closing strains of distorted guitar seamlessly segue into the pseudo-tribal rhythms of Simon and Garfunkel's "Cecilia." But where the a cappella singalong break of "Cecilia" takes place, the drums are replaced by the rhythms from the introduction of U2's "Sunday Bloody Sunday." The match between both songs is so congruent that once Simon and Garfunkel's beat returns, the beats of both songs still overlap perfectly. Also functioning as binding glue here is "Get Low" by Lil Jon and the East Side Boyz (feat. Ying Yang Twins), which offers vocal exclamations across the multiple samples, ensuring that the listener still is able to make the transition comfortably along with the mashup. In the next ten seconds, the mashup moves from Grateful Dead's psychedelic rock of "Casey Jones" directly into INXS's new wave sensation "Need You Tonight." Again, the transition is made possible by Gillis's immaculate layering; while one song transitions into another, the ongoing layers of other samples ostensibly bridge the musical gap. In the closing seconds of the mashup, INXS's groove is supplemented by the "sneeze" yell that signifies The Clash's "Should I Stay or Should I Go," along with some LL Cool J thrown in for good measure. "This Is the Remix," indeed.

These representative mashups indicate that few of these samples exist in any definable or predictable system; they are as disparate as Gillis's taste for music is eclectic. Indeed, many of the samples that play concurrently originated from opposing genres. Still, when they are mashed up in such a manner, there is no question that they belong together. This apparently self-evident perception comes from the rhetorical potency of such a mashup. When clashing artists and genres are layered together in a congruous way, the clash is still apparent at an abstract level, but the listener can simultaneously oscillate from one to another when the DJ reframes its incongruities as congruities.

Exorcism by Misnomer

While discussing perspective by incongruity, Burke coined the term "exorcism by misnomer." This is a transformational technique that demonstrates the power of misnaming something. To gain some context, Burke was conceptualizing perspective by incongruity in the context of psychoanalysis when he began referring to exorcism by misnomer. (Notably, he also continued his discursive remixing performance by using a religious-cum-secular term "exorcism" to name this idea.) In psychoanalysis, there is never a shortage of diagnoses for afflictions, but those "weighted" diseases may also stigmatize the patient and frame the disease as incurable. To circumvent that weightedness and offer relief, Burke suggests that those diagnoses can receive a "downward conversion" from threatening to treatable by calling them something that they are not. By so doing, those diseases appear perhaps more curable by altering relevant perspectives of patients and doctors.

Applied to rhetoric, exorcism by misnomer delegitimizes some rhetorical artifact by calling it exactly what it is not. One of Burke's examples of exorcism by misnomer is particularly instructive: A child is terrified by a monster in the corner of his room, but his mother comes in his room and reassures the boy that the monster is really only a pile of old coats. Therefore, she "exorcizes the demon" by calling it something else. This powerful discursive act creates a "downward conversion," stripping the monster of its power to terrify by calling it old coats: "One casts out demons by a vocabulary of *conversion*, by an *incongruous* naming, by calling them *the very thing in all the world they are not*: old coats."[70] At the core of the process—we're talking about Burke here, remember—is the human motive to explicitly attempt to reduce the status of the artifact. Exorcism by misnomer has that power. Burke argues that in naming something, it illustrates how one feels about a thing. As an example, if one calls someone a villain, then he or she is evil. The opposite is true when someone calls another a hero.[71] The name of something changes attitudes, and changing attitudes leads to changing behaviors. Thus, by misnaming a thing, one exorcises its demons.

Possession by Misnomer

There is an important subset of perspective by congruity. This subset, which I call *possession by misnomer*, is creative, innovative, and able to function as a tool of social critique. Possession by misnomer is a valuable critical tool because it complicates our ideological understandings of the text through remix. Much as Burke used "exorcism by misnomer" as a subset of perspective by incongruity, so is possession by misnomer a subset of perspective by congruity. Unlike Burke's exorcism by misnomer, however, the musical equivalent in remix propels the act beyond the process of exorcism. Burke called "exorcism by misnomer" rhetorical because the act of misnaming something had the power of ridding that thing of its power. This process of downward conversion entailed something once considered pious or exalted becoming secularized—converted to a lower status—by calling it something else. Possession by misnomer presents the obverse, in which the new name bestowed on the thing being debunked gains a new power of its own by virtue of the association. Therefore, continuing Burke's example from earlier, exorcism by misnomer happens when the mother of the frightened child calls the "monster" in the shadows of the dark room only a pile of old coats. However, possession by misnomer is also interested in how "old coats" can suddenly become something interesting by its new association with the erstwhile "monster." Put simply, the conversion downward for the monster is also a conversion upward for the old coats. In remix, the ideological exorcism of the original source clears the way for a new possession to take place and a subsequent reconsideration of the sample that now possesses its place.

Possession by misnomer takes place frequently in the mashups of Girl Talk. Revisiting "In Step" can help illustrate the concept. For example, pairing the one-hit-wonder rapper Drama with legendary rock 'n' roll pioneer Roy Orbison on his song "You Got It" is a bold decision. Salt-N-Pepa's "Push It" over Nirvana's "Lithium" is a sampling masterwork, but still not as subversive as debunking Nirvana's critically acclaimed mystique or Kurt Cobain's alternative rock legacy. Finally, placing Ludacris over Brian Wilson and the Beach Boys' hyper-influential and beautiful "God Only Knows" is tantamount to heresy. And yet, importantly, none of these spliced pairings exist in aesthetic conflict with each other. They are placed in a musical space where their congruities make the mashups succeed.

Though the concept of authorial intent has fallen out of common practice when critically explicating cultural texts, against all odds it remains germane to discussions of post-parenthetical phenomena like mashups. Gillis has hinted at the deliberate embedding of something resembling possession by misnomer in his work:

> Pop music or music from different genres seems untouchable, you know Elton John seems untouchable. Obviously, they create that, and they make . . . they force that idea in your mind that these people are superstars, they're untouchable. So just being able to just manipulate and do whatever you want [like put] Elton John in a headlock, and just you know put a beat behind him and pour a beer on his head.[72]

Aesthetically speaking, these deliberate heresies have their purposes. In part, they are analogous to the functions of avant-garde art in that each of them questions the arbitrary classifications of art. Moreover—and more importantly to our digital age of information superabundance—these texts vie for our attention. A good remix has this function; it blurs the division between the critically revered (relative to rock 'n' roll) Beach Boys, Nirvana, and Roy Orbison with Ludacris, Salt-N-Pepa, and Drama respectively.[73] Possession by misnomer may shock critics into questioning the pedestals that they have constructed for these artists.

A mashup by remix artist Mighty Mike offers another demonstration of the process of possession by misnomer. In "Imagine a Jump," Mighty Mike samples the vocal track of Van Halen's "Jump," and layers it on top of the musical track to John Lennon's "Imagine."[74] For those who are familiar with each song, the pairing seems inexplicable. Both songs are familiar, even iconic, yet each song is taken from an opposing genre: "Jump" is eighties-era hair metal; "Imagine" is protest rock. At first blush, the listener only sees the incongruity between the songs. However, the mashup actually sounds *good*; the reason that it works so well as a mashup is because the tempo, beat, key, and pitch of both songs, when combined together, are all congruent.[75] This musical exemplar puts forth three instructive rules for making the most effective mashups: (1) Use unifying beats and keys; (2) Use familiar songs with high allegorical potential; and (3) Draw on opposing genres as resources for their samples. However, the aesthetic congruity is not the only notable aspect of the mashup; the manipulation of the "weightedness" and cultural connotations of each artist by the mashup demonstrates the rhetorical utility of possession by misnomer.

To fully understand the rhetorical dimension of "Imagine a Jump," one must first have a basic understanding of each of the songs being sampled. In other words, the allegorical potential of "Imagine a Jump" is key to its rhetorical function. John Lennon's "Imagine" has become sacrosanct, a paean to his efforts at promoting peace during his lifetime. Lennon worked hard to cultivate the ethos of a pacifist in his post-Beatles years, and "Imagine" is a powerful plea for world peace. The song also doubles as his swan song, essentially evoking the tragedy of his death. Perhaps for these reasons, "Imagine" is critically adored, considered recently by *Rolling Stone* magazine as the third greatest song of all time.[76] Former U.S. president Jimmy Carter even considered the song impactful on an international scale, remarking in an interview that "Imagine" functions similarly to a national anthem for some countries of the world.[77] The poignant song evinces tragedy while aspiring for world peace. In distinct contrast to the noble aspirations of "Imagine," however, the ethos of Van Halen in "Jump" is derived from hedonism. The innocuous metal pop song is simply about having fun and being spontaneous. Because of these differences, and due to the allegorical potential of remix, the juxtaposition of each of these songs in the mashup is heresy of the highest order to rock cognoscenti. This repulsion is essential, however, for possession by misnomer to take place.

As in "Imagine a Jump," possession by misnomer changes a prevalent orientation by allowing other ideologies to possess the remixed texts. Possession by misnomer not only removes (exorcises) whatever cultural connotations exist in the source material, it introduces new ones, most of which will be quite opposite to the source. This possession can either completely replace the original or create an incongruous synthesis of both. Because of the congruity of these songs, and the choice of the remix artist to mash them up, it debunks the reverence of "Imagine" and its concomitant implied respect for Lennon. It also strips the song of its idealistic ideology regarding world peace. By contrast, it valorizes Van Halen by using their most famous song as the sample to replace the lyrics of "Imagine." It injects the whisky-soaked signifiers of Van Halen and "Jump" into "Imagine," thus changing the original message. Enacting the cultural logic of remix, it took the DJ-as-rhetor to make this congruity between the songs apparent. To be truly transformative, a mashup needs to make a novel pairing of seemingly incongruous samples and surprise its audience with how similar they can be.

Possession by misnomer, however, is not only useful in its ability to knock down the reputation of classic songs a few notches. Amplifying the arbitrariness of musical classification is only part of its rhetorical function. Its capability to extract and withdraw ēthē can also be applied to other media, as illustrated in "Right Wing Radio Duck," or applied to scholarship, where the author's arguments can be manipulated and mashed up with contrasting arguments to debunk one or validate another. As such, this method can be useful for social protest. The choices of candidate or policy by the dissenting group will likely garner attention and status by its perceived ubiquity and association with its remixed counterpart.[78]

The operative term in this definition is "perceived." Possession by misnomer, as subsidiary to perspective by congruity, grabs our attention. This fact, given the concept of rhetoric for the digital age that I've been advancing in this book, deserves further reflection. Recall the Lanhamian argument that contemporary rhetorical texts are the ones that can grab and sustain one's attention. The perspective by congruity engendered in these texts is rhetorical because these texts vie for our attention. But this fact is not exclusive to the aesthetic choices of the DJ, however; it can call attention to other issues like the structure and ideologies in social controversies. As mentioned, remix is not only a productive art, it is a tool for amplifying congruities in incongruous texts. When applied to other contexts, the same result can occur as in a musical mashup.

Perspective by congruity can be a productive analytic when expanded to realms beyond music as well. As an interpretive lens used in critiquing advertising, for example, perspective by congruity can evince important insights about advertising's gendered dimensions. The Gendered Advertising Remixer is an example of this potential. Jonathan McIntosh, the self-designated "pop culture hacker" who created "Right Wing Donald Duck," created the Gendered Advertising Remixer to "help empower youth of all genders to better understand, deconstruct and creatively take control of the highly gendered messages emanating from their television sets."[79] To assist in this effort, the website allows the user to take preexisting toy commercials that are aimed at youth, and use a free drag-and-drop remixer embedded right into the website, to recombine the audio of commercials aimed at girls and the video of commercials aimed at boys, for example. By participating in the remix process, the user can see the gendered element of advertising directed toward children amplified.

The potency of perspective by congruity as a tool of social critique suggests a few points similar to the argument I have advanced thus far regarding the aesthetics of Girl Talk's mashups. First, like Girl Talk's strategic congruities, the Gendered Advertising Remixer attracts the viewer's attention. Because of the incongruous combination of audio and video, it directs attention to the standardized structure of the ads. In fact, because of the formulaic nature of the samples, they align almost perfectly; there are traveling, building, and narrative points that occur simultaneously in both clips. Second, the remix reveals sharp differences between ads aimed at boys and girls. Their juxtaposition amplifies how different they are (even while maintaining virtually the same narrative structure), thus revealing the gendered dimension of children's advertising today. Girl Talk's mashups function similarly, evincing key identifying characteristics of the genres from which the samples were taken. For example, the rapped lyrics sampled tend to be profane and hypersexualized; the pop music tends to be unified by the systematic use of catchy and melodic hooks; the rock 'n' roll samples betray a strong guitar presence; the hip-hop samples display the importance of beats. Thus, reminiscent of Burke's argument, the connecting traits of the genres sampled not only provide a unifying generic identification, but also a sharp division away from other clashing genres. Third, the Gendered Advertising Remixer reveals how playful social critique can be when it is performed with remix. It is a humorous, instructional experience that also teaches important insights about the nature of advertising. Girl Talk's mashups are playful through their use of generic clash, and act as a master class to aspiring remixers about the nature of digital sampling. Finally, the interface of the Gendered Advertising Remixer demonstrates how remix is getting progressively easier to do as barriers become lowered. There is no previous remix experience or knowledge required to perform the remix; it is as simple as clicking a button. In fact, even the video "Right Wing Radio Duck" demonstrates how easy it is to remix on YouTube. When the user visits the video clip, he or she may notice that to the bottom-left of the clip, there is a button labeled "Remix this video!" Upon clicking it, the user is taken to a new page similar to video-editing software. On this page, videos can be edited and spliced en route to making a new mashup. Perspective by congruity is most apparent in remix via mashup aesthetics, but it can be observed and used in other contexts as well.

The Rhetoric of Girl Talk's Mashups

In his writings, Kenneth Burke observes the constitutive power of rhetoric in creating worldviews. Groups adapt shared understandings about certain relationships, which, in turn, are reflected by their own realities. Other groups have different interpretations, and thus create other salient relationships, which create their respective realities.

> Our minds, as linguistic products, are composed of concepts (verbally molded) which select certain relationships as meaningful. Other groups may select other

relationships as meaningful. These relationships are not *realities*, they are *interpretations* of reality—hence different frameworks of interpretation will lead to different conclusions as to what reality is.[80]

Burke goes on to say that once a group ascribes meaning to these relationships, it either invents new terms to understand it, or manipulates old terms in new ways to describe the relationship and finally legitimize them with the others.[81] Importantly, Girl Talk's mashups also follow the rhetorical logic of Burke's argument, thus posing an intervention into the copyright debate.

In his mashups, Gillis creates "meaningful relationships" between multiple musical samples. In the process of selection and mashing up, he deftly uses the unique affordances of digital media to create a "strange assemblage of related ideas," which translates into a novel mashup.[82] This task surely has an aesthetic dimension, but Girl Talk's choices also carry the rhetorical imperative of communicating a worldview to an identifiable group, one of copyright reform. The rhetorical potency expands beyond copyright reform advocates as the circumference widens to anyone else who listens to his mashups. In other words, Girl Talk's aesthetic choices are rhetorical in that they reorient the attention of the audience away from legal questions surrounding the practice to aesthetic questions surrounding the congruity of the mashups. By so doing, his mashups shift the terms of the debate away from "stealing" to the creative juxtapositioning that characterizes the mashups.

Here's how the process works. When Girl Talk uses perspective by congruity, he not only persuades the audience that the clashing songs belong together, he does so through their congruity, thus erasing the dissonance embedded in the very idea of sampling. In some ways, Girl Talk's use of aesthetic means to a rhetorical end is similar to mine in this chapter. Much as I have spent the majority of my discussion on issues other than the staid questions regarding the legality of remix, Girl Talk's mashups focus on the neglected aesthetic dimensions of the remix and deflect the audience away from legal considerations. This strategy is reminiscent of a model of argumentation in which the orator is responsible for using language in a way to create a version of reality that will support whichever arguments he or she is constructing. Provocatively, Kenneth Burke described this process as such: "Even if any terminology is a *reflection* of reality, by its very nature as a terminology it must be a *selection* of reality; and to this extent it must also function as a *deflection* of reality."[83] Orators select from a wide array of arguments in their inventional process to reflect reality as they select it (or desire the audience to see it), while choosing which aspects to deflect away from the audience's collective consciousness. Thus, the orator's task of using this *dissuasive* function of argumentative discourse is to move the audience to accept certain ideas while rejecting others as unacceptable.[84] The outsized aesthetics of Girl Talk's mashups suggest a rhetorical purpose similar to this.

This shift in orientation is best examined through the parallels of classical rhetoric with the philosophy of digital remix. This model of appropriateness over ethics is endemic to pre- and post-parenthetical norms. This model of selecting samples rooted in their "due appropriateness to the [mashup] at hand" is a post-parenthetical application of the classical Isocratic notion of kairos.[85] Gillis's selection of samples is based on their aesthetic appropriateness for the overall mashup, without explicit regard to potential ethical or legal issues. However, the *kairotic* imperative of selecting samples based on their appropriateness for a mashup presents a disjunction between kairos and the generic clash of the source materials: strictly based on their origins, these samples were never really considered that appropriate to be paired in the first place. However, the belief that all materials are available for the benefit of art, culled from the open-source ideology of the post-parenthetical era, presents the challenge to make something beautiful and unified out of something disjunctive. Thus, despite the apparent disconnect for the kairotic belief in appropriateness and the clashing genres of the music, Girl Talk samples the sources anyway. Once the mashup is complete, it prominently exhibits the elements of novelty and surprise to enhance the rhetorical function of the aesthetics in the mashup. Girl Talk's mashup, facilitated by his process of digital invention, ultimately performs its rhetorical function of sublimating the ethical issues into its transcendent aesthetic presentation via its use of perspective by congruity. Moreover, Girl Talk's effective use of possession by misnomer solidifies his aesthetic intervention into the copyright debate. When he debunks great songs and converts them downwards from their previously exalted status as closed intellectual property, the process aims to help the audience shift its attention away from the modernist concept of property. Instead, the hedonism of disposable pop propelled by infectious beats is converted upward into the place previously held by the discussion on property. Thus, in a Burkean sense, Girl Talk's use of linkages and relationships between samples creates this interpretation of reality.

The process also depends on rhetorical tropes. Girl Talk's effective use of kairos, novelty, surprise, and perspective by congruity reveals some characteristics about the nature of remix culture. Recall that the codified language of liberalism—a universalist moral vocabulary that originated with Kant's categorical imperative—is now largely at odds with the practices of the post-parenthetical era. Remix culture indicates that there needs to be a new understanding of appropriateness when it comes to post-parenthetical practices. Whether that refers to the Aristotelian mandate of prudence or the Isocratic notion of kairos remains a matter of debate. However, by focusing on the aesthetics of the remix—its kairos, smooth transitions, unifying beat, and other elements leading to its perspective by congruity—there is something happening in public culture larger than judgment about whether a mashup is aesthetically beautiful or acceptable. This shift relates to the rhetoric of inventional choices superseding legal or ethical considerations that are embedded in the very idea of the Western liberal tradition. This post-parenthetical shift toward digital invention focuses accountability more on the agency of the digital software than the scene of remix artists being interpellated into the state and corresponding legal system. The modern language of the debate and the open-source practices of remix culture continue to grow further apart.

The application of Kenneth Burke's lexicon to the mashups of Girl Talk (and the subsequent rhetorical tropes that emerge as a result) demonstrates a few ways that remix can be rhetorical. I have argued that the debate about remix needs to shift away from its legal implications to its occluded rhetorical potential. In this case study, the rhetorical potential of remix is revealed via the aesthetic dimensions of Girl Talk's mashups. In his successful employment of appropriateness, novelty, surprise, perspective by congruity, kairos, and possession by misnomer, Girl Talk is shifting the debate away from legality to aesthetics. In short, his mashups do the work for him.

Conclusion

In this chapter, I have used the mashup albums of Girl Talk as a representative anecdote of both open-source culture and the adaptation process of aesthetics to a postmodern digital age. In doing so, I used the rhetorical tropes of "perspective by congruity" and "possession by misnomer" as tools for providing insight into these phenomena. There certainly are other groups that operate within the same orientations as Girl Talk and perhaps even exemplify the competing tensions in remix more clearly than he. However, it is my hope that this chapter has at least offered a hypothetical stone upon which we can step in our quest to traverse the murky waters of remix and rhetoric.

CHAPTER 4

Epaesthetic Rhetoric

Remix and Auto-Tune on YouTube

In late July 2010, an attempted rape happened in Lincoln Park, a housing project complex in Huntsville, Alabama. Kelly Dodson had been sleeping in her second-story room when a man allegedly broke in and tried to sexually assault her. Hearing Kelly's scream, her brother Antoine was able to rush in and try to fend off the intruder, but the man escaped. The next day, reporter Elizabeth Gentle and news cameras from Huntsville's WAFF-TV arrived in Lincoln Park to report on the crime. As they briefly filmed Kelly telling portions of what had happened, Antoine, "with a mixture of anger, defiance and flamboyance," decried the crime.[1] Staring defiantly at the camera, he declared:

> Well, *obviously* we have a rapist in Lincoln Park. He's climbing in your windows, he's snatching your people up, trying to rape them, so you all need to hide your kids, hide your wife and hide your husband, 'cause they're raping everybody out here.[2]

The intruder also left "evidence of his visit"; the story cuts back to Antoine, who speaks directly to the perpetrator: "We got your t-shirt, you done left behind fingerprints and all, you are so dumb, you are really dumb, for real . . . you don't have to come and confess that you did it. We're looking for you, we—we're going to find you. I'm letting you know now. So you can run and tell that, homeboy."[3] Explaining Dodson's passionate delivery, WAFF's news anchor Mark Thornhill introduced the story with "emotions were running high."

To be sure, Dodson's delivery of his warning was impassioned. So impassioned, in fact, that it attracted the attention of Michael Gregory, the resident composer of the Gregory Brothers, a Brooklyn-based group of musicians best-known (then) for their web channel "Auto Tune the News." The group, consisting of Michael and his brothers Andrew, Evan, and Evan's wife Sarah, *auto-tuned* the newscast into the clip "Bed Intruder Song."[4] This video was featured as part of their YouTube channel, which took notable and often-controversial news stories (usually commentary by talking heads or rants made by members of Congress or the Senate) and juxtaposed them with banal or bizarre news stories. "Bed Intruder Song" was an immensely popular online phenomenon, becoming the most-watched YouTube video for 2010.[5] That popularity continues, as it is approaching 150 million views as of this writing. It was also released as a hip-hop single, cracking the Billboard Hot 100 chart that same month and moving up to number 16 on iTunes's pop charts and number 3 on iTunes's R&B chart.[6] The Gregory Brothers shared these profits with Dodson; in an interview with *CBS News Sunday Morning*'s David Pogue, Michael explained, "Yeah, we went 50–50 [with Dodson] just like co-writers would go . . . [he was] the unintentional lyricist."[7] Elaborating further in another interview, Michael Gregory said:

> We're really breaking "unintentional singing" ground, so we're trying to set precedents by making it so that Antoine, or whoever that artist might be in the future, has a stake not only as an artist but as a co-author of the song. It's like you said: He wrote the lyrics, he's the one who put it out there. What we're doing on iTunes and on any other sales, we're splitting the revenue after it gets through Apple down the middle.[8]

Given these earnings and other revenue for merchandise Dodson sold on T-shirts (with the catchphrase "Hide Yo' Kids, Hide Yo' Wife" emblazoned on the front), he was able to move his family out of the projects and into a new house.[9] Despite his crucial role in providing the raw material with which the Gregory Brothers could work, it was their technological manipulation of speech into music that facilitated the movement of his rant into the center of public culture.

The Gregory Brothers, called "some pranksters in New York" by the *Washington Post*'s Philip Kennicott shortly after the video went viral, make their living by using technology to alter the spoken word into sounding like song.[10] This practice—called "auto-tune"—was originally developed to use in the recording studio to manipulate singers' voices to stay on pitch. This practice has also notably been used as an aesthetic embellishment in music as well; Cher's 1998 mega-hit "Believe" famously used auto-tune to manipulate the sound of her voice, for example. However, the Gregory Brothers use the same technology to alter the spoken word and vocal inflections into their corresponding musical notes. They then lay a backing track of chords and rhythm on top of the auto-tuned delivery, and the transformation from oratory into song is complete. Presumably because they use the technology for something other than auto-tune's original function, they have come to call the practice "songifying." This process was described by Richard Lanham in this way: "Now anyone can take sounds from alien context, translate them on the screen into their visual equivalents, and stretch and bend them at will. Such bending and sampling, long a staple of electronic musical composition, is rapidly becoming part of everyday expression."[11]

Online video is an important component of remix culture. Discussions of remix often neglect to mention remix in a nonmusical context, yet YouTube is a thriving locus of remix and digital culture. In fact, Axel Bruns argues that the user's propensity to remix is part of the innate appeal of the medium: "YouTube . . . provides an excellent opportunity to trace the emergence and development of cultural memes from the initial, notorious video clip to a host of mashups, parodies [and] reinterpretations."[12] Auto-tune contributes another component to remix culture apart from the better-known remix techniques like sampling and mashups. A rhetorical perspective recognizes how auto-tune capitalizes on the once-nebulous distinction between music and speech. This concept has long been articulated in the works of Isocrates and Aristotle up through modern experimental artists like John Cage.[13] Auto-tune is a natural tool for remixing the human voice because the spoken language has an inherent musical quality and rhythm or meter to it that auto-tune amplifies.[14]

To be sure, the process of auto-tune is highly creative, and the Gregory Brothers (also known as "schmoyoho," a YouTube channel with over three million subscribers) are the best-known auto-tuners in the world thanks to their online presence. Despite this popularity (or, more accurately, because of this popularity), their videos have long fallen under the cloud of controversy. The *Washington Post*'s

Philip Kennicott, for example, was not amused by "Bed Intruder Song," entitling his piece "Auto-Tune Turns the Operatic Ideal into a Shoddy Joke," which included calling the video itself "[a] man's anguish, digitally altered to amuse you."[15] He's not too far off the mark, given that Michael Gregory said in an interview with the *New York Times*, "Mostly we started doing the videos because it amused us."[16] Though Michael never specifically linked that comment with "Bed Intruder Song," his brother Evan later defended their choice of source material in an interview on *CBS News*. Interviewer David Pogue posed a question to them about those people providing the responses that were ultimately auto-tuned: "Aren't we mocking their unsophistication?" Evan responded, "We're not making a judgment on whether a person is kind of low class or high class or making a fool of themselves or, or, or not, but a lot of those interesting turns of phrases that are memorable and make a musical hook come from unusual situations."[17] Certainly the Gregory Brothers have insulated themselves against accusations of discrimination against the people in their source-material videos in several ways, including the fact that they split their profits with those people in the videos.

Still, their choice of source material presents troubling issues regarding the politics of representation. There are complex power relations involved when white artists remix videos (and thus appropriate narratives) of African Americans speaking about trauma. Amber Johnson, for example, argues that this video "appropriates a stereotype that denies [Dodson's identity] authenticity by reducing it to coonery."[18] This is all the more disturbing because the overwhelming reception of the auto-tune as comedy inhibited progress on the investigation of the actual event; once the auto-tune of Dodson's news footage went viral, "Social commentary ceased asking about the rapist, and regarded the incident with nonchalance."[19] The video may also be considered an illustration of a systemic issue; some scholars have argued that racial stereotyping and discrimination are "part of the architecture and language of technology."[20] For the above reasons and more, "Bed Intruder Song" has been the subject of much scholarly criticism.[21]

The Gregory Brothers have created other troubling auto-tunes as well. In "Backing Up Song," for example, a white woman who witnessed a convenience store robbery recounts the ordeal in perhaps the catchiest of their auto-tunes.[22] In "Sunny D and Rum," a white woman sings a new song that she "just thought of," an ode to drinking Sunny Delight mixed with rum.[23] In another popular video, "Winning—A Song by Charlie Sheen," the eponymous celebrity reveals his egotistical, meandering philosophies about fame and drugs. The common thread connecting all these videos is spectacle. Certainly, most of those people in the auto-tunes do speak with a degree of passion and thus provide easy fodder to be auto-tuned. But other issues abound in the selection of those auto-tuned—issues of race, class, and mental illness. The question about race is ever-present in videos like "Bed Intruder Song" and "Dead Giveaway." It is a matter of debate if any of these individuals being auto-tuned are struggling with their mental health. Class, however, seems to be an important component of the spectacle. The woman in "Sunny D and Rum," for example, appears to be obese and is missing multiple teeth. Dodson and his sister are living in the projects. Charlie Sheen, while certainly the wealthiest of any of those in the clips by far, is a cautionary representation of the hedonistic excesses of fame and the debilitating effects of drug use. Thus, troubling issues emerge from each of these videos. Ultimately, though, these horrors are circumnavigated by another type of aesthetic: the structure of song. The *oscillatio* trope inherent in remix allows the beauty and the horror to exist simultaneously, thus providing the requisite conditions for the sublime.

In this this chapter I will focus primarily on the aesthetics of the "Bed Intruder" video, grounding the discussion in rhetoric and the philosophy of art. To that end, most of the following analysis will explore the aesthetic concept of "the sublime" in the post-parenthetical era. First, however, I discuss what Richard Lanham considers to be the dominant trope of contemporary digital culture: *oscillatio.*

There is a rhetorical trope, rooted in both avant-garde art and technological processes, called *oscillatio*. The term was coined by Richard Lanham in his 2008 book *The Economics of Attention*, though he used the same idea in an earlier book, 1993's *The Electronic Word.* Oscillatio refers to the process of moving back and forth from one thing to another: mostly, between looking *at* something and looking *through* something. A simple example of this process would be the reader of a book oscillating between looking at the font and spacing of the typed words on the page and comprehending the ideas and narratives expressed by those words.

This process of oscillation is essential to understanding digital media and its associated attention economy. Explaining, Lanham argues that the digital age has evolved attention structures from "stuff" to "thinking about stuff." Ephemeral information systems have shifted into taking precedence over the material artifacts of the physical world. The individual has become privy to these new digital norms and can therefore accept that oppositional aesthetic processes can exist simultaneously: "climax and anticlimax, repetition for emphasis, parenthetical enclosures to establish special spaces, and puns to compress dissimilar worlds of meaning

. . . At the center of the pun is oscillation, bi-stability."[24] Oscillatio means that these binaries can exist without collapsing into each other.

The savvy individual develops the oscillatory capability by understanding that meaning at multiple levels can occur simultaneously. For example, literate individuals generally look at print not to appreciate its typography, but rather to read it, to attempt to comprehend the message expressed in the words. Lanham explains this attitude: "Print should be like a crystal goblet that contains a fine wine: transparent but containing; metaphysically invisible. You do not see the print but look through it to the heady meaning swirling within."[25] However, in the medium of digital expression, readers increasingly are invited to oscillate, to notice not only the meaning contained in the words but also the "expressive surface," the manner in which the typography is displayed. Certainly this idea can be applied to the hyperlinks that permeate online spaces; the user is invited to *literally* use the words on the screen as digital portals into worlds of further meaning. Thus, he or she looks at the word itself, not only for the semantic meaning of the word, but also through the word with the understanding of its role as a conveyer of additional information.

I add to Lanham's argument that oscillatio is essential not only to the digital age, but to classical rhetoric and aesthetics as well. The rhetorical canon illustrates this place of the trope in oratory. The orator, for example, uses all five canons to craft a speech, using invention, delivery, memory, arrangement, and style. Additionally, the orator also takes into account the Aristotelian proofs of *ethos*, *pathos*, and *logos* when crafting the speech. However, while the orator and the audience may not notice each of these components working concurrently, at some point they oscillate between the argument expressed in the speech and the manner in which it was made. In other words, the listener must oscillate between acknowledging the rational dimensions of the speech while appreciating the style of the presentation, via its use of figures of speech. Therefore, rhetoric involves a constant oscillation between logos and pathos, or rational argumentation and stylized aesthetics.

Similarly, rhetoric and aesthetics are not mutually exclusive because they work in conjunction, oscillating between different sides of the same coin. Remix captures this movement between rhetoric and aesthetics and thus troubles the distinction between both. This movement might be manifested in "Right Wing Radio Duck," where the video uses an aesthetic means to a rhetorical end, or in the mashups of Girl Talk, where the aesthetics of the sonic collages *are* the rhetorical elements. In auto-tune, the rhetorical messages are compounded (and occluded) by the potency of the aesthetic structure.

The musical elements of auto-tune actually detract from the ideologies inherent in the messages, thus becoming more rhetorical for their effort at obfuscation. All of this oscillation is possible in remix, according to Lanham, because of the atomization of music into sound samples: "As a result [of remix], the act of listening becomes acutely self-conscious. People become connoisseurs of sound. Their listening habits always oscillate between the sound and the music."[26] But with the Gregory Brothers' remixes, listeners oscillate between the communicative meanings of the words, the semiotic connotations of the visuals, and the sounds of the music—sometimes the music overshadows the others. Auto-tune oscillates as well between its musical and visual dimensions. Though this was not initially the case, the fact that auto-tune is now inextricably connected with those individuals in the video, the "unintentional composers," means that the visual element is just as important as the sonic one. This oscillation that inheres in remix becomes particularly relevant when observed through its constituent parts: *epaesthetic* rhetoric and the sublime.

Despite my connection between classical rhetoric and oscillatio, Richard Lanham generally frames the trope of oscillatio as a late-modern invention. In fact, his exemplars of economists of attention are generally avant-garde artists rather than classical purveyors of rhetoric-*qua*-rhetoric. Lanham argues that rhetoric in the networked era is synonymous with attracting attention. As such, he dedicates a large amount of his discussion on the attention economy to people who know how to attract attention: avant-garde (and pop) artists like Marcel Duchamp, Christo, Andy Warhol, and the Dadaists/Surrealists/Italian Futurists.[27] When the vanguard artist Duchamp, for example, placed a urinal inside of a prestigious art gallery—a piece called *Fountain* that is still prominently displayed in the Paris modern art pantheon the Pompidou to this day—his motivations were certainly subversive. Notable here, though, is that the very act exuded a real display of oscillatio. The art critics and consumers could scoff that it was not real art because it was so banal, but Duchamp could respond by questioning the arbitrary nature of what truly constituted art. But, on the other hand, if the critics and consumers began adoring the piece because of Duchamp's sterling reputation as an artist, and perhaps because of this genius decided to see the inherent beauty of the mundane, he could laugh at them for admiring something as ordinary as a urinal. Thus, "A maximum of commentary was created by a minimum of effort."[28] Though *Fountain* is generally cited as an example of an artist getting the attention of the people, it also illustrates how art can function in an oscillatory manner.

Using Lanham's discussion of experimental art-as-rhetoric as impetus, I dedicate the following discussion to John Cage as an economist of attention par excellence. In discussing some of his compositional techniques, I intend to demonstrate how Cage exemplified the rhetorical use of oscillatio and the intellectual curiosity that spawned a progeny of remix artists.

Avant-Garde Musical Composition as Technique of Oscillatio

Aesthetically and ideologically, remix is grounded in the avant-garde modern music movement of the twentieth century. In 1906, for example, Charles Ives released "Central Park in the Dark," a seven-minute cacophonous collage of atonal string chamber music. This collage was a philosophical antecedent to the digital sampling movement decades later. Early modern musical composers experimented with sound collages because recording technologies allowed them the ability to capture sound and use it. In 1946, composer Pierre Schaeffer pieced together recordings of trains running on railroad tracks, whistles sounding, and conductors yelling to make a sound collage that imitates rhythms of more conventional-sounding songs.[29] This type of sound collage is nevertheless an innovative precursor to the commercial sound collages that took place throughout the rest of the century.

"Found sounds" were often integrated into sound collages. This compositional process, dubbed *Musique concrète* and dating back to 1948, would use the sound of trains and other ambient noises to create a new type of song.[30] Although *Musique concrète* may be considered a direct precursor to remix, the controversies that surround sampling tend to gravitate away from environmental sounds and toward the unlicensed use of commercial music samples. Still, *Musique concrète* was controversial in the way that it challenged the listener's understanding of what music was supposed to be. Incidentally, this rhetorical function of *Musique concrète* would be echoed in the auto-tunes that would be created decades later. But for their time, this use of oscillatio was fundamental to the interpretation of these and similar works.

Remix is not only a rhetorical extension of the aesthetic vanguard, but is progeny of the sonic happenstance of modernity. When industrialization proliferated in the mid-nineteenth century, a new series of sounds infiltrated public culture. These new sounds—perceived as merely commonplace today and thus largely ignored—were considered at the time an unwanted sonic assault. The people making these aesthetic judgments had previously taken part in an agrarian society, and as a result, had been largely accustomed to the familiar bleating of their herds of animals. With the advent of the Industrial Revolution, however, there was now "a constant din of construction and pounding, of the shrieking of metal sheets being cut . . . of ear-splitting blasts from huge steam whistles, sirens, and electric bells that beckoned and dismissed shifts of first-generation urbanized laborers from their unending and repetitive days."[31] As Aldous Huxley would describe it, the twentieth century would become "the Age of Noise," a time when silence would be defeated by the technological developments of the era.[32] The conquerors of silence, it would turn out to be, were clocks, whistles, and sirens. These everyday noises grew so deafening to the unaccustomed workers that they developed the fear that noise would drown out the human voice. Jacques Attali explains this fear by noting that noise is associated with the idea of the weapon: "In its biological reality, noise is a source of pain . . . Diminished intellectual capacity, accelerated respiration and heartbeat, hypertension, sound in the environment. A weapon of death."[33] In short, the erstwhile agrarian culture upon which these sounds had intruded was not equipped to cope with the sonic changes. I would argue that this sonic intrusion was so alarming because it occurred largely before avant-garde art. In the age of noise, no one had taught the people how to properly oscillate yet. The avant-garde movement would take the charge.

Naturally, these sonic-induced anxieties were embraced and exploited in the works of experimental artists. According to a cultural history of modern sounds, Greg Goodale notes that the Italian Futurist artists were hyper-focused on onomatopoeia in their art, for example. As a result, words were interjected into their art like the machine-gun-sounding "taratatatatata," "pik-pok-poom-toomp" and "splish splash zong-zong-shaaak-shaaak." Their rephrasing of banal sound was given credence through its oscillation between the mimesis of sound and the work of art. Explaining the poet Filippo Tommaso Marinetti's motivations for using onomatopoetic language, Goodale states: "To be effective, poetry could not be composed of pretty words and subtle ideas but rather . . . vivid and immediate sounds . . . Sound was the key to understanding and controlling modernity."[34] And control modernity it did—along with the masses. Goodale argues that twentieth-century propaganda—long recognized in accounts of media history for its visual properties—was largely dependent on its sonic component: "Sound was a more effective agent of control than Nazi visual icons."[35] Sound worked powerfully during the twentieth century to unsettle the masses or move them into a sonorous envelope of comfort. These powers were exonerated and/or incriminated in the art of the time. In either case, the power of noise not only provided important fodder for twentieth-century experimental art, but it also helped inject the trope of oscillatio into public culture.

John Cage

John Cage was an incredibly influential composer of experimental music during this time. His work is often cited because of his controversial contributions to this corpus of vanguard music. He is also important for inclusion here because of his attitudes toward music and innovation. As part of his illustrious body of work, Cage composed music using the guiding framework (or anti-framework) of networks of chance.[36] He argued that music could be composed by any combination of sounds and in any context and illustrated this point with his 1939 composition *Imaginary Landscape*, which consisted of him using multiple radios and phonographs at varying speeds and frequencies played simultaneously.[37] He also would create "aleatory compositions" that "could be played in many different ways, depending on the choices of the performers," certainly paving the way for remix.[38] And, as stated by Ken Jordan and Paul Miller (aka DJ Spooky), all of this was "wholly original, uncharted musical terrain, one that is unthinkable without networked computers" that helped pave the way for "the traditional distinction between 'artist' and 'audience' [to begin] to melt away, as the 'listener' also becomes a 'performer.'"[39] As the audience listened to these compositions, as with much experimental art, there would be an element of interactivity where it would cognitively create the musical meaning out of these fragmented and chaotic sound streams. Cage's compositions amplified the oscillation inherent in art, from art being a calculated, painstakingly crafted exercise to one that simply harnessed the opportunities put forth by chance and randomness.

Cage also experimented with musical concepts like duration, silence, and noise to create his compositional mélanges. This experimentation functioned as an impetus for an exploration of art as a series of oscillations. Perhaps his most controversial piece was entitled *4'33"*, consisting of exactly four minutes and thirty-three seconds of silence. The point of this composition was to invite the audience to oscillate from focusing on the *foreground* to the *background*—to realize that the sounds of the audience coughing, shifting in the seats, or the rain hitting the roof of the concert hall are just as musical as successions of notes arranged in harmony. Naturally, when Cage's composition was "performed," it would bewilder many audiences. Video clips of Cage performing this or other experimental works often show the chuckling of the audience afterward.[40] Indeed, Richard Lanham argues that avant-garde aesthetics generally evoke similar oscillatory reactions in audiences: "Music was reduced, as John Cage was later to reduce it, to pure sounds, randomly collected or generated . . . What happens when you do this? Two things . . . You get mad and you start to laugh."[41] Richard Kostelanetz framed the act this way: "[The original audience] missed the point. There's no such thing as silence. What they thought was silence, because they didn't know how to listen, was full of accidental sounds."[42] The foregrounding of the sound of the audience was a strategy to remind the listener that art is a social construction, not solely an aesthetic one.[43] In short, "[Cage] wanted us to hear ourselves hearing."[44] This oscillation between figure and ground would become foundational to the practices of sampling and remix.[45] Writing, in part, about Cage, composer John Zorn argued that Cage created his own rules, which helped initiate an open dialogue between the composer and the performer.[46] This same notion of dialogue can be applied to contemporary remix, as it can be a dialogue between the composer and the performer, the performer and the audience, the composer and the audience, or any of the above with the art.

Cage's art also holds other important implications for the present discussion on auto-tune. Cage believed that like auto-tune, the *sound* of language was at least equally as important as the *content* of language. Cage's experimental compositions began in music and spilled over into his invention of speech. In these speeches, he doggedly pursued the primacy of form over content in language—an idea akin to Marshall McLuhan's influential ideas in media ecology.[47] He explained his reasoning in this way: "If, in a speech, one allows musical means to come into play[,] the speech becomes something to experience rather than something to just hear about."[48] The sensual experience of speech was appealing to Cage; to him, the form became just as important (or more so) than the information shared. Because the concept of aesthetics is frequently ascribed to an erotic process, or an understanding of the beauty of nature and art in a corporeal fashion, Cage's focus on the sensuousness of speech presents a point of convergence between aesthetics and rhetoric. In other words, his artistic contributions make him an essential contributor to any discussion on how rhetoric and aesthetics can help us better understand remix.

Cage not only applied the musical elements to speech (pitch, rhythm, and tone, for example), but he became obsessed with other elements as well, like duration.[49] Much as the beat is a constitutive element of popular music, Cage considered the words uttered per minute in a speech to have a similar function. Indeed, in his "Lecture on Nothing" and "Lecture on Something," he illustrated this analog by mathematically dividing the structure of the speech into exactly equal parts. He saw the significance of equal parts silence and words in speech as the same as rhythm in music. In other speeches, he delivered 30 one-minute mini-speeches; or he delivered four simultaneous lectures; or he exclusively used the vocal intonations that occur when one is posing a question.[50] These speeches were generally characterized as nonsense because the audience did not understand how important oscillatio is to experimental art.

The purpose of addressing the artistic contributions of John Cage is not only to demonstrate how his work expanded the compositional parameters of music, but especially to view him as a predecessor to current practices in remix. His art illuminates the dimensions of remix today: He used technology as a way to manipulate sound; he used a "call and response" model of voices and sounds coexisting in an ongoing dialogue (though some of these dialogues were more calculated than others); he used fragments of sound to create a larger mosaic of sound, thus creating a new notion of what music could be; and he used playback machines (tape loops and radios, for example)—traditionally used for the reproduction of sound—as means of production. He epitomized the philosophy of composer Edgard Varèse, who famously called music "organized noises."[51] This almost comically understated definition of music is amplified by the aesthetic sensibility of digital sampling. These unorthodox compositional statements were met with baffled reactions by the public at the time, but have since been rehabilitated and framed as seminal works in the history of modern music.[52]

Music as Rhetorical

In this section, I focus on what brings music and speech together and how that union is specifically illustrated in remix. There has been a modern oppositional relationship between rhetoric and aesthetics, and remix provides an inviting context within which to connect rhetoric and aesthetics back together. To conceptualize logic and beauty as discrete in the context of rhetoric—as an either/or dichotomy—is a missed opportunity. Rather, rhetoric and aesthetics should exist in a mutually beneficial *both/and* relationship.[53] This discussion will be essential in providing a template for how remix can function as *epaesthetic* rhetoric: a union of epistemic rhetoric (speech) and aesthetic rhetoric (music). I proceed here with caution, as many theorists of language argue that comparing music and language is a fruitless endeavor. Linguistic theorist Ann Clark cautions, "To read music as a language is to make music a means, not an end, and hence is to undermine the real significance of music [as] an alternative to language."[54] This underscores the difficulty of theorizing music as a language, or language as a type of music. However, I do not consider music to be an alternative to language, or a language itself, but a constellation of grammars, nondiscursive symbols, and emotional stimuli that, when functioning together in harmony, can produce a persuasive object.[55] There are certain shared affinities between both, and remix can amplify those similarities. One of the purposes of this book is to argue that rhetoric and aesthetics are more similar than the rhetorical tradition generally acknowledges. One site where this similarity is particularly apparent is music. This is a relatively novel claim today because, despite this similarity, rhetorical criticism is a rare method for examining music.[56]

Though we are accustomed today to seeing music and language as separate, there was a time in the fifteenth and sixteenth centuries that composers used the principles of rhetoric to guide their musical compositions. They did this because they did not have a sufficient musical lexicon from which they could draw to describe their compositional process. George Buelow explains: "The union of music with rhetorical principles is one of the most distinctive characteristics of Baroque musical rationalism and gave shape to the progressive elements in the music theory and aesthetics of the period."[57] Indeed, numerous years later, composers gradually stopped the use of rhetorical figures in music as music's own lexicon became standardized.[58]

Historically, music has functioned similarly to rhetoric.[59] Instead of the orator preparing his or her message with rhetorical figures, however, musicians would prepare their messages through using the elements of music like melody, rhythm, harmony, tone, and timbre. This is not necessarily a novel concept: Renaissance-era composers explicitly used Aristotle's proofs as a grammar to compose their own music. Like orators, the musician also "manipulates a symbol system (sound, rhythm, words, and tempo) to react to and modify the dominant philosophical, political, religious, and aesthetic values of both general and specific audiences."[60] Composers had a reputation to uphold; if they wished to assure their audience of their "moral rectitude," they would choose to avoid using "lascivious" dance rhythms in their music.[61] This attitude is illustrated in a quote from Claudio Monteverdi's 1638 book, in which he writes, "The end of all good music is to affect the soul . . .

music, naturally inborn in our being, ennobles or depraves his morals."[62] Gerald LeCoat interprets this musical demonstration of ethos as similar to the Ciceronian topos of modesty. Musicians also had an understanding that to produce pathos, one had to make a part of the musical melody particularly high, thus making it more poignant.[63] The melodic structure of a song could affect the listener in concrete, physiological ways.[64] They also knew that the type of instruments used would evoke certain moods and trigger various types of emotions in the listeners. They also used logos to provide the correct sonic balance to evoke the desired moods in the listener. The musician and the orator are similar in more ways than one, in that the musician essentially becomes a "harmonic orator" who uses *tonal topoi* "in order to appear plausible to the listener."[65] Echoing Lloyd Bitzer's "The Rhetorical Situation," Irvine and Kirkpatrick argue, "The artist is clearly functioning in a rhetorical manner as he attempts to adapt his musical message to the value structure of the perceived audience."[66] In these interweaving and complex ways, musicians are performing persuasion each time they compose or write new music.

During the Baroque period of musical composition—especially with German composers—rhetorical figures even provided the terms with which musical composition could be defined. George Buelow argues that these historical similarities between music and rhetoric can be traced to the direct influence that rhetoric played in a European education. Even as students were inculcated with the rhetorical figures, they were applying these same terms to the text-bound practice of music. Over time, these terms became applicable even to music without accompanying lyrics. In the early seventeenth century, German musical theorist Joachim Burmeister released several works that became influential in establishing the musico-rhetorical tradition; most notable among those was his *Musica Poetica*, published in 1606. In this text, Burmeister introduced the novel idea of musical figures. Music theorist Patrick McCreless argues that Burmeister chose to address music by using rhetorical figures because it was a certain way to "restore music theory to intellectual respectability; what better way to do so than to map the academically prestigious discipline of rhetoric onto music?"[67] In appropriating the rhetorical canon for use in a musical context, for example, musical composers were able to use the same logic of rhetoric to guide the intricate process of composition (as well as, in one notable case, contest the perception of rhetoric as purely stylistic and, thus, without substance).[68]

A Tropological Analysis of "Bed Intruder Song"

In table 1, I list a number of musico-rhetorical figures, demonstrating a Renaissance-era link between musical compositional techniques and the lexicon of the rhetorical tradition. The rhetorical and musical figures included in table 1 demonstrate several loci of connection between both rhetoric and aesthetics that can be observed in remix. "Antitheton," for example, is a figure similar to perspective by congruity. "Hyberbole" also has a similar function to perspective by congruity, in that it magnifies the standard aesthetic structure of songs by mashing them up together. However, there are two musico-rhetorical figures that deserve further discussion. First, "asyndeton" (conflated with its related figure "ellipsis") is a stuttering and skipping aesthetic hard-wired into mashups. Second, the figure "mimesis" is rooted in the rhetorical tradition, and yet is equally applicable to contemporary remix. I include the following brief discussion not only because these tropes provide a locus of music, remix, and rhetoric, but because they demonstrate the utility of the idea of *epaesthetic* rhetoric.

Asyndeton

In *On Rhetoric*, Aristotle notes that the use of *asyndeta*, the deliberate omission of connecting words, is more appropriate in speech than in writing.[69] An example that Aristotle gives of this device in use is: "I have spoken; you have listened, you have [the case], you judge."[70] As demonstrated here, the asyndeton can be used as a dramatic variation in the orator's delivery of speech. Its purpose extends, however, beyond mere dramatic flourishes to higher aesthetic purposes. For, despite its apparent fragmented form, asyndeton creates a semblance of unity. Aristotle explains that "asyndeta have a special characteristic; many things seem to be said in an equal space of time; for the connectives make many things seem one."[71] These connectives, the *syndesmoi*, allow fragmented utterances of many disparate ideas to be linked together into a seeming whole.[72] These syntactic links, however, are not as important as the function of omission here that asyndeton offers. In addition to missing syntactic links, asyndeta may omit *logical* unifying links, which prompts the audience to consider the fragmented discursive statements in the larger holistic context. Thus, the hearers of the speech provide a logical unity to the fragments, the act of which, in turn, offers them a certain pleasure.

Like the Aristotelian idea of proportional metaphor, the asyndeton teaches its audience by making learning pleasurable. This classical stylistic device illustrates

TABLE 1. Rhetorical Tropes and Musical Figures

TERM	RHETORICAL FIGURE	MUSICAL FIGURE
Anadiplosis	The repetition of the last word of one clause or sentence at the beginning of the next. (Silva)	The repetition of a closing melody at the beginning of a new section. A double mimesis. (GB)
Anaphora (Repetitio)	Repetition of the same word at the beginning of clauses. (Silva)	Repetition of a melodic statement on different notes in different parts. (GB) Imitation in some (but not all) voices of a polyphonic piece. (PM)
Antitheton	A figure of thought also known as Reasoning by Contraries. Using one opposing statement to prove the other. (RAH)	A musical contrast, to express things contrary and opposite, occurring successively or simultaneously. (GB)
Antithesis	When spoken style is built upon contraries. Example: "In peace, you keep demanding for war; in war, you yearn for peace." (RAH)	When a few passages are contrasted with each other to bring out the main subject more clearly. (PM)
Asyndeton	A presentation in separate parts, conjunctions being suppressed. This figure has animation and great force and is suited to concision. (RAH)	This is the trope that remixed compositions use. Similar to ellipsis, Asyndeton is used here because it holds more specific rhetorical connotations.
Climax	The figure in which the speaker passes to the following word only after advancing by steps to the preceding one. (RAH)	Repetitions of a melody in the same part a 2nd higher. (GB) Repetition of a melodic fragment on another scale degree. (PM)
Ellipsis	Omission of a word or short phrase easily understood in context. (Silva)	Omission of an otherwise essential consonance . . . An unexpected new direction taken by a passage that has led up to an expected conclusion. (GB) Breaking off of a passage that has begun but does not finish. (PM)

Note: The information for this table was taken from *Rhetorica ad Herennium*, in *The Rhetorical Tradition: Readings from Classical Times to the Present* (2nd ed.), ed. Patricia Bizzell and Bruce Herzberg (New York: Bedford/St. Martin's, 2001), 243–82 (RAH); Gideon O. Burton, "Silva Rhetoricae," 2016, http://rhetoric.byu.edu (Silva); Gerard G. LeCoat, "Music and the Three Appeals of Classical Rhetoric," *Quarterly Journal of Speech* 62 (1976), 161 (GL); Patrick McCreless, "Music and Rhetoric," in *The Cambridge History of Western Music Theory*, ed. Thomas Christensen (Cambridge: Cambridge University Press, 2002), 857–58, 863–64 (PM); George J. Buelow, "Rhetoric and Music," in *New Grove Dictionary of Music and Musicians*, ed. Stanley E. Sadie (London: Macmillan, 1980), 795–800 (GB); Michael Spitzer, *Metaphor and Musical Thought* (Chicago: University of Chicago Press, 2004), 186 (MS); Robert P. Morgan, "Schenker and the Theoretical Tradition: The Concept of Musical Reduction," *College Music Symposium* 18, no. 1 (1978), 82 (RPM); and Greg Goodale, *Sonic Persuasion: Reading Sound in the Recorded Age* (Urbana: University of Illinois Press, 2011), 72 (GG).

TERM	RHETORICAL FIGURE	MUSICAL FIGURE
Epanalepsis	Repetition at the end of a line, phrase, or clause of the word or words that occurred at the beginning of the same line, phrase, or clause. (Silva)	Repetition at the end of a melody or a whole musical section from the beginning. (GB)
Epistrophe	Repetition of the same word at the conclusion of clauses. The opposite of anaphora. (Silva)	Repetition of a closing section at the end of other sections. (GB) When the ending of one passage is repeated at the end of another passage. (PM)
Heterolepsis	Does not appear in rhetoric. (RPM) However, I would call the rhetorical figure prosōpopoeia analogous to heterolepsis. Speaking as someone else. (Silva)	The taking up of another voice. The process of leaping from a dissonant to a consonant voice, or vice versa. A purely musical figure. (MS)
Hyperbaton	Upsets the word order by means of either Anastrophe (reversal of order) or Transposition. (RAH)	Removal of a note or musical idea from the expected order for underlining of the text. (GB) Transfer of a note or phrase from its natural position to a different position. (PM)
Hyperbole	A manner of speech exaggerating the truth, whether for the sake of magnifying or minifying something. (RAH)	A melodic passage that exceeds the normal ambitus of a mode either above or below. (GB) Overstepping of modal ambitus in upper register. (PM)
Interrogatio	Reasoning by question and answer. It reinforces the argument that has just been delivered. (RAH)	A musical question. (GB)
Mimesis	The imitation of another's gestures, pronunciation, or utterance. (Silva)	Noema (homophonic sections) in some parts while others are silent. (PM) Musicians imitated nature's rhythms in music in order to stir up the passions of the listening audience. (GL)

how fragmentation and unity can be considered both rhetorical and aesthetic. As Elizabeth Blettner argues, the rhetorical function of the asyndeton is its anticipation of the hearer's more metaphysical desire for holism: "The listener may attain a binding conviction through the pleasurable perception of easily intelligible wholes. By grasping what is delivered as many, instead of one, he may be led to bind the diverse, readily discordant parts of his soul into a single harmonious whole."[73] Though this primordial urge may certainly be a component of asyndeton's rhetorical potential, its value is not limited to its unifying ability. Its aesthetic function featuring ellipses should also be considered.

Asyndeton is more than a rhetorical trope; Michel de Certeau argues that asyndeton is one of the dominant tropes in the spatial construction of everyday life.[74] The act of walking through the city is an example of how frequently asyndeton manifests itself as lived spatial ellipses. When walking through the city, a child can spatially experience the sensation of asyndeton. She may skip over segments of the sidewalk, circumventing small connecting paths and dodging puddles of water that overlie the concrete panels. The child's walking patterns could be best interpreted as a flow, despite their avoidance of the traditional connecting path. This anecdote amplifies a fundamental paradox of asyndeton—it allows for a unified flow of fragmented segments.[75] Its ellipses-driven practice not only amplifies its fragmented structure, but it also challenges the importance of *the very idea* of continuity. Perhaps the child deviates from the mandated path; so what?[76] She can still arrive at her destination eventually. The point is that asyndeton, considered as a spatial trope, demonstrates its utility in a nonlinguistic context.

The construction of "Bed Intruder Song" also parallels the logic of asyndeton. The auto-tune begins with Dodson speaking about the rapist in Lincoln Park. Suddenly, the auto-tune begins in earnest when Dodson's diatribe turns into song. Lyrically, the narrative continues unhindered until the utterance "So y'all need to hide your kids, hide your wife," which then repeats two more times before he ends the musical phrase with "And hide your husbands 'cause they're raping everybody out here." The musical phrasing repeats anew with Dodson telling the alleged rapist, "You don't have to come and confess, we're looking for you. We gon' find you," the last part of which repeats again. He finishes out the section with "So you can run and tell that, run and tell that, run and tell that, homeboy, home-, home-, homeboy." This iconic beginning of the auto-tune illustrates the use of asyndeton as a connector between the clip's aesthetic and rhetorical dimensions.

The Gregory Brothers create and unify narrative fragments by appropriating vocal snippets of Dodson and re-creating the narrative. The unified narrative of the song belies the unusual pairing of fragments of the dialog in the clip. As the final line is transferred into writing—"homeboy, home-, home-, homeboy"—Dodson's dialog becomes fragmented, stuttering, and repetitive, divorced from the usual characteristics of vernacular speech. As such, were the speech not auto-tuned, it would sound mechanical and artificial, devoid of logic. The transformation of the speech into song, replete with rhythm and melody, provides the logic to cognitively link the statements together into a cohesive lyric. The insertion of ellipses in the speech makes the fragments function as an enthymeme, because despite the fragmented and repeating narrative, the imposition of a melody and a beat invites the audience to connect to the auto-tune by cognitively linking it to a formula for previous pop songs. In this way, the auto-tune functions as *epaesthetic* rhetoric, using its aesthetic components to trigger the cognition associated with epistemic rhetoric. The use of asyndeton also provides the auto-tune with its rhetorical heft. By atomizing, repeating, and essentially reframing Dodson's dialogue as musical lyrics, the disturbing message of the original speech is overshadowed and perhaps even ignored, thereby lessening its impact. This incongruity between the message of the source material and the final auto-tuned product, and the subsequent occlusion of the former by the latter, is a rhetorical act made possible by asyndeton.

Mimesis

The function of music as mimetic to human emotion reveals a strong rhetorical element in music. Philosopher Susanne Langer argues that patterns of tension and release occur in music, and that subsequent emotional responses by the listener occur because music imitates physiological processes in humans.[77] For instance, the strong, fast tempo of a song imitates the tensions, shocks, and instabilities in life. Thus, the associated reaction may take place within the listener. On the other hand, music can calm the listener by making intermusical resolutions—resolving dissonant chords within the music will likely correspond to calm feelings within the listener. Thus, music has similar objectives as rhetoric in the linguistic context; it wants to infiltrate the consciousness of the listener, which, not coincidentally, is also a function of rhetoric.[78] In rhetoric, orators embed ideologies in their speeches, which are then transmitted through the use of rhetorical figures. Likewise, the composer of music has a worldview that she or he encodes by using the elements of music, like melody, harmony, tempo, rhythm, style, and form. These elements work in a parallel fashion as the rhetorical figures in speech.

Music does more than simply invite the listener to reflect or be entertained; music does, indeed, infiltrate the consciousness of the listener, but often in more subtle ways than argumentation. When the artist inserts a rhetorical message that is couched within the elements of music, the listener will be less aware that persuasion is taking place. The reason for this lies in the nature of music. Because it is typically regarded simply as entertainment, its rhetorical element is usually overlooked: "When listening to a message couched in music, one is less prepared to argue in opposition to the projected message."[79] But because its rhetorical dimension is often overlooked does not mean that music cannot persuade as effectively as language—on the contrary. Music carries persuasive messages, but those messages are even more intense when in the musical context because music adds emotional gravitas to the message. The musical message can be more effective than words alone because music is ineffable, a nondiscursive symbol. Further, the musician has a greater freedom of expression for his or her message than perhaps the orator would.

The Gregory Brothers transmit affect through their mimetic use of rhythm in their auto-tunes. The beat that accompanies "Bed Intruder Song" uses concise fills, frequent repetitive use of the bass drum, and later handclaps to evoke a generic sense of old-school hip hop. In other words, its use of rhythm clearly mimics a hip-hop song. This mimetic aspect is essential to its rhetoricity; James Irvine and Walter Kirkpatrick argue that "rhythm is the element [of music] rendering all music rhetorical."[80] Rhythm amplifies music's rhetorical dimension to such an extent because rhythm can produce a tangible change—one that is capable of being both psychological and physiological—in the listener and in the artist. There is, however, another reason that rhythm renders music rhetorical and that is its function as "*a carrier of rhetorical impact*."[81] Spoken another way, rhythm can "render [the listener] more susceptible to the rhetorical aspects" of the messages embedded in the music.[82] This rhythmic potency occurs in two ways: First, rhythm is mimetic in that it imitates the physiological rhythms of life, thereby appealing to the body on a corporeal level. Second, rhythm functions at a psychological level by appealing to the listener's cognitive need for order in a spatio-temporal sense. I would add that because rhythms are mimetic to the rhythms of the body and nature, when it impels order onto the musical composition, that order is symbolically transferred into the lived experience of the listener.[83]

If rhythm has the capability to induce psychological and physiological changes in the listener, remix has an even greater potential to do so. Remix can uniquely foster those same changes within the listener because its functionality is more robust than that of rhythm. One of the rules for making effective (rhetorical) mashups is to use unifying beats and keys. The beat is key to remix because it offers a means whereby the perspective by congruity can take place. Irvine and Kirkpatrick, in fact, wrote about this very process; rhythm has the ability to evoke an "experiential capacity" within the listener—a memory of a comparable musical message from a prior listening experience—that ultimately can lead to a change in attitude. A familiar chord progression from a previous song (it's hard to get away from these in popular music, after all), similar lyrics, or the like: each of these can trigger musical associations in the audience. But it is this linking between the familiar and the unfamiliar in music—and the resulting tension—that can result in a cathartic experience for the audience.[84] Music can amplify familiar meaning when the artist makes unfamiliar compositional decisions and helps the listener hear them against previously experienced music.[85]

Irvine and Kirkpatrick argue that rhythm is rhetorical because it helps propel existing tensions throughout the song to a resolution. I modify this definition slightly to account for the place of the beat in "Bed Intruder Song." Their definition should not mean that rhythm necessarily provides a resolution to the tensions evinced throughout the song; rather it only underlies them, existing as accompaniment as they structurally unfold through time. As post-parenthetical music often structurally parallels the philosophies of the digital culture that produces it, I do not believe the rhythm is a conduit for reconciling these contrasting tensions. Recalling the prior discussion on perspective by congruity, the unifying rhythm and key enthymematically (and emphatically) emphasize the congruity of both components without acknowledging the division. There does not need to be a rhythmic resolution because there is nothing to reconcile. The allegorical function of remix is so hardwired into the process that the composition becomes entirely holistic via the participatory role of the listener.

Ultimately, the Gregory Brothers' use of the tropes of asyndeton and mimesis in "Bed Intruder Song" illustrates how remix can connect rhetoric and music. Related to this connection, remix also can function as a hybridized type of rhetoric composed of two previously contrasting rhetorical motifs: epistemic and aesthetic.

Aesthetic Rhetoric

For much of the latter half of the twentieth century, the idea of rhetoric being epistemic was popular in the field. This idea originated from Robert Scott's 1967 article, which framed rhetoric as a discourse capable of generating knowledge. This epistemic perspective asserts that truth and knowledge are not fixed and based upon a verifiable scientific reality, but rather created moment by moment through social interaction. Though Scott's argument was immensely popular—with ideas roughly paralleling Peter Berger and Thomas Luckmann's influential book of the previous year, *The Social Construction of Reality*—some critics dismissed it as simply an example of the pejorative term "perspectivism."[86] Still, the concept of rhetoric constituting knowledge (rather than simply reflecting it) gained traction within the field of rhetoric.

In 1993, Steve Whitson and John Poulakos wrote a response to Scott's epistemic view of rhetoric wherein they proposed a new form of rhetoric, one in which aesthetics is the primary factor in framing the argument. Using an aesthetic rhetoric requires that the orator uses the music of spoken sounds and an affective language from which an audience can be aroused. At the core of this argument was their condemnation of epistemic rhetoric as being incomplete. Using Friedrich Nietzsche as an intellectual guide, the authors asserted that aesthetics provided an alternative to the epistemic bias in rhetoric. They attempted to sublimate, not bifurcate, epistemology into sensuousness: "The epistemic endeavor is a derivative of something greater: primordial desires, irrepressible passions, and blind drives."[87] In so doing, they presented a novel approach to rhetoric, one that prioritizes its indemonstrable elements rather than its scientific and logical qualities.

In the final words of the article, however, the authors lamented that they advanced these radical views while only using the language of the status quo: epistemic rhetoric. Explaining, they wrote, "The conventions of academic writing militate against the kinds of [aesthetic] prose Nietzsche would have endorsed."[88] Perhaps as a response to this challenge, two years later they published an article in the same journal that appears to perform an aesthetic presentation of prose. As such, the article was written in snippets of text, almost in the style of a discursive remix. It tried to break from the epistemological model of rhetorical critique by becoming a montage of aphorisms, titles, and memorable prose—with very few academic citations. In concluding their article, the authors playfully speculated about the future while remixing some terminology:

> Two thousand and four hundred years from today readers of the history of rhetoric will probably read in the *Journal of the Idle Ages* an article of this sort. "The Academy of Rhetorical CD-ROMology recently discovered a fragmentary text whose title is 'Rhetoric as Epi[ ]ic.' Philologists are bitterly divided on the issue of the missing letters. One camp reasons that the term is 'Epidemic'; another supports 'Epinoetic.' A third camp combines the arguments of the first two camps, and conjectures that, most likely, rhetoric during the Idle Ages was understood as a disease of the mind.[89]

Following their lead, I remix a term of my own here, arguing that remix—as rhetoric—is *epaesthetic*. I remixed this term by combining the two key words of the debate together when referring to rhetoric: "epistemic" and "aesthetic." Much as it is a bridge between so many rhetorical and aesthetic concepts, remix is also a bridge between both types of rhetoric. Before advancing the concept of *epaesthetic* rhetoric, however, I shall briefly discuss what an aesthetic rhetoric rooted in Nietzschean thought might look like.

Nietzsche argued that human understanding does not emerge from epistemologically valid truths but rather from aesthetically generated images. An assessment of aesthetics often stalls at the sensual surface level for some auditors of art; Nietzsche would be inclined, it seems, to see this process as analogous to the epistemological process as well. In lived experience, human understandings of truth are generated not from objective truth but rather aesthetic appearances that have later become crystallized. In other words, those things taken to be profound truths were once only surface-level aesthetic assemblages that solidified into their current configurations over time. Thus, when considering "truth" as the means of revealing knowledge, argued Nietzsche, we are mistaken because reality and its corresponding truths are only composed of the now-petrified artistic representations. The epistemological validity of these representations is irrelevant; the value of these representations, rather, is contingent on their aesthetic successfulness. The same applies to rhetoric as an aesthetic enterprise:

> For Nietzsche, rhetoric is not an epistemological undertaking but rather part of a greater artistic act—the act of ordering the chaos of life. This act produces signs

> that function *not* as truth but as beautiful veils masking the chaos in which people live . . . Signs are attempts to endow existence with beauty and to make us forget that behind this fabricated beauty lies only chaos.[90]

The acquisition of knowledge, then, consists not of rhetorically constructed realities, but of an ongoing interaction with aesthetic images turned petrified truths. These aesthetic representations not only embody sensuousness, they also serve as buffers to insulate their auditors from a life that is certainly less than beautiful.

Much as Nietzsche's art is central to life as a veiled coping mechanism, aesthetics are central to rhetoric as a means of satisfying the audience's aesthetic appetites. Not surprisingly, Whitson and Poulakos's brand of aesthetic rhetoric is markedly different from Scott's epistemic rhetoric. Rather than attempt to frame the practice as rational or cognitive (and thus perpetuate the rehabilitation process of a discipline still smarting from Romantic stone throwing), aesthetic rhetoric does not shirk its aesthetic connection. Sensuousness pervades every aspect of aesthetic rhetoric, with its heavy emphasis on the linguistic equivalent of the bodily senses: "It substitutes the sounds, the smells, the textures, the flavors, and the sights of the world with a sensual language that surpasses them."[91] This rhetoric attempts to arouse the audience at a corporeal level, thus offering a mimesis of language-induced pleasure. Due to its immediacy, it is best served to an audience in oral fashion, one in which the audience can *hear* the music of language en route to a non-(or pre-)cognitive ingestion of the performance of language. In short, the sound of the language outweighs the message communicated by it.

The Nietzschean mandate advanced by the authors in their argument—to create a rhetoric that surpasses the other remaining senses—is a particularly formidable one. Rhetoric can be compelling and impactful, as evidenced by some of its vocal critics, but to be vivid enough in speech to surpass the holistic system of the five senses (especially in the traditionally drab halls of academia) is a daunting task indeed. Perhaps this is why writings on rhetoric are slow to take on the charge. But the overall injunction to create a more aesthetic rhetoric is still not entirely new; it actually reveals shades of the pre-parenthesis and the importance of oral performance still at work. It also depends largely on the interaction of audience and orator, wherein the rhetoric becomes heavy on affect, pathos, and rhythm. In sum, aesthetic rhetoric emphasizes the same similarities between music and language that I discussed above.

Nietzsche's critique is valuable for my purposes because it not only *rhetoricizes* aesthetics, but it also *aestheticizes* rhetoric. Its connection between both evokes the Enlightenment aesthete Alexander Baumgarten, who repeatedly expressed ideas of (1) how aesthetics help people learn things sensately, and (2) how rhetoric and poetics are separated by "only a matter of degree."[92] It also evokes the argument that art is the expression of aesthetic ideas, and the expression of aesthetic ideas takes place through rhetoric. Kant, in fact, argued that rhetoric and aesthetics are similar in that they both can cause delight, similar to musical composition.[93] To be sure, there are exciting possibilities for considering rhetoric anew by using Nietzsche's notions of aesthetics and rhetoric.

The connection made here between rhetoric and aesthetics is pivotal to the discussion I have been advancing throughout this whole chapter—perhaps I could simply mention its parallels with remix and leave it at that. However, remix-as-rhetoric does even more than connect rhetoric and aesthetics. In the context of rhetoric, remix bridges the ostensibly opposite ideas of epistemic rhetoric and aesthetic rhetoric into a hybrid of both that I call *epaesthetic rhetoric.* In discussing what this term means, remix will offer some insights and exemplars.

Epaesthetic Rhetoric

Epaesthetic rhetoric entails a mixing together of the aesthetic and sensual dimensions of language with its cognitive elements. As I mentioned earlier, remix simultaneously combines both an affective, embodied component (its danceable beat) with an inherently cognitive component (its referentiality). The unifying rhythm of the mashup provides the affect, and the allegorical nature of the mashup uses enthymematic logic to unite the audience with the remix artist, thus enacting a cognitive dimension of remix. This oscillatory pleasure of auto-tune is perhaps best articulated through the literary term *jouissance.*[94] This term, introduced into the academic vernacular by literary scholar Roland Barthes, describes a corporeal sensation of intense pleasure (usually translated as "bliss"). Readers can experience this pleasure when they interpret a text and feel that they have taken some role in the co-construction of that text with its author. In other words, the reader might feel a "loss of self" into that text.[95] Much like the Barthesian notion of *jouissance,* auto-tune works on both affective and cognitive levels simultaneously. In the musical context, auto-tunes are characterized by their beats. The beat is the textual unifier; it allows for the decontextualized and auto-tuned vocals to become joined together in a sense of aesthetic uniformity. Through these rhythmic elements of the music, the audience derives pleasure in a corporeal sense. *Jouissance*, therefore, can be considered a sensation stimulated by the transmission of affect. This rhythm-induced *jouissance* in remix further demonstrates its Nietzschean character—by imposing a unifying rhythm over the chaotic fragments of disparate samples, it imposes order upon the uncertainties of life.

To recap, remix as *epaesthetic* rhetoric not only "focuses on the human body as an excitable entity," and thus uses vivid imagery, it also invites the audience to cognitively make linkages and provide omitted information to make the rhetorical discourse more complete.[96] Whitson and Poulakos argue that aesthetic rhetoric "draws its strength from seeing an audience affected by its message."[97] Remix is dependent on the same process. The commonplace between the audience and the DJ reflects this same basic quality, one in which the DJ not only draws his or her strength from the interchange, but shapes the actual text accordingly. However, the point of divergence for *epaesthetic* rhetoric from a strictly aesthetic rhetoric comes from its overtly cognitive dimension. Aesthetic rhetoric necessarily "forgoes the attempt to communicate a particular message exactly, and strives to contain an impulse."[98] Like the precognitive impulses of affect, the meaning of the message is preceded by the transmitted affect. However, the two need not be mutually exclusive. *Epaesthetic* rhetoric, rather, anticipates an oscillatory understanding of both sides of the continuum, one in which each can exist concurrently without detracting from the other or needing to be reconciled. In this way, *epaesthetic* rhetoric exhibits a logic rampant in remix culture, positing that aesthetics and cognition—or style and substance—can coexist in an oscillatory relationship. Put another way, *epaesthetic* rhetoric uses aesthetic means to reach an (often) epistemic end.

To an extent, all argument arrives at epistemic conclusions through aesthetic presentations. The writing style of Kenneth Burke, for example, exemplifies this point. The process of working through his unfiltered arguments is sometimes akin to taking a wandering, scenic journey to arrive at a conclusion that is epistemically valid and holistically useful. In this context, remix culture challenges the distinction of rhetoric being either epistemic or aesthetic.

Epaesthetic Rhetoric in "Bed Intruder Song"

"Bed Intruder Song" demonstrates *epaesthetic* rhetoric at work. Dodson's cautionary arguments serve as a reminder that the world is a violent place, and his dialect, intonations, and clothing are rich with semiotic signification. The red do-rag in his hair, combined with his black tank top and unwieldy hairstyle are popular signifiers of poverty; contemporary racial politics fills in the rest of the picture by using his visual portrayal as fodder for an overdetermined representation of a poor black man living in the projects. Each of these aesthetic components of representation functions epistemically because they evoke enthymematic connections. Despite the horrors of Dodson's auto-tuned representation, however, the sheer sensuousness of the clip reveals a strong element of the beautiful. The auto-tune heavily employs an affective hip-hop beat, an impassioned delivery, consonant vocal harmonies, clearly delineated sections connected by smooth transitions, and provocative use of minor chords.[99] Even Dodson's indignant gestures begin to resemble dance moves once the music begins.

The sheer emotion of Dodson's delivery also shines through because of the remixers' successful application of poetic devices. In an interview, Evan Gregory explained part of the appeal of Dodson's delivery: "The song is memorable and compelling for the same reasons a conventional song is . . . He's conveying emotion and a strong personality, and that's what we latch onto in a pop performance."[100] In that emotional performance, the verbal articulation of open vowel sounds provides the remixers with room to work their craft. The Gregory Brothers also employed other poetic devices in the clip. Through their editing, they isolated rhymes from the deliveries, then aligned them at appropriate intervals so as to mimic the lyrical nature of a song. For example, they composed a "bridge" after the hook by using reporter Gentle's statement "The man got away leaving behind evidence," followed by Kelly Dodson's "I was attacked by some idiot in the projects." The rhyme here is explicit, but its inclusion in the auto-tune invites the audience's participation in co-creating the assembled utterances and reconfiguring them as a pop song. What is most notable here, however, is the co-creation of poetic devices by both the remixer and the remixed. The Gregory Brothers exploit the musical timbre of Dodson's voice by making implicit connections between its musical and impassioned quality and that of a pop song. However, Dodson's original utterance used certain vowel sounds conducive to auto-tune transformation. When the individuals in the clips use words that unintentionally rhyme, the remixers isolate those and amplify them, thus revealing their occluded musical potential.

Each of these beautiful elements contributes to the overall rhetorical dimensions of the clip because the beauty occludes the horror of the speech and images being auto-tuned. It enacts oscillatio by demonstrating both the beauty and the horror simultaneously, giving the appearance that both elements appear to work in conjunction. Despite the disturbing source material, the song is appealing because of its catchy melodies and infectious beat, but it also offers something else more sinister—the perverse pleasure of schadenfreude. Viewers are conscious of the horrors embedded in the auto-tune, but rather than moving to action, the song's beautiful element lulls them instead into laughing at it and singing along. In this way, the *epaesthetic* rhetoric of "Bed Intruder Song" is a site of struggle between both constitutive motifs.

Because of its emphasis on oscillatio, the *epaesthetic* rhetoric of remix is a natural extension of twentieth-century experimental art. In fact, the works of the artistic avant-garde have frequently been labeled as canon by DJs and remix artists. In a series of interviews Aram Sinnreich conducted with these DJs, he was struck by how often they compared their craft to the vanguard of the art world. He concluded that these DJs chose this rhetorical tactic in order to bring an aesthetic credibility to remix. The connection is therefore explicit: Though the experimental composers and artists of the twentieth century were often marginalized for their art, their true genius has become more apparent with the passing of time. The remix artists may perceive this to be the case with their work, or they may even be perceived as such by critics. *New York Times* writer Zachary Lazar has likened Girl Talk to another Pittsburgh native, Andy Warhol, because of similar artistic vision: Warhol "blurred the usual distinctions between shallow and deep, trashy and sublime (and who broke through with a 'sample' of Campbell's soup cans)."[101] Drawing this parallel between avant-garde art and remix is not that far off; it is notable that the connection Lazar makes between both is firmly related to an oscillation between opposing terms. Further, his dichotomies of shallow/deep and trashy/sublime suggest another important component of oscillatio: the sublime.

The Sublime

The trope of oscillatio is not only embedded in the practices of experimental artists and *epaesthetic* rhetoric, but in a concept from the philosophy of art called the sublime. Contrary to its vernacular usage, the sublime is something separate from common perceptions of beauty; the sublime is related to experiences in which auditors of art or nature are so overwhelmed by an aesthetic experience that they are reduced "into a state of awe and trembling . . . [In this situation, they] cannot properly conceive of, cognize, the thing presented to [them]. Hence the mixture of pleasure and pain built into the experience."[102] It is the inability to rationally process the experience that registers those feelings of awe. The sublime is also inextricably tied to ambivalence, oscillating between pleasure and pain, beauty and horror, order and disorder. The terror involved in the sublime is in and of itself ambivalent, "a rapid alternation of attraction and repulsion."[103]

The theoretical progenitor of this concept is also a figure from the rhetorical tradition, Longinus, who argued in his thesis *On the Sublime* that confrontation with the unknown and threatening in art is that which evokes feelings of wonder and awe within us.[104] In the mid-eighteenth century, Edmund Burke expanded on this idea by seeing the sublime as a mixture of both pleasure and pain. In confronting the unknown in art and nature, Burke equated fear with terror, which is "the ruling principle of the sublime."[105] Implicit in these conceptions is an oscillation between opposing terms. Several decades after Burke, Immanuel Kant made this tension explicit, arguing the sublime was "a radical experience of disagreement, in which the synthetic power of imagination is defeated by the experience of an infinite, which sets up a gap between the sensible and the supersensible."[106] This definition essentially brought the sublime to a liminal space between the comprehensible and the infinite, the pleasurable and the painful, and (especially in art), the representable and the non-representable. Jean-François Lyotard extended its relevance into the postmodern age, calling it "this contradictory feeling [of] pleasure and pain, joy and anxiety, exaltation and depression."[107]

This liminal existence makes the sublime in art especially prone to interpretation and yet still recalcitrant to those interpretations. In this way, the sublime bears a particular resemblance to avant-garde art. Avant-garde art requires interpretation because of its provocative aesthetic characteristics (or lack thereof). As theorist Daniel Herwitz notes, historically "the avant-garde [artists] already relied on words to spell meaning into their reductionist gestures . . . The true task of aesthetics became to understand this double game the avant-gardes were playing, [the tension] between reduction and manifesto."[108] However, like the sublime, avant-garde art transcended the restrictions of meaning. Silence, emptiness, or erasure in art made art philosophical, an exercise in which the auditor became a philosopher by using interpretation to bestow meaning upon the work. With this refusal also came transcendence, a certain affective pleasure for the person who interpreted and therefore imbued the work of experimental art with meaning.[109]

Similar to the (anti-)meaning in avant-garde art, the referentiality of remix is crucial to its persuasive potential. Though it is certainly correct that no previous knowledge of the songs being sampled is necessary for an audience to enjoy the remix on the dance floor, the audience can still glean a real pleasure from knowing the songs that are being sampled beforehand. Likewise, this breakdown of meaning in the text and subsequent participation in the enthymeme by the audience can lead to *jouissance*.

Another rhetorical element of the sublime emerges when it is used for political purposes.[110] Scholars in the Frankfurt School were especially attuned to this possibility. They routinely scrutinized art to discover its political dimensions. Walter Benjamin, for example, saw a danger in exploiting feelings of the sublime in art in order to obtain allegiance to an individual or an ideology. Herwitz calls this rhetorical process "subliming." When employed, subliming entails the appropriation of the sublime by propaganda into making the masses unilaterally bestow their abstract and ineffable feelings of awe onto an individual. This exploitation of the sublime is clearly dangerous, as it can move the public to place too much power, even divinely inspired feelings of allegiance, upon that leader. Therefore, this function of the sublime can be rhetorical due to its pervasive cultural consequences. Jean-François Lyotard argues that avant-garde art's attempt to evade any sort of common standard of taste was a way for artists to reclaim their art from (a)politicized art like propaganda or kitsch:

> There have been certain "realisms" . . . that have tried to reintroduce symbolism, to offer the public accessible works of art which will allow it to identify with specific ideas (race, socialism, nation, etc.). We know these attempts always call for the elimination of the avant-garde . . . The avant-garde . . . manages to neglect utterly [this] "cultural" responsibility for unifying taste.[111]

The abstraction of avant-garde art is a refusal to be appropriated and presented to the public as any cultural or political signifier. However, rather than being apolitical, this move by the avant-garde is indeed a rhetorical move calculated to persuade the masses of the art's seeming independence from ideology.

Both *epaesthetic* rhetoric and the sublime have oscillatory functions: the former addresses the convergence of epistemic rhetoric and aesthetic rhetoric in remix and the latter describes the tension between concomitant dichotomous conditions, like beauty/terror or joy/apprehension. "Bed Intruder Song" uses *oscillatio* in both cases. It combines the (re)cognition of musical structure with the beauty of the song, not quite sublimating one into the other but allowing both to exist simultaneously. The video is also sublime in a related way; it displays the horror of the violent attack and evokes troubling racial dynamics between source and artist. It also uses musico-rhetorical tropes in its presentation that make it aesthetically appealing. Other auto-tune videos by the Gregory Brothers showcase these *epaesthetic* and sublime dimensions as well, like the popular video "Double Rainbow Song!!"[112]

The Sublime in "Double Rainbow Song"

In the early literature on the sublime, much of the discussion addresses how the condition takes place when one is observing the staggering grandeur of nature. The sublime is activated when the individual meets the limits of comprehension while viewing the beauty and enormity of natural phenomena. When the human faculties become insufficient to truly process the experience, the sublime occurs. Rare natural phenomena are particularly effective in triggering these feelings.

Such an experience happened in early 2010, when Paul "Bear" Vasquez filmed a rare event from the vantage of his front yard, located near Yosemite National Park in California. In the video, Vasquez is clearly awestruck by the experience of viewing a double rainbow glistening near a mountain in the distance. His ecstatic reaction is apparent in his shaky filming, which suggests he is so overcome by emotion that he's struggling to stay calm. As he films the serendipitous event, he starts commenting on what he's seeing in hushed, almost reverent tones: "Whoa, that's a full rainbow, all the way. Double rainbow . . . it's so intense!" However, in the three and a half minutes that follow, he excitedly raises his voice, in pitch and in volume, culminating in ecstatic yelling. He weeps repeatedly, overcome, as he films. Words seem to fail him as he attempts to explain what he's seeing: "It's so bright and vivid, oh! It's so beautiful [*sobbing*]!" His gasping commentary is spontaneous and joyful, an exclamation verging on prayer; at one point, he asks "What does this *mean*?" Indeed, in interviews afterwards, he likened it to a religious experience, saying that "God wanted to give a message to humanity."[113] The video quickly went viral, helped along by late-night show host Jimmy Kimmel's tweet that it might be the "funniest video in the world."[114] The Gregory Brothers also noticed the video. Their auto-tuned version, "Double Rainbow Song," was uploaded to YouTube three days after Kimmel's tweet.

The music of "Double Rainbow Song" is intense, like the source material. The video begins with Vasquez's breathy, hushed vocals attempting to narrate what he's experiencing. A piano softly accompanies him, using a chord progression that will repeat again in the chorus. The chord progression is vi-IV-I-V (in the case of this video, it's B minor-G-D-A), a sequence of chords that is used enough in pop music that it's been dubbed a "sensitive" chord progression.[115] As such, the chordal accompaniment amplifies the emotional tenor of Vasquez's experience. This compositional choice lends an epic feel to the auto-tune, enhancing the impact of the emotional delivery. The pulse of the beat that accompanies the song is insistent, especially once the intensity of Vasquez's auto-tuned delivery elevates—though there is a respite from the beat during the ostensible bridge section when it is replaced by the sound of chimes.

The composition of the auto-tune also uses several rhetorical tropes referenced earlier in table 1: mimesis and anaphora (or *repetitio*). First, "Double Rainbow Song" uses mimesis as an important component of the compositional structure. The musical phrases have to be structured in such a way that they imitate the rhythms and cadences of Vasquez's verbal exclamations. With the former, the composer/remix artist has to contend with the irregular meter of Vasquez's verbal statements before he or she can determine the accompanying beat. Regarding the latter, auto-tune compositions work backwards in some ways from the usual compositional process. Rather than creating a melody that will fit the existing chord progression, the inherent melody of the speaker's words need to conjure up a natural chord progression to accompany it. Likewise, the spoken words of the source material (i.e., Vasquez's passionate declamation) need to have a structure imposed in order for the auto-tune to follow pop music logic. Therefore, the remix artists enhance the anaphora suggested by the material. Although Bear Vasquez does repeat himself numerous times, the Gregory Brothers amplify that repetition substantially. In the chorus, for example, he repeats "double rainbow all the way across the sky" several times, much like a hook would sound in the chorus of a pop song. In the bridge, his question "What does this mean?" initiates two musical statements. Anaphora is evident in the auto-tune; in all, the 89-second-long video contains the phrase "double rainbow" eleven times.

This brief analysis is included here to address the use of the sublime in these auto-tunes in different ways. "Bed Intruder Song" balances the horror of representation with the beauty of the song; "Double Rainbow Song" offers a remixed representation of a sublime event to enhance the immediacy of the reaction to it. To be clear, "Double Rainbow Song" is not a sublime text in the same sense as Vasquez's experience of the double rainbow back on that day in early 2010. Like the other Gregory Brothers videos, "Double Rainbow Song" is a winking parody of Vasquez's original emotional video. In this unique case, however, the technical affordances of digital media and the creative affordances of remix coalesce to offer an enhanced version of the sublime event. Vasquez laments in the original video that "I can't even capture it on my camera!" The representative limitations of mediation mentioned here inhibit the audience's true experience of the sublime. However, the auto-tuned video can still represent it in a surprising way, enhancing the original video by accompanying it with an emotional chord progression and employing repetition to amplify the speaker's ineffable experience.

An Ethics of the Sublime

Though the sublime in auto-tune is novel, it is not unprecedented in remix. In fact, the tensions between terror and beauty in "Bed Intruder Song" parallel those in Fatboy Slim's 1999 hit "Praise You." For those unfamiliar with the remix, "Praise You" samples the song "Take Yo' Praise" by Camille Yarbrough, an African American woman who wrote and sang the song during the civil rights movement. However, the sample of her voice is thoroughly transformed in the Fatboy Slim remix. Her voice is manipulated, androgenized (it "digitally neuters Yarbrough . . . render[ing] the voice asexual"[116]), deprived of historical context, and given a skipping stutter as if to emphasize to the listener that her voice is indeed being sampled.

Rather than seeing any tension between the source and the manipulated sample, however, listeners generally responded by celebrating the song. One listener said, "I think one of my friends described 'Praise You' best when she said it felt like one of those songs you cruise around town with all your friends listening to and doing fun, crazy stuff . . . it's just a fun song."[117] Incidentally, this same sentiment was echoed when "Bed Intruder Song" became popular on the Billboard hip-hop charts. One of the comments below the clip on YouTube emphatically approved of the song in a manner similar to this: "I love this song. It's perfect for this summer, just to listen to as I drive down the freeway, with the windows down, and the wind in my hair, singing along at the top of my lungs." The dissonance between the actual context of the source material and the remixed versions demonstrates the rhetorical power of the musical aesthetics in these songs.

Continuing in his critique of "Praise You," musicologist Mark Katz argues that Fatboy Slim disempowered Yarbrough by decontextualizing her performance in such a way and "whiten[ing]" the song by changing its title from "Take Yo' Praise" to "Praise You." Yet Yarbrough, interviewed for Katz's book, revealed that she was not particularly distraught by the remix; she was somewhat ambivalent about it becoming such a dance anthem, but did not consider that fact to devalue her original performance in any way: "I can still do that song as I do it. And so what [Fatboy Slim] did [with the sample], that's on him; what I do, that's me."[118] Still, others felt that it was disturbing that she "spoke so forcefully to us about racism and injustice [in the original recording, and yet] did not see that she herself had been exploited."[119]

The above case illustrates a few troubling implications of the remixed sublime. Similar concerns need to be raised about the ethical ambiguities surrounding "Bed Intruder Song." For example, Dodson responded to the auto-tune in this way: "I love it . . . We laugh and joke about the videos . . . We watch it every day." But he also demonstrated oscillatio by acknowledging the seriousness of the original event: "I want people to realize that this is funny. It is funny—I'm not going to lie, 'cause we're laughing too. But this is a serious matter . . . I really thought that when I went into Kelly's room, he was choking her life out of her. I was terrified . . . It was so crazy. But God allowed me to save her and that's what I did."[120] This general ambivalence about the auto-tune followed in the 2010 BET Hip Hop Awards, when Antoine Dodson "performed" his auto-tuned tirade with the assistance of Michael Gregory on stage. Following the performance and subsequent laughter, the host of the show, Mike Epps, said to the predominantly African American audience, "Antoine Dodson and Michael Gregory, real talk. For real. I know that was messed up, but they was able to buy their mama a house and get them out of the projects with that song right there. I don't know how long they goin' to live there [laughs with the audience], but a . . . So go run and tell that, homeboy."[121] As the auto-tune circulated, the viewers of the clip seemed to acknowledge its disturbing dimensions, but still ultimately smiled at them.

The sublime is one important element that makes discussions of remix culture more dynamic than its legal dimensions. In concluding his discussion of "Praise You," Mark Katz argues that perhaps the politics of digital sampling are more nuanced than they seem: "'Praise You' does not allow us the luxury of a blanket condemnation (or celebration, for that matter); it can be understood as derivative *and* novel, exploitative *and* respectful, awkward *and* subtle."[122] Though claiming this position effectively frees him from making a definite pronouncement, Katz is really only illustrating the respective places of the sublime and oscillatio in contemporary remix culture. In his book *Mashed Up*, Aram Sinnreich supports the same assumption as Katz, concluding that remix has introduced more gray space in between the poles of what used to be black/white dichotomies. In the post-parenthetical era, the observer must acknowledge the influx of gray space in between the previously defined oppositional poles. As such, the ethical dimensions of remix are sometimes nebulous. However, that gray space is not as pervasive as some would argue. Because oscillatio is so prevalent in remix culture, these texts illustrate that both poles exist concurrently in a dialectic relationship. Unlike Sinnreich's argument, it is not the nature of the binaries in the debate that has changed, but the *audience* that has changed. It has changed by learning how to move between looking at one and then looking at the other. Who has trained the people to do this? Avant-garde artists.

Poetics and Parentheses

Remix offers several points of convergence: of emotion and intellect in a musical context; of DJ and audience; of music and speech; of epistemic rhetoric and aesthetic rhetoric; of pain and pleasure, among others. Broadly, remix is a contemporary bridge between musical aesthetics and rhetoric. I use the word "contemporary" because this is a bridge that is in the process of being constructed anew; historically, there was no need for one because the gulf that divides music and rhetoric did not always exist. This bridge is nowhere as apparent as in the case of auto-tune, which specifically presents a case whereby we can see oscillatio take place between each of these oppositional terms. I add to the discussion another important point about auto-tune. The bridging of these terms is representative of a larger connection I made in an earlier chapter: the connection of the post-parenthetical era to the pre-parenthetical era. I believe that this connection is especially apparent in the term "poetics," a classical hybrid of speech and art.

In the rhetorical tradition, the classical term "poetics" referred to a hybrid of rhetoric and art that is no longer as ubiquitous in common contemporary vernacular (beyond highly specialized terminology for literary wonks like "prosody"). Because poetics was so inclusive, it included a slippage between language and music. In Aristotle's *Poetics*, he noted that form extends to the rhythm and meter of language or dance, which can be rhetorical.[123] Plato likewise argued to the sophist Gorgias that "poetry is a form of rhetoric . . . if you strip from all poetry its music, rhythm, and meter, the residue would be nothing else but rhetoric."[124] Isocrates wrote that a person could "captivate the audience" with "a voice and a clarity of utterance" that confidently communicates a clear message by "the music of his words."[125] Indeed, the sophists of his time used a "poetic, nonrational prose" that amplified the sensuous qualities of words and sound. This included rhythm, meter, speed of delivery, intensity, sound textures, and pitch variations in words. The *telos* of this study was, in fact, to examine how a "prose-speaker could use effects of rhythm and assonance to influence his audience."[126] This once-studied affective style often slips into the margins, however, because it was loudly superseded by Plato's "nonpoetic, rational prose," thus paving the way for Cartesian notions of non-emotional rationalism.[127]

In the contemporary era, auto-tune shares the same characteristic as poetics: a blurring of the distinction between speech and music. The Gregory Brothers use clips that are easily manipulated because they are articulated in emotional ways. The more expressiveness in the voice and the more syncopation in the verbal delivery, the better the auto-tune candidate. In selecting their candidates in this way and auto-tuning their language in the way they do, the Gregory Brothers are enacting the classical concept of poetics anew. Just as the post-parenthetical era returns to pre-parenthetical norms in its culture of collective creativity, so it does in its primacy of poetics.

CHAPTER 5

Projecting Voice in the Digital Age

Remix, Śūnyatā, and Prosōpopoeia

In the early twenty-first century, remix artists took advantage of sophisticated studio techniques to help individuals deliver unlikely performances. In 2004, the dead John Lennon debuted a postmodern iteration of his vocals from the tender ballad "Julia" to accompany Jay-Z's "Dirt Off Your Shoulder." In 2010, the deceased father of golfer Tiger Woods returned to life just long enough to chastise his son on television for his extramarital affairs. These ventures, driven more by creativity and commerce than by any need for closure or catharsis, have a precedent in ancient cultures. Millennia prior to the prevailing sampling practices of remix culture, ancient rhetoricians, mindful of Horace's observation that "the voice once sent forth cannot return," discussed the rhetorical strategy of making an abstract or absent essence concrete or present by providing it with a voice.[1] In the first decade of the first century BCE, the anonymous Roman author of the *Rhetorica ad Herennium* explained that "*conformatio* [literally, *giving form to*] consists in representing an absent person as present, or in making a mute thing or one lacking form articulate, and attributing to it a definite form and a language or a certain behavior appropriate to its character."[2]

Because there is no literal English cognate of the term conformatio, this rhetorical practice of prosōpopoeia is often conflated with "personification." Despite its common usage in ancient Roman literature, the term is usefully reconceptualized to analyze contemporary digital culture.[3] As the (re)presentation of a once-absent voice, the rhetorical figure of prosōpopoeia (προσωποποιία)—literally, "face-making"—is one of the essential tropes of remix.

Similarly, the act of remixing is much richer than merely personifying. When the trope is envisioned as an ancient antecedent for contemporary remix, prosōpopoeia is linked to a cluster of additional terms like *voice making*, *voice restoration*, and *voice projection*.[4] Cicero and Quintilian hint at these dimensions by explaining that *prosōpopoiiai* are "bolder" than speech and require "stronger lungs."[5] As part of its powerful potential for giving form, though, prosōpopoeia can give voice only to a person or a thing that has no voice. Historically, the term entails more than simply assuming the mannerisms of a person or thing; it must restore an essence that was previously lacking to a thing.[6] What, then, do we make of prosōpopoeia after postmodern critiques of essentialism? The argument of this chapter is that to best understand this projection of voice and its relationship to the lack of textual essence, another cultural tradition is needed to explicitly address the essencelessness of remix in a contemporary, digital context. To find overlays between disparate philosophical traditions, this chapter mashes up ancient Greek and Roman rhetorical theories of prosōpopoeia with the ancient Mahayana Buddhist philosophy of śūnyatā. Śūnyatā, the ancient philosophical construct that communicates a simultaneous lack of essence and fullness of possibility, can be a valuable resource for understanding the complexities of how remix plays with form. Like any good remix, the juxtaposition of the different intellectual "tracks" represented by prosōpopoeia and śūnyatā draws out heretofore-unexplored components of each.

Remix shares essential characteristics with prosōpopoeia. By its very definition, remix uses prosōpopoeia every time a remix artist spins vinyl records on a turntable or copies and pastes samples of music into a digital mashup. Though it is the rhetorical counterpart of some of the creative strategies of remix, prosōpopoeia does not layer multiple voices on top of each other in the same manner as a musical remix. When prosōpopoeia projects voice into a new appropriate context, however, the appropriation of the voice combined with the new situation creates a new, recombinant voice in place of the original voice. As a result, that new voice may be more rhetorically powerful than either of its constituent voices alone.

In this chapter, I aim to focus on remix as a practice that is concerned with *essence*. When conceptualized in this way, remix not only "speaks" the absent recording artists' songs, it also opens new possibilities by distilling external voices and influences into the body of the speaker. Put another way, the reason that prosōpopoeia works with remix is because of its philosophical debt to śūnyatā: the essencelessness of the spoken voice is what allows it to be filled by the projection of other voices.

Remix mashes up various voices according to their appropriateness and familiarity—the kairos discussed earlier in the book. When the DJ or remix artist creates a mashup, he or she is responsible for choosing the appropriate voices to be sampled and the parts of the composition to be added upon or subtracted from.[7] This is a tricky maneuver because remix artists must allow the original essence of the song to remain intact and yet transform it sufficiently to be considered something novel. This is a rhetorical process, in that the remixer chooses certain songs to sample while deflecting others. Remixers will consider the final product as successful if they, as rhetors, are able to sufficiently sustain the audience's attention as well as help persuade it that the remixer's aesthetic choices were appropriate. There is a level of prestige gleaned by DJs when they find an obscure sample and reintroduce it into the limelight in the form of a great mashup. DJs call it "crate digging," a way to demonstrate to the audience musical proficiency, that the DJ not only has a vast knowledge of songs but also even specific (and perhaps forgotten) parts.[8] Because vinyl-record culture is unwieldy and often highly esoteric, remix pervades every aspect of it.

Remix is also at the core of academic scholarship. In fact, the act of research is comprised of equal parts prosōpopoeia and crate digging. The point to be made here is that academic scholarship is thoroughly *prosōpopoetic*—citation is merely the animation of an absent voice. Because all scholarship is remix, all scholarship is *prosōpopoetic*. Because scholarship aims to build upon past arguments and findings, scholarship considers itself empty of completed essence and full of potential, ready to be used again in the service of epistemology. Both prosōpopoeia and śūnyatā will be applied to remix as rhetorical tropes in this chapter.

Remix and Śūnyatā

Remix highlights an important rhetorical function of contemporary digital artifacts: the ease with which the absent are reanimated, repurposed, and remixed demonstrates how artifacts lack essential properties. This absence of essence recalls the words of the second-century philosopher Nāgārjuna. Nāgārjuna theorized śūnyatā, Sanskrit for "emptiness," as a Buddhist approach that sees existence as all-encompassing and hollow at the same time.[9] Nāgārjuna's invitation to understand śūnyatā demonstrates the tantalizing potential of the idea: "For whom emptiness is possible / For him all is possible."[10] To the remix artist, the possibilities for creative production are innumerable for the same reason.

Śūnyatā defies the traditional concept of emptiness and the value ascribed to essence. Rather than embodying a lack of essence, śūnyatā should be considered a stripping away of all external complications, including the complications posed by meaning, thus freeing the text to become the starting point for something new. Śūnyatā is more closely associated with a swelling or hollowness than an absolute emptiness. It is neither a being nor a non-being: "Buddhist emptiness in its very etymology holds a hint of fullness that is lost in its English translation."[11] That swelling is addressed by numerous explications of śūnyatā through the metaphor of an expanding seed. Nāgārjuna explained the emptiness of perceived reality in this way: "all phenomena are devoid of inherent existence . . . because the inherent existence of all phenomena is not to be found in causes, conditions, aggregations or individualities."[12] Unpacking these provocative stanzas, David Ross Komito explains that every phenomenon is dependent upon being caused, having a condition, being joined together, or being taken separately. The joining together of one phenomenon with its essential conditions is the *aggregation* of which Nāgārjuna wrote and makes their discrete *individualities* impossible to examine. With a sprout, for example, a seed is the cause, and the water and earth are contributing conditions that aggregate with the seed to allow the sprout to take shape.[13] Key to understanding the connection is acknowledging the interdependence of each of the factors—not simply the nature of their individualities, but rather, their essences in totality. As Michael G. Barnhart explains, "śūnyata was dependence; that all things were empty meant that all things were mutually (and thoroughly) dependent."[14] Nothing can emerge in front of the rest if everything is interdependent. Thus, all phenomena are empty of essence, traditionally understood.[15] By contrast, as philosopher Gay Watson argues, Western intellectual traditions have a difficult time comprehending the nature of śūnyatā because of their cultural fetishization of meaning and the master narratives of Authority and Absolutes, inspired by Platonic thought.[16]

Remix artists also consider all potential samples as interdependent. When a song is recorded and released to the public, like the seed of śūnyatā, it swells into fruit that is available for any perceptive passerby to pick, plant, and cultivate. Because of the relatively affordable and intuitive digital composition technologies available, remixers consider recorded songs to be raw materials just waiting to be mashed up. Like Nāgārjuna's insistence on the lack of "inherent existence," remix culture flattens authorities and multiplies absolutes until the seed of new forms of creation can swell unhindered. In this way, remix culture directly challenges norms of authorship enshrined in the codified language of copyright law.

Both remix and śūnyatā have a potential to be subversive. Remix attempts to resist hegemonic aesthetic conventions by subverting them, even turning the critical eye upon itself when appropriate. In 2013, Daft Punk, a duo known for making unashamedly derivative music, challenged the myriad digital capabilities of recording technology by being explicitly analog.[17] In their album *Random Access Memories* (*RAM*), the duo subverted the trend of sampling influential artists and digitally mashing them together by inviting a few of those actual artists into the studio to collaborate and create new analog music. Ironically, Daft Punk "de-black-boxed Remix" and created a real-life remix without digital samples.[18] Though they used no samples, they still facilitated a variety of prosōpopoeia by inviting other recording artists to provide vocals. Fundamentally, then, the emptiness inherent in both śūnyatā and remix, unfettered by anchoring essences, enhances the subversive potential of prosōpopoeia. This subversive potential is sympathetic to the mask-wearing purpose of prosōpopoeia; the mask will fit any face if the face's features are ever-changing.

Prosōpopoeia

Prosōpopoeia is a powerful, yet peculiar, rhetorical trope. For literary critic Paul de Man, prosōpopoeia is "the master trope of poetic discourse," as it describes the very act of reading.[19] The functions of the trope have been the subject of controversy. Exceeding the contemporary parameters of the symbolic act, the poetic usage of prosōpopoeia in the nineteenth century initiated a microgenre called the "corpse poem." Diana Fuss claims that the act of "giving voice to the voiceless cadaver" allows the poet to use "literary fictions that seek to revivify and reauthorize the dead."[20] Giorgio Agamben acknowledges that those endowed with voice have the capability to act as pseudo-witnesses for those who no longer have one. He quickly adds, however, that this *lending* of voice is no different than the fictive *imposition* of one.[21] Despite its potentially controversial dimensions, the ability of prosōpopoeia to reanimate the dead is only one aspect of its rhetorical function. Fundamentally, prosōpopoeia is about projecting voice. This concept is apparent in Adam J. Banks's writings on African American rhetoric and "back in the day" narratives of African American history, culture, and struggle, which he explains are imposed upon current texts, such as hip hop that "helps heal the disruptions of black experience."[22] He says, "The 'back in the day' narrative becomes remix, sampling, layering, and revising multiple, sometimes contrasting elements of black culture in a productive synthesis for right now."[23] Thus, prosōpopoeia projects voice for the purpose of imbuing remixed text with deeper meaning.

The ability of prosōpopoeia to project voice to another person or thing is a critical component of its definition. In the bundle of ancient Greek handbooks that preserve the *progymnasmata* (preliminary rhetorical exercises), several teachers address the exercise in similar ways. Some of the accounts distinguish between variations of the term depending on the identity of the orator and the audience. While one of the progymnasmatists, Theon, broadly defines the term as the act of attributing appropriate speech to another, other ancient pedagogues consider prosōpopoeia as the attribution of voice to more than absent speakers. While addressing the rhetorical figure of personification, the author of *Rhetorica ad Herennium* explained that it could "be applied to a variety of things, mute and inanimate."[24] Save Theon, the progymnasmatists distinguish variants of speech for the absent, like *eidōlopoeia* (image, idol, or ghost making; that is, a speech for a god or dead person) and *ēthopoeia* (character making; that is, a speech for a living person).

Though this chapter generally focuses on prosōpopoeia, the ancient variant ēthopoeia offers additional insights into the various voice makings that prevail in remix. Ēthopoeia, or "character making," is concerned with the persuasive possibilities of character portrayal, rather than its mere fidelity.[25] Performing ēthopoeia entails representing one individual with another for the purpose of dramatic characterization. This act can exhibit a discourse that is deeply rhetorical because it impersonates the individual to exploit his or her ēthos.

Cicero's *Pro Caelio* is one such example. In this defense speech, recognized since then as a "first-rate piece of acting," Cicero attempts to absolve Marcus Caelius of several charges.[26] Among these charges is the attempted poisoning of Caelius's lover, the infamous Clodia. Cicero, relishing the opportunity to embarrass the sister of one of his own enemies, chastises her while using the persona of her long-deceased ancestor Appius Claudius Caecus.[27] Prior to this mask-wearing discourse, Cicero acknowledges that he is choosing to let the dead speak so that he can invoke a harsher tone appropriate to the grievousness of Clodia's immoral act:

> I will first inquire of [Clodia], whether she prefers me to deal with her severely, solemnly, and in an old-fashioned manner, or mildly, gently, and in a modern way. If in the old grim mode and method, then I must call up from the dead one of those full-bearded men of old—not with a trim modern beardlet that she delights in, but a rough one, like those we see on old statues and busts—to rebuke the woman and speak instead of me.[28]

Twisting the knife, he then shifts to impersonate Clodia's absent brother to continue the rebuke.[29] In prefacing his rhetorical onslaught, Cicero tells Clodia that her brother is "a perfect man of the world; who loves you most dearly." He then invites her to "Imagine him saying to you, 'Sister, why are you making such a to-do? Why have you lost your senses?'"[30] Cicero's *prosōpopoetic* prosecution was so devastating that Quintilian later celebrated Cicero's stylistic use of "force for rousing emotion."[31] Cicero's masterful technique was so successful in achieving its rhetorical objective that it prompted Clodia to be subsequently "laughed out of court."[32] Cicero's in-court mashup of his own ideas with the simulated mannerisms of Appius illustrate the potency of the recombinant voice; because of the iconic status of the sonic properties of the original source material, the voice that resulted from Cicero's rhetorical act was more powerful than his alone.

Tropes in Action

Contemporary remix deploys prosōpopoeia for rhetorical purposes. The familial voice in Cicero's *prosōpopoetic* defense offers a point of consonance with a 2010 television commercial by Nike about one of the company's most famous spokespersons, professional golfer Tiger Woods. At the time the company created the ad—informally called "Did You Learn Anything?"—news coverage of Woods was ubiquitous due to his many marital infidelities. Inspired by the milieu, the ad begins with a camera slowly closing in on Woods's expressionless face, while a recording of his father's voice apparently urges Woods to take responsibility for his actions: "Tiger? I am more prone to be inquisitive to promote discussion. I want to find out what your thinking was. I want to find out what your feelings are. And did you learn anything?"[33] The remixed recording is especially poignant because Woods's father, Earl, had passed away four years previously.[34] The *prosōpopoetic* familial pleading of the ad is reminiscent of Cicero's invocations over two millennia before.

By reanimating the elder Woods's fatherly evocations, Nike uses prosōpopoeia and thus exploits Earl Woods's paternal propriety. The advertisement implies that Woods's actions gravely disappointed his father, yet rather than offering a Ciceronian shaming for his behavior, it becomes a vehicle for recuperating his image on the eve of his return to competitive golf. The first phrase of the recording indicates that Woods's actions warranted a clear explanation, though it simultaneously invites a dialogue—an invitation for a cathartic learning moment. The remixed voice of the deceased speaks to Woods in a familial accord that affords permission for the viewing public to voyeuristically participate in expressing its own feelings vicariously for the betrayal of sorts. The aesthetic representation of Earl Woods's voice, offering a fidelity to the speaker that Cicero never could have accomplished in the ancient Roman court, created a *prosōpopoetic* remix that could both chastise and rehabilitate simultaneously. The aesthetic arrangement of the samples of Earl Woods's voice, coupled with the fidelity of portrayal made possible by the digital technology, amplifies the rhetorical potential of prosōpopoeia beyond its analog constraints. A contrast of this type of remix with an ēthopoetic remix can help make this point clearer.

The "character making" ēthopoetic text is analogous to prosōpopoeia, but a close reading of the ancient term reveals a crucial point of divergence. In the ancient text *Lysias*, Greek literary critic Dionysius of Halicarnassus focused on the persuasive compositional element of ēthopoeia as opposed to the progymnasmatic emphasis on suitable characterization. Dionysius's ēthopoeia was unique because it emphasized the creation of a persuasive ēthos, one that was stylistically concise and compellingly performed. According to Kristine S. Bruss, most noteworthy of Dionysius's emphases was the importance of "lifelike, charming composition," a manner of aesthetic arrangement that was ostensibly improvised. Despite its clearly aestheticized structure, this ēthopoetic manner of composition is called "artless," because the arrangement of the text should not be "contrived or formed by any conscious art . . . [but rather give] the impression that this arrangement has not been deliberately and artistically devised, [that it] is somehow spontaneous and fortuitous."[35] This emergent distinction between prosōpopoeia and ēthopoeia offers clarification into the structural variations of remix and their associated appeals.

Some remixed texts tend to be *prosōpopoetic* while others are ēthopoetic—the distinction emerges from how the text is arranged. An ēthopoetic remix is the equivalent of a musical cover; it retains the basic sonic properties of the original song but aims to create a "lifelike, charming" representation rather than a portrayal that is completely accurate. Thus, the ēthos of the original artist(s) continues through a straightforward reimagining of the song.

Though it is emphasized in Dionysian ēthopoeia, this "art of artlessness" is not a necessary component of prosōpopoeia.[36] Appropriateness is lauded as the most important dimension of prosōpopoeia. In *Pro Caelio*, Cicero would change his tone of voice and nonverbal delivery to faithfully impersonate the mannerisms of the character he wished to evoke.[37] Theon and his fellow pedagogues in the *Progymnasmata* spent the majority of their lectures on the "propriety of portrayal," in taking on the form of voice of characters or things.[38] Indeed, their discussions of the trope, as well as Quintilian's, focus on the minutiae of the task, including what age-appropriate colors of apparel the orator should wear when impersonating other individuals.[39] Details of such an endeavor were meticulously outlined so that the character being impersonated could retain a semblance of its ethos in the perception of the audience.

The practice of taking on the voice of another happens frequently in online remixes. One notable example of *prosōpopoeia*—and the best that I've discovered—is the video "Paul McCartney Rabbit Hole" by the master remixer Swedemason.[40] One reason this video is noteworthy is because it offers both a master class in sampling and a powerful illustration of the rhetorical power of taking on another's voice. At its most basic, this video is an extensive *pwning* of Paul McCartney's various interviews over decades, put over an infectious techno beat. But as the mashup clip progresses, it becomes apparent that its objective is not to merely make McCartney's words rhyme and work as the lyrics to a song; the clip actually is a means for Swedemason to talk about his thoughts on remix, through the voice of McCartney. At one point, McCartney is remixed to say "Swedemason, that's my name / I'm ahead of the game." He continues, later on, with a manifesto about remixing authority in the digital age:

> I'll halftime the drum machine / tell you all about how I've been / down the McCartney rabbit hole / took samples people'll say I stole / but I'm not stealing anything, man / I was just doing what the computer can / and this allows me to do what I do / and if you still don't like it, screw you / Producers today have so much choice / but they're too respectful of my voice / You can speed it up, use an

effect / Swede's got a healthy lack of respect / He's a naughty boy, what can I say / He's gonna do it anyway / He's been studying all those years to go "donk" / So I got mashed and wrote this song / Plonk

The video is rhetorically potent, in part, because it uses the rhetorical trope possession by misnomer. There is a tension continually circulating through the text between the technical mastery of the remixer and the authoritative voice of the former Beatle. Swedemason speaks through McCartney, the most important and influential pop musician still living. It's an audacious stunt, to be sure—but to make McCartney appear to endorse Swedemason's shenanigans makes the video even more provocative.

As discussed in earlier chapters, remix exhibits a strong concern for appropriateness. In selecting samples of songs, the best remixers appropriate appropriately. These standards of appropriateness can be witnessed in the musical articulation of a remix. Just as language has a grammar, music has elements crucial to its aesthetic representation. Among them are tempo, chords, pitch, beat, and phrasing. Just as Cicero altered the tone of his voice when he assumed the persona of Appius Claudius, remix artists must alter the pitch of the samples appropriately, slow down the tempo or speed it up, and impose a coalescing beat on top. Remix artists perform a similar dialectical task each time they sample materials and mash them up into a distinctive mosaic.

To meet the standards of appropriateness, remixers rely on śūnyatā to see the potential interdependence of the texts, a contingent collection of song snippets that can function as the starting ground for further artistic creation, while simultaneously conveying the extant social and aesthetic associations inherent to each of the songs. For example, a sampled song that included recorded sound by The Beatles might contain any number of the following musical and/or cultural associations: the British invasion, the political and social tumult of the late sixties, and the assassination of John Lennon. In the case of remix, the allegorical potential of the samples may be amplified and simultaneously effaced as these musical fragments are accompanied by charged associations even while reframing them with new juxtapositions.[41] In addition to having a sense of the interdependence of all of these factors, the remixer must have an astute ear to find aesthetic connections where others would likely never look.

The dialectical logic of remixes—oscillating between the familiarity of the sampled material and the novelty of the mashup—is illustrated in the case of

Danger Mouse's *The Grey Album*. More importantly, the album illustrates a tension between *prosōpopoetic* and ēthopoetic types of remix. In this 2004 album, a mashup of Jay-Z's a cappella tracks from his *Black Album* and selections from The Beatles' *The Beatles* ("White Album"), remix artist Danger Mouse uses aesthetic appropriateness to explore the gray area between allegory and clean slate.[42] Though his experiment succeeds better in some tracks than in others, Danger Mouse appropriates musical samples from the iconic album and transforms them so convincingly that they appear to be appropriate backing tracks to Jay-Z.

Despite its abundance of samples, *The Grey Album* is an example of an ēthopoetic remix. An illustrative song off of the album is "Dirt Off Your Shoulder," which samples John Lennon's "Julia." Lennon's original track, perhaps the most tender and haunting track on "The White Album," is an homage to both his deceased mother (Julia Lennon) and his partner (Yoko Ono). Placing its original authorial meaning and quiet, haunting chords aside, Danger Mouse adds a stuttering and frenetic drumbeat behind the original samples while savagely splicing them into new configurations. The final effect is stunning, as the intensity of the chords and beat coupled with Jay-Z's rhymes work in unexpected ways. Additionally, unsettling elements of the mashup emerge through the unlikely pairing; on top of the original song's fingerpicked chords, Lennon's repeated vocal utterances are disembodied and incomplete in the mashup, evincing a haunting quality that becomes more amplified given the premature deaths of Lennon and his mother. Further, the incongruous pairing of the two songs makes some uncomfortable associations for Beatles fans who hold Lennon's legacy to be sacrosanct: not only is Lennon's song transformed into a nearly unrecognizable sample, Lennon's voice is drowned out by Jay-Z's. The relationship of the voices is ambiguous enough that Jay-Z's voice can be dually interpreted as valorizing Lennon's original song as the greatest, or as essentially proclaiming the artistic superiority of Jay-Z over Lennon.[43] The literal layering of Jay-Z's voice over Lennon's resuscitates Agamben's fears that any sort of prosōpopoeia is an imposition of the living's voice over the dead. However, the concerns of Beatles and Lennon fans from their reading of the remix may be rooted in expectations relating to the type of remix from Danger Mouse. This might occur when fans want a *prosōpopoetic* remix but get an ēthopoetic remix instead. The arrangement of the sample did not strive for a replication of his voice but reanimated it through ēthopoeia.

As evidenced in the case of *The Grey Album*, the appropriateness of the samples is paramount to the text's aesthetic and rhetorical success. Yet the conflation of competing ēthē that is derived from the congruity of musical form and incongruity of extramusical associations further enhances the rhetorical value of the mashup. For example, one entertaining aspect of remix is its nuanced assemblage of music samples from competing genres.[44] Hip hop and classic rock mashed together can be surprising; blends of smooth jazz and heavy metal can create a sense of the carnivalesque.[45] Functioning in more profound ways than its mere entertainment value, the congruent mashing up of samples from traditionally incongruent musical genres demonstrates more of the rhetorical power of the practice. Though this species of layering does not directly parallel the prosōpopoeia of ancient times, its musico-rhetorical use throughout history illustrates how incongruity and prosōpopoeia converge in remix. Ultimately, the appropriateness of the character's representation (or the violation thereof) has been one of the most compelling dimensions of prosōpopoeia in both ancient and networked eras.

The congruity of ostensibly clashing genres in remix cues us to another dimension of śūnyatā: an emphasis on *process* rather than *product*.[46] Nāgārjuna taught that once one could grasp the true meaning of emptiness, one could transcend conventional ways of thinking about reality and perceive the true reality enveloped within the external reality dictated by one's mortal (and thus incomplete) understandings.[47] Śūnyatā, the middle path between permanence and nihilism, was to be achieved through a rigorous process resembling contemporary argumentation:

> [Nāgārjuna] developed a process of dialectical reasoning which exposed contradictions in ordinary thought and which, by reducing all claims to pairs of negations, sought to dislodge thinking from such extremes, thereby freeing the mind to achieve enlightenment. According to this procedure, when it is recognized that opposing poles of thought may be negated by reasoning, the mind is able to acknowledge that reality is neither of them, and is able to experience *sunyata*.[48]

This process of intense interrogation was also designed to penetrate through what the Mādhyamaka School called the "concealment reality" of empirical experience that obscured true reality. This true reality could only be discovered through this rigorous process of intellectual reasoning and reflexive negation. Nevertheless, this discursive process of "abolishing analysis" and the discovery of the true reality "through the [destruction of] the empirical one" was no easy task, nor was the overall objective immediately evident.[49] The monolithic structures of empirical reality were difficult to overcome because they set the parameters for the discussion, after all. Therefore, the school believed in employing aggressive argumentation tactics to challenge the contrary theses. These included using the reductio ad absurdum fallacy or addressing the rival schools' claims by continuously negating rather than engaging them.[50] The individual's phenomenal perception of reality needed to be challenged through a "destructive dialectic" so that the "ultimate truth" could emerge from the obstructions surrounding it.[51] Ultimately, the process of liberating the self from the illusion of empirical reality is the same as the goal of obtaining a true understanding of śūnyatā.

Remix also focuses more on the process than the final product. Similar to the open-source culture that enabled its growth, remix is situated within a discourse that privileges the process of production and circulation even more than the content itself. A key component of the practice is the DJ's demanding challenge of digging in crates, finding creative ways to mash up the subsequent samples, and *prosōpopoetically* assessing the allegorical aura attached to each in order to please the audience. An appreciation of a remix is closely tied to an understanding of how many hours of work it took the remixer(s) to put it together. For example, former NBC anchor Brian Williams's broadcasts have been remixed by Jimmy Fallon's *The Tonight Show* staff numerous times to make Williams appear as if he is rapping famous hip-hop songs.[52] These remixes are not only entertaining, they are also a testament to the tedious process of discovering the appropriate vocal snippets from hundreds of hours of film and compiling them into a two-minute rap. Further complicating the process, in the "Rapper's Delight" video at least, Williams needs to appear to rap colloquialisms that certainly would never appear on an evening news broadcast.[53] The remix artists need to edit the clips with such precision that the words would sound appropriate for their new musical context. Additionally, the rap includes other NBC news anchors and commentators in supporting roles, sometimes rapping in unison with Williams. Part of the delight of the clip certainly is the incongruity of seeing Brian Williams rap the iconic song; another part of the delight stems from knowing that a person (or team of people) would go through such effort to make the clip. Though a "real" clip of Williams rapping the song would certainly entertain as well, the remix is more memorable because of the levels of prosōpopoeia at work; the remixers have imposed their own voices by selecting the Sugarhill Gang song, the clips of news broadcasts, and Williams himself as the unwitting rapper. The projection of voices and ēthē in the remix are imbued with more aesthetic value (hence more *prosōpopoetic* power) because of the painstaking process of finding and remixing the appropriate samples. Hence, like śūnyatā, the process of getting there is even more impressive than the remix understood on its own merits.

Conclusion

Remix is one of the most common practices of the networked era.[54] It represents an amalgamation of persuasive tropes, writings, and philosophies from secular and religious societies spanning both hemispheres and thousands of years. Linking these disparate elements is the belief in the never-ending potential of the text, empty of essence, ready to receive a voice. Poet Emily Dickinson once ruminated about this vivacity of language, declaring that "A word is dead when it is said / some say / I say it just begins to live / that day."[55] Sonic artist Christian Marclay applies the same sentiment to remix: "recorded sound is dead sound, in the sense that it's not 'live' anymore . . . I'm trying to bring it back to life through my art."[56] Following Marclay's articulation of śūnyatā, remix considers a text to be lacking essence when it is not in flux. Through the digital facilitation of prosōpopoeia made possible by remix, the once-dead text is transformed, thereby filling its emptiness, or lack of vivacity, with new life. That new essence, in turn, fends off further "death" in favor of an encompassing and theoretically never-ending cycle of textual recirculation.

Using the elements of music as its repertory of persuasive resources, the task for the remix artist is to create a coherent text out of many that, by definition, are tremendously fragmented. Therefore, the remix artist will select samples of songs, videos, or images that provide a starting place for a transformative articulation of the available material. In order to attempt this creative task, the remix artist must envision the texts' potential for transformation and, thus, sees the raw materials as a palimpsest; the materials being sampled already contain the essence of the soon-to-be text but are also absent of the social (and legal) imposition of completeness.

Still, the vocalization that imbues absent or inanimate form with essence, prosōpopoeia, only partially describes the rhetorical function of remix. If a rhetor is giving voice to another, it is because that other is not present or cannot speak. This practice of assuming the voice of the absent is heuristically valuable for contemporary discourse. It can be considered a social practice intended to grant voice to marginalized, incapacitated, or deceased populations; this rhetorical maneuver can be empowering or forbidding.[57] But certain conditions must exist for it to take place. Anciently, Cicero could only grant voice to Clodius because there was no essential voice of Clodius to hear in the trial. In the ancient case's networked counterpart, Nike gave Earl Woods a voice because his opportunity to share it had passed. Put differently, prosōpopoeia is only plausible for an audience if there is no essence of the voice being projected.

Prosōpopoeia, however, is not theoretically sufficient to account for the essencelessness of texts—a crucial dimension of mashup logic. For this reason, a turn to the ancient Buddhist tradition of śūnyatā is needed to complement the discussion. In order for a text to be remixed, it must first be simultaneously considered as lacking essence and yet entirely interdependent with all other texts. Remix projects voices onto texts that are perceived as lacking one. These essenceless texts are considered discrete and complete. Much as prosōpopoeia projects form onto an absent individual by giving him or her a voice, remix reanimates its samples by mashing them up in novel ways. In other words, digital prosōpopoeia is possible because the text is philosophically bracketed by śūnyatā.

It is śūnyatā that considers the finished text empty of essence because its constituent hooks and melodies have not yet been sampled. In other words, a completed text is dead because it is only brought to life through its artistic appropriation. In so doing, remix injects the text again with a contingent essence. Like a seed's relationship with its nourishing surroundings, the song's constitutive musical elements are all interdependent, as are the entire population of human creative texts.

CHAPTER 6

From Allegory to Anthology

Stranger Things and Nostalgia

To watch the popular show *Stranger Things* (which debuted on Netflix in 2016), a pop culture neophyte might be forgiven for thinking that it's a show from the eighties. From the beginning title sequence, the show's debts to eighties pop culture are apparent: the opening theme uses a pulsating synth theme reminiscent of the soundtracks of John Carpenter's films, the title font recalls the cover of Stephen King's book *Needful Things*, and the ambulatory shots of portions of the title are similar to the introduction in Tim Burton's 1989 film *Batman.* The score of the show is a large part of its nostalgic draw; throughout the seasons, the score (composed and performed by Kyle Dixon and Michael Stein of Austin-based electronic band S U R V I V E) showcases an uncanny similarity to the work of seventies and eighties composers Giorgio Morodor, Harold Faltermeyer, and Tangerine Dream.[1] The plots of the three seasons are sprinkled with narrative Easter eggs from eighties films like *Poltergeist*, *Alien*, *Raiders of the Lost Ark*, and *E.T.* Even the actors cast for supporting roles are actors known primarily for their work from the eighties and nineties: Winona Ryder, Matthew Modine, Sean Astin,

Paul Reiser, and Cary Elwes. *Stranger Things*, in other words, unironically deploys remixed tropes to create a love letter to eighties entertainment.

Stranger Things may be the most visible example of remix and rhetorical tropes in contemporary entertainment. The show is a cultural phenomenon; the first season was nominated for 109 awards.[2] When Netflix dropped the second season on its streaming service, *Stranger Things* quickly become the most tweeted-about show in Netflix history. The first episode of the second season was watched by nearly 16 million people in the first three days after it was made available—over 350,000 people watched the entire season in a day.[3] The third season of the show debuted to even larger numbers, with the season being viewed by 64 million households in its first month on the platform—the most viewed season of the show on Netflix.[4]

In addition to its cultural relevance, *Stranger Things* is discussed here because the show is evidence of the persuasiveness (and pervasiveness) of remix in contemporary entertainment. As stated earlier in the book, remix has an allegorical dimension to it; however, remix occasionally crosses the threshold from allegory to something more—a text that is not just referential, not just intertextual, but hyper-referential. In other words, remix can make a text take a turn from *allegory* into *anthology*.[5] The difference between each can be attributed to the degree of intensity and speed with which the references are made by the text. In an early scholarly article about the show, Myke Bartlett found the amount of references in *Stranger Things* to be staggering: "Certainly, what makes the show so irresistible to children of that decade [the eighties] is that it isn't just paying homage to one or two films, but rather to all of them."[6] Accordingly, I will treat *Stranger Things* as a case study for showing how remix can use rhetorical tropes, combined with an anthology of textual references, to create powerful storytelling techniques.

The transition from remix-as-allegory to remix-as-anthology is on display in *Stranger Things*; but this is not the first time a text has been created from a dizzying number of references. The literary critic and semiotician Umberto Eco has written about how the classic film *Casablanca* could also be considered an anthology because of its prolific use of archetypes. In two similar essays, Eco essentially claims that *Casablanca* is mediocre, a mishmash of recycled archetypes combined with a tired plot.[7] Although the film has been lauded for decades as a masterpiece—a film expert in the film *Adaptation* notoriously calls the script for *Casablanca* the greatest screenplay ever written[8]—Eco argues that these inflated opinions of the greatness of the film are derived from *Casablanca*'s wholesale appropriation of every cinema archetype in the book:

> So all those moments of inspired direction that wring bursts of applause for their unexpected boldness actually represent decisions taken out of desperation . . . Forced to improvise a plot, the authors mixed in a little of everything, and everything they chose came from a repertoire of the tried and true.[9]

He continues by asserting that *Casablanca* is more than one film—it's an anthology, composed of extant archetypal stories and characters from many other films. In this way, the film becomes a repository made sublime through its unabashed usage of recycled archetypes.[10] Eco considers this transformation in the status of a text from banal to sublime to be related to the difference between quantity and quality: the more recycled archetypes the text contains, the better. He explains:

> When the choice of the tried and true is limited, the result is a trite or mass-produced film, or simply kitsch. But when the tried and true repertoire is used wholesale, the result is an architecture like Gaudi's Sagrada Familia in Barcelona. There is a sense of dizziness, a stroke of brilliance . . . When all the archetypes burst in shamelessly, we reach Homeric depths. Two clichés make us laugh. A hundred clichés move us.[11]

Part of the upward movement of the status of the text, therefore, is due to the evocative referential power of the sources being remixed. Eco compares the referential power of intertextuality to that of a traveler hearing the names of mythical stops in the subway, names that "not only stand for physical places, but become the catalyzers of collective memories."[12] In the same way, a film composed wholly of recycled archetypes "provokes in the addressee a sort of intense emotion."[13] The use of (extreme) intertextuality within a text can make it resonate with an audience in ways that a text alone seldom accomplishes. This lasting resonance is related to the emotions within the audience that were derived from its recognition of those already-cherished archetypal stories and characters.

Eco also considers this type of film to be evidence of texts existing within a postmodern "cult culture."[14] The claim, of course, implies that not all viewers will recognize the allusions made by every text. Noël Carroll, in an often-cited essay, argues that the recognition of cinematic allusions is an important component of the film-going experience. Carroll saw movies in the seventies and early eighties as conforming to what he called the "two-tiered structure of communication."[15] Within this system, filmmakers created movies that catered to a group of youthful moviegoers who favored films that could offer them an entertaining escape. A second group, however, who had acquired higher levels of cinematic knowledge that the first group (the "inveterate film gnostics in the front rows"), craved films that were more "hermetic, camouflaged, and recondite"—in other words, this portion of the audience wanted films that satisfied their desires to feel like part of the film cognoscenti. Still, there were yet other viewers who didn't easily fit into either of these types of viewers. This third group were nonplussed by the films that appeared to simultaneously appeal to both of these audiences. They recognized the paradox inherent in a film studio creating a "dumb" film (to appeal to certain audiences) with "intelligent" cinematic allusions (to appeal to other audiences).[16] As a result, this third group sought something else from their entertainment, films that, as a backlash to the two-tiered system, appealed because of their "deathly sincerity."[17] It will be my contention here that *Stranger Things*, as a remixed text, appeals to each of these audiences; as an anthology of eighties entertainment references, it uses remix to wield nostalgic appeal to the reference-savvy audience, fulfills generic conventions for the uninitiated audience still unaware of the show's vast repository of references, and employs an appealing brand of sincerity for the viewers who appreciate cinematic mashups but crave a more authentic humanism over the potentially shallow strategy of pastiche. Put another way, this entertainment characterized by its premium on human connection and relationships appeals to the audience suffering from postmodern fatigue. *Stranger Things* uses remix to offer a range of pleasures for disparate audiences.

In this chapter I (re)introduce a few rhetorical tropes that help explain the appeal of *Stranger Things*, both on a textual/rhetorical level and in terms of its potential reception by the audience.[18] The vast majority of scholarship on the show—predictably—focuses on its use of nostalgia. While any discussion of this show (or other similar remix films like *Super 8*) must include its use of nostalgia, I choose as a point of departure to examine how nostalgia functions from a tropological vantage point—how does *Stranger Things*'s use of remix and rhetorical tropes make the nostalgia so potent with this particular text? The following discussion will focus on three tropes associated with classical rhetoric and Greek philosophy: *enthymeme*, *eudaimonia*, and *suasoria*. The show's use of nostalgia is a rhetorical move—it uses the *enthymeme* and *suasoria* to prime the viewer for a *eudaimonic* experience. Looking at *Stranger Things* from the framework of rhetorical tropes (and not merely from the analytical lens of nostalgia) offers new insights about how remix can persuade an audience.

Applying these rhetorical tropes to the text of analysis, this chapter concludes with the assertion that *Stranger Things* resonates with viewers through its use of remixing and recycling well-known cinematic, sonic, and aesthetic tropes from eighties entertainment. However, the show's rhetorical objective—persuading the viewers that the show is worth their time in an age of innumerable shows and cluttered viewing platforms, that is—goes beyond its use of nostalgia. Whereas nostalgia has long been associated with remix and the emotions it evokes, it also has been reduced merely to its use of irony because of its association with a postmodernism redolent of pastiche. The nostalgia of *Stranger Things*, however, is a remixed nostalgia, a unique, updated variety that conforms to a recent trend of literature and entertainment sometimes referred to as "the new sincerity." I argue that remix (and its enthymematic logic) primes the viewers (via *suasoria*) to be moved to feel a satisfaction associated with nostalgia which can lead to a deep sense of contemplative longing (eudaimonia). An overview of remix and the enthymeme will set the stage for the discussion.

Enthymeme

The *enthymeme* is a rhetorical trope present in remix. As a subcategory of Aristotle's logos, the enthymeme is particularly important because it is dependent on the interaction of the orator and the audience. Translated from Greek, "enthymeme" means "something in the mind." Aristotle called the enthymeme the rhetorical equivalent of the syllogism, an inductive logical reasoning process that took place within the realm of dialectic.[19] However, while the syllogism provides both the premises and the conclusion of the logical thought process, the enthymeme omits one of them, thus allowing the audience the opportunity to provide the missing component of the argument. In this way, the enthymeme is a persuasive strategy because speeches "with enthymemes excite [a] more favorable audience reaction" than those without.[20] Isocrates also used this concept in his discourse, calling the enthymeme "a striking thought," used to adorn a speech.[21] "For Isocrates, the best and most effective enthymemes will in some sense come as a surprise . . . and will seem to stand apart from or go beyond what precedes them."[22] By inviting the audience to participate with the creation of the argument, the orator is able to create a persuasive argument that is pleasing to the listeners.

Considered aesthetically, the enthymeme suggests that an audience can participate in the formal construction of psychological reactions to art. Kenneth Burke explains that one aspect of the appeal of aesthetics is its effective evocation of feelings of participation within the audience:

> It is the suspense of certain forces gathering to produce a certain result. It is the suspense of a rubber band which we see being tautened. We know that it will be snapped—there is thus no ignorance of the outcome; our satisfaction arises from *our participation* in the process from the act that the beginnings of the dialogue lead us to feel the logic of its close.[23]

Enthymematically, when the artist (or orator) is able to successfully conjure up the audience's emotions—fear, surprise, humor—it does not come at the expense of the audience's intellect. Its success is predicated upon the audience's belief that it participated with the artist in summoning those emotions. Therein is registered one of the pleasures of art.

The enthymeme is one reason nostalgic, remixed entertainment like *Stranger Things* resonates with its audience. Part of the thrill of consuming the remix is the recognition that the audience has when it notices a sample, quote, motif, or trope used elsewhere, especially if the text does not attribute the citation. Similar to the notion of *jouissance* discussed earlier, an enthymeme evokes a sense of pleasure from the reader (or viewer or listener) of the remix when that person makes connections that are not explicitly there. In *Understanding Comics*, Scott McCloud argues that the reader of comics appreciates the movement of the action within the panels—but is even more excited by the space *between* the panels; this is where the reader is able to interject parts of the story that are left out by the artist and writer.[24] John Fiske—by way of Roland Barthes—explains *jouissance* as the moment of bodily pleasure the reader experiences when "text and reader erotically lose their separate identities and become a new, momentarily produced body that is theirs and theirs alone."[25] This strategic withholding of the puzzle pieces is an excellent narrative strategy, commonly referred to in cinematic theory as the "2+2 theory." Explained by Pixar director Andrew Stanton, "never give the audience '4.' Instead, compel them to come to '4' on their own."[26] Thus, the creator(s) of the text use the enthymeme to compel the audience to feel as if it is a participant in the deciphering of the text.

Stranger Things and the Enthymeme

As a text, *Stranger Things* uses the enthymeme to persuade the audience. The text is saturated with intertextual references—visually, narratively, and sonically—to the point of being an anthology. It not only uses these references to conjure up emotions related to nostalgia; it uses them to advance the plot via enthymeme. Beginning with its sonic references, the show selects familiar songs that evoke feelings associated with the recognition of the source, as well as thematically relate to the narrative purpose of that scene. Perhaps most famous is the show's repeated use of "Should I Stay or Should I Go?" by The Clash—the repetition of which becomes a plea from the interstitial Will Byers (Noah Schnapp) to his mother Joyce (Winona Ryder), as he is helplessly trapped between two dimensions. New Order's "Elegia" (meaning "lament for the dead") accompanies Will's funeral in Season One. Oingo Boingo's "Just Another Day" introduces Season Two, with a message that's hard to miss: welcome to another day in the life of a small Midwestern town. The concluding scene from Season Two also contains an appropriate popular song: "Every Breath You Take" by the Police. The song not only accompanies the geekily romantic Snow Ball dance, it represents an ominous message from the Shadow Monster to the kids. The show allows the audience to interact with the text, appreciating the show through the framework of their own love of popular culture.[27]

Along with its viewers, *Stranger Things* embraces the nostalgic desire for an older time—and older technologies. The archaic technologies in the show are often pivotal for the success of the characters—a makeshift radio tower allows the team to save the day in Season Three.[28] Walkie-talkies and ham radios are the principal means of communication for the kids—even supernaturally—in Season One. And cassettes and cassette-playing stereos feature prominently early on in the show. These featured technologies are not surprising in a nostalgic text. After all, nostalgia has been used in previous texts as a way to lament the progress of technological advancements (and its inevitable push toward a "technological apocalypse").[29] Others have argued that *Stranger Things* resonates in the current climate because it embraces the analog era (and, by implication, repudiates the age of the internet and perpetual surveillance).[30] The nostalgia of *Stranger Things*, then, is not only a product of its pop culture references. Sound culture scholar Megan Fariello suggests that the use of defunct technologies in the show, the "techno-historical acoustic," is one of the reasons for its nostalgia:

> I am suggesting a new use of sound has emerged that indicates a shift in audience engagement . . . The techno-historical acoustic works as a catalyst to memory. Sound is often associated with its ability to produce memory, and this works both for the characters on screen and for the audience, especially because of these media's settings or engagements with the past. It is a two-part experience for the audience, since they are being called to remember both aspects of the diegesis and an actual historical past.[31]

The "two-part experience" referred to in this quote recalls the enthymeme. The diegetic sounds produced by archaic technologies on the show activate a nostalgia not only for the songs, but also for old technologies mediating the songs. The mediating technology on the show thus contributes to the tapestry of nostalgic responses by the viewers to the text.

But this argument about the technologies in the text does not sufficiently explore these implications beyond sound—the nostalgic potential of the enthymeme is made more powerful as the textual references grow progressively denser. The signifiers of the eighties in *Stranger Things* are found in the vast number of references from other movies from that time, as well as the soundtrack, score, fashion, hairstyles, and architecture. References are layered on top of other references, making the intertextuality more robust as each new season is released. Because the enthymeme leverages unstated connections, the more densely the archetypes and allusions are layered in the text, the more potentially powerful the enthymeme will be. Therefore, as the viewers progressively recognize the references, the palimpsests of past memories gradually become more pronounced and the viewer experiences ever-greater feelings of nostalgia. The implication for rhetoric here relates to how the text is constructed—if the text is a mashup of a torrent of other textual references, it allows for more room for connection and recognition by the audience. The enthymeme, then, is a rhetorical device with much potential for remix.

There are many other references in *Stranger Things* that function as homage to entertainment from the eighties, but they are far too numerous to mention here. More relevant to our discussion is *how* the show uses remix and nostalgia. *Stranger Things* uses the enthymeme to provoke emotions associated with the remixed texts, thus producing a sense of nostalgia within the viewer. To better understand how remix can harness nostalgia, we will discuss another concept from the writings of Aristotle, the notion of *eudaimonia*.

Eudaimonia and Nostalgic Representations

Although eudaimonia originated in ancient Greece (it is roughly translated to mean happiness, fulfillment, or blessedness), it has become a term used in entertainment psychology scholarship for understanding reasons why people might consume their entertainment. Entertainment has been often understood as a means of escape from current stifling conditions (this argument will become even more apparent in our discussion of nostalgia further on). The escapist motivation for preferring certain entertainment has been described as "hedonic." Hedonic motivations for consuming entertaining media are related to hedonism, a desire within the viewer to engage in sensation-seeking, overcome loneliness, and/or regulate suboptimal mood states.[32] *Eudaimonic* media, on the other hand, provokes other, more nuanced sensations within the viewer that cannot be simply reduced to "enjoyment." This is media that can lead to contemplation, reflection, and a mixture of positive/negative affective responses. As such, eudaimonic media leads to appreciation more than enjoyment, "a perception of deeper meaning, the feeling of being moved, and the motivation to elaborate on thoughts and feelings inspired by the experience."[33] These types of affective outcomes suggest that viewer responses to eudaimonic media often border on ambivalent, such as when a sad movie can evince pleasurable sensations among its viewers.[34]

Eudaimonic media is also associated with the notion of tenderness, an affective state within which contemplation and self-reflection exist alongside feelings related to empathy, warmth, and kindness.[35] This explains the ambivalence that can characterize eudaimonia; the poignant reflection that emerges from self-reflection can be instigated by the feeling of memory and closeness, along with its dialectic of irretrievable loss. The condition that entertainment scholar Mary Beth Oliver has referred to as "tenderness" is similar to the phenomenon articulated by the German word *sehnsucht,* a wistful sensation of longing for something that is gone even while paradoxically feeling the resonant warmth of its erstwhile presence. Inspired by Aristotle's definition, eudaimonic motivations for selecting media content might be centered in the desire for insight, self-reflection, and "contemplations of poignancy or meaningfulness (e.g., what makes life valuable)."[36] For our purposes, this eudaimonic motivation offers a point of theoretical convergence with nostalgia.

Nostalgia

While nostalgia means many things, the discussion of the term to follow focuses on its similarity to eudaimonia. Recent literature on rhetoric, nostalgia, and technology suggests that remembering can be considered a rhetorical means for reaching eudaimonia.[37] Nostalgia is a portmanteau of the Greek words *nostos* and *algos*, meaning "to return home" and "pain" respectively.[38] Thus, nostalgia can be seen as a homesickness, a yearning for a home or a time that is now lost. Linda Hutcheon explains, "It is the very pastness of the past, its inaccessibility, that likely accounts for a large part of nostalgia's power."[39] This irrecoverable past often assumes a halcyon appearance in memory because it can become idealized (and therefore sanitized) in contrast to the undesirable present.[40] Nostalgia is something that is *felt* more than perceived in something, according to Hutcheon—there is a clear affective element to it.[41] And this poignant sensation of sorrow and longing can be an impetus for creating great art (although some would argue that nostalgia spawns kitsch[42]).

The feelings that accompany nostalgia seem to be anchored to a time that perhaps feels more stable and authentic than the present.[43] Hence, there is often a nostalgic glow that surrounds cultural texts from someone's own life. Referring to popular music, essayist Chuck Klosterman says, "If you unconditionally love something from your past, it might just mean you love that period of your own life."[44] Indeed, recent scholarship seems to confirm this connection between text and associated (extramusical) memories with a phenomenon called "cascading reminiscence bumps."[45] In this 2013 study, Cornell psychology scholar Carol Lynne Krumhansl and student Justin Adam Zupnick found that popular music from one's late adolescence had the greatest impact on individuals throughout their lives because of the strong emotions and memories that proliferate during that developmental time. Provocatively, even the pop music from the listener's *parents'* generations evoked a similar reminiscence bump, or spike in feelings of nostalgia.[46] The suggested implication is that indirectly consuming the parents' favorite songs also yielded nostalgia, despite the fact that these songs were likely released before the births of the listeners. Incidentally, my students have a similar nostalgic response to *Stranger Things*, even though most of them were not alive during the decade of the eighties; Kayla McCarthy calls this an "appropriated nostalgia."[47] One possible reason why this nostalgia can cluster around media from a time before the life of the viewer is due to the status of remixed texts as *pastiche*—texts understood to reference not an actual historical period, but rather (inter)textual representations of that time.

Pastiche

A writer in the *New Yorker* has called *Stranger Things* "a pastiche of eighties pop culture."[48] However, this description is somewhat reductive because it does not take into full account what pastiche means and what *Stranger Things* actually does. As discussed in an earlier chapter, pastiche is an element of recycling cultural texts that emphasizes representation, full of style but void of substance. In a sense, pastiche defiantly confirms the same critiques of style that preceded the transition from the world of *stuff* to the world of *fluff*.[49] Unmoored by material referents, pastiche exists as an idiosyncratic representation that revels in its artifice. In a meaning coined by Fredric Jameson in his influential book *Postmodernism*, pastiche is like parody, but not quite; where parody is an engagement with a text, undergirded by a tenacious "satiric impulse," pastiche is drained of humor and any textual history is effaced.[50] Rather, pastiche is a "cannibalization of all the styles of the past" that shuns historical referents in favor of simulacra. Pastiche texts, then, sidle into the space carved into existence by postmodernism. If the past is nothing more than a repository of allusions, style-heavy pastiche can offer the past what it wants: not history, but pop history.[51] *Stranger Things* certainly uses elements of pastiche as a textual device, but the show also complicates it.[52]

Postmodern pastiche envisions nostalgia in a negative light. To wit, Jameson argues that nostalgic films open up missing pasts "for aesthetic colonization" and subsequently present a version of the thing in a glib, ironic way. Pastiche, in other words, is not interested in accurately representing the past, but rather in presenting a stylistic version of *pastness*, the "1930s-ness" or "1950s-ness" of the past.[53] To be sure, both Jameson's postmodern pastiche and Hutcheon's nostalgia are interested in "pastness"; but a crucial difference between both is the presence of irony (in pastiche) or its absence (in nostalgia). The "blank irony" of pastiche is lacking in historical authenticity or warmth; it happens when two meanings (or codes) "come together, usually with a certain critical edge," often aiming that critical edge directly at the artery of nostalgia: its emotional lure.[54] Hutcheon argues that the irony of pastiche does indeed acknowledge the affective potency of nostalgia, but uses it, instead, to subvert the nostalgic logic that the past can be revisited through poignant memories and tender contemplation.[55]

Because of the incisive objectives of postmodern pastiche, there has been an emerging clamor from writers and filmmakers alike to counter it.[56] Like the third tier of moviegoers referenced by Noël Carroll earlier, a number of viewers crave the "deathly sincere" in their entertainment, and filmmakers often accommodate this request. This "affective and personally invested" trend of textual production, organized loosely around this call to action, is sometimes called "the new sincerity."[57]

Stranger Things, like pastiche, is not interested in accurately representing the historical past. Unlike pastiche, however, it is interested in using remix to mine the emotions that come from revisiting a nostalgic re-creation of that mediated past—it wants the viewer not to visualize an authentic "eighties" but rather the Spielbergian eighties—a decade that only existed on the screen. Still, it's an eighties that was filled with innocence and geeky awkwardness, a (begrudging, yet endearing) commonplace between many people. It deploys textual references to enliven past representations and inject an authenticity into the characters. In other words, *Stranger Things* not only uses remix to pull emotions out of the viewer associated with the anthology of references in the show, deploying nostalgia to help the viewer reach toward eudaimonia; *Stranger Things* also uses remix to recreate "the new sincerity" in its episodes, a tonal decision conspicuously absent in postmodern pastiche. Therefore, the text *uses* pastiche in the service of *remixing* pastiche, thus adding a nostalgic color back into the blank corpus of postmodern texts.

The New Sincerity

The notion of "the new sincerity" is more closely related to eudaimonia and nostalgia than it is to pastiche. Like postmodernism, the new sincerity should also be seen as a response. Whereas the irony of pastiche countered the indulgent feelings of nostalgia, the new sincerity (sometimes called "post-irony" or "post-postmodernism") is a response to pastiche.[58] Responding to the double-coding of pastiche, writer David Foster Wallace called on others to aesthetically uphold "single-entendre values," despite the potential "yawn, the rolled eyes, the cool smile" from the postmodernists that would inevitably accompany that aesthetic.[59] To subscribe to the new sincerity aesthetic meant to be earnest and authentic, and acknowledge that words could be sincere.[60] It should be noted that this aesthetic did not necessarily mean a repudiation of postmodern values, but an opening up and allowing for more feeling within the text.[61]

Despite its origin in the early nineties, the new sincerity gathered steam in fiction following 9/11, when the perceived nihilism of postmodernism seemed to fall out of fashion.[62] Although irony still proliferated in popular televisual entertainment (*Seinfeld*, *Arrested Development*, and *30 Rock* are notable examples), other shows like *The Office*, *Parks and Recreation*, and *Community* were also emerging—shows that made a point of emphasizing human connection and authentic, vulnerable expressions of emotion. *Community*, in particular, is an interesting case study because of its apparent oscillation between parody and sincerity; the show frequently references archetypes from entertainment and gleefully acknowledges when it resorts to the same tactics. Still, however, the show reiterates its title in every episode when it reminds the viewer of the importance of human connection and good that exists in everyone. Frequently, the core characters hug and support each other rather than responding with ironic detachment (as in *Seinfeld*, for instance).[63]

Stranger Things, also, is an allegory of many different references—although it is a much starker example of pastiche than *Community* is, due to its unblinking appropriation of the multitude of references for their use-value, not commentary. Still, *Stranger Things* presents the ensemble of characters in a mostly positive light, as caring for one another and banding together as good in the face of evil. What's more, *Stranger Things* showcases positive tropes frequently; Jonathan (Charlie Heaton) and Steve (Joe Keery) are progressively sensitive and confident throughout the seasons, illustrating the trope of the "new emotional male protagonist."[64] The characters openly and unironically demonstrate their affection for each other throughout, as seen in the dance at the Snow Ball at the conclusion of Season Two. There is very little misogyny or racism evident in the attitudes and dialogues between characters, and kids are punished by Eleven (Millie Bobby Brown) for being bullies.[65] Further, the relationship between Sheriff Hopper (David Harbour) and Eleven, whom he takes in and raises as his daughter, is flawed yet heartwarming. Hopper, in particular, is presented as sensitive and emotional throughout the entire series. Even relatively minor characters, like Bob Newby (Sean Astin), engage in heroic acts of self-sacrifice. *Stranger Things*, in other words, presents the core characters as sympathetic and concerned with human connection—the warmth of their portrayal is an important foil to the darkness of the evil monsters that pervade each episode.

As an aesthetic, the new sincerity can amplify the nostalgic power of the remixed text; not only do viewers experience the associated emotions with the referenced source material, they experience eudaimonia from the warmth of human connection portrayed in the text. As mentioned earlier, the notion of eudaimonia has been adapted by media studies scholars to reflect the effects media can have on its audience. But its modern usage in media scholarship has become separated from its rhetorical origins. When Aristotle wrote about eudaimonia, his arguments focused on envisioning the term in the context of living a good, contemplative, virtuous life.[66] Socrates spoke about eudaimonia as a goal, a perfect happiness—a way for a human to overcome an unjust life by adopting ethical codes, which can lead to living a life, governed by self-control, in a just society.[67] Usually, in Greek literature, eudaimonia is discussed in the context of ethics and politics. But in the *philosophia* of Isocrates, the political, ethical, and the rhetorical were interconnected.[68] Thus, Isocrates wrote about eudaimonia with rhetoric in mind. As explained by classicist Werner Jaeger, "The purpose of Isocrates' rhetorical culture is to produce perfection in human life, the state which he, like the philosophers, calls *eudaimonia*, happiness."[69] In his *On the Peace*, Isocrates articulates his idea of eudaimonia at the Hellenic state level:

> Let me ask, then, whether we should be satisfied if we could dwell in our city secure from danger, if we could be provided more abundantly with the necessities of life, if we could be of one mind amongst ourselves, and if we could enjoy the high esteem of the Hellenes. I, for my part, hold that, with these blessings assured us, Athens would be completely happy.[70]

For Isocrates, the use of logos, communication, and "the acknowledgment of common values" is a pathway to the "objective good" of eudaimonia.[71] Relationships, to Isocrates, are essential for happiness.[72]

Stranger Things draws its rhetorical strength from the common values shared by the showrunners and the viewing audience, thus evoking nostalgia en route to eudaimonic reception. Eudaimonia is not just a media effect, it is an element of a rhetorical text, invented and organized because of a rhetorical exigency, aiming for a particular impact upon the audience. Picking up again on the "tender affective states" dimension of eudaimonia mentioned earlier, the discussion now shifts to address the final rhetorical trope, *suasoria*, as a means of exploring how history, nostalgia, and eudaimonia may intertwine.[73]

Suasoria, Historical Context, and Affective Priming

Suasoria refers to a type of rhetorical exercise that was performed by students in ancient Roman schools. This term, used in the writings of Seneca and Quintilian, referred to a role-playing exercise where the student of rhetoric would be asked to speak in character on a topic related to a historical theme or dilemma.[74] This pedagogical activity was a type of declamation, a voice-training exercise; as such, the speakers could often get loud and emotional in their deliveries—an aspect that Quintilian laments about in his *Institutio Oratoria*.[75] Although this exercise was not as difficult as the *controversia* exercise that would follow, it was demanding due to its historical specificity.[76] In giving hypothetical advice to past leaders in moral crises, as they would in these types of deliberative situations, students would need to be intimately aware of the historical context surrounding the dilemma. Still, the student sometimes opted to remix the history; Seneca wrote about "Cicero" facing the choice of whether to ask forgiveness of Antony or burn his own writings—no evidence exists that Cicero was ever actually faced with these choices.[77] Although these exercises were rhetorical, they also were poetic and contemplative, verging on theatricality and entertainment before further rhetorical work could be done.[78]

In the preceding example, we can see that *suasoria* also involved the use of a previously discussed trope: *prosōpopoeia*, or speaking in the first person as another historical figure.[79] Because context was key, in order for speakers to effectively perform the exercise using the voice of another, they needed to learn the historical context of the situation, the appropriateness and timeliness of their responses (*kairos*).[80] The appropriateness of the performance also depended upon their knowledge of the listening audience—these speeches could not exist without context, and the audience was fundamental to the appropriateness of the speech. In the *suasoriae*, "Appeals to *pathos*, then, as well as to *ethos*, had to be modified in accordance with time, place, and the imagined character of the audience named in the case."[81] In fulfilling the audience's desires to hark back to a defined time and space in history, the *suasoriae* accommodated a sense of nostalgia. Summarizing the role of *suasoria* as declamation, with a decidedly musical twist, Mendelson argues that "declamation is a dramatic exercise in occupying the space of the other, in giving voice to a person who speaks in a different key, of 'identifying' to the point of consubstantiation."[82] *Suasoria* is a rhetorical trope relevant to this discussion because it is concerned with history, entertainment, and speaking in the voice of another—or, as I have argued previously, remix.

Related to the trope of *suasoria* is the word "suasive" (defined by the New Oxford American Dictionary as "serving to persuade") and the related "suasion" (defined as "persuasion as opposed to force or compulsion"). I read these terms as being analogous to the media phenomenon of priming the audience, or preparing the conditions whereby the audience can be receptive to the persuasion that is to follow. Elsewhere, I have argued that sonic media facilitates a suasory experience as it transmits levels of affect that can prepare its listener to be moved.[83] Likewise, the nostalgic materials remixed in *Stranger Things*, presented to the audience enthymematically, creates a suasory condition whereby the text leverages the resulting emotions felt within the audience to facilitate a state of eudaimonia.

The *suasoria* of remixed nostalgia works in more ways than affective priming; understanding the heritage of the original Roman rhetorical trope in the context of remix can yield further insight. Returning to Carroll's tiers of film viewers from earlier, the episodes of *Stranger Things* are entertaining enough to satisfy the escapist motivations of its young audience without reverting to pastiche. But it also offers the Easter eggs to those who appreciate the texts of the eighties. In this way, the show takes the trope of *suasoria* very seriously—it knows its audience and it wants to reward them for their knowledge of eighties pop culture. *Stranger Things* uses kairos and prosōpopoeia by creating an appropriate fictional plot and characters for this already-established intertextual universe. In this way, *Stranger Things* is a form of *suasoriae*, entertaining and priming its audience to be moved via its referential pathos. It creates a eudaimonic experience for the audience through these references, incited by the enthymematic logic of the show.

Conclusion

Stranger Things is an example of how a torrent of recycled cinematic, sonic, and aesthetic tropes from eighties entertainment can be mashed up to create an anthology masquerading as a single text, one that is more compelling than a sum of its parts. Although past research on *Stranger Things* typically gravitates to its use of nostalgia (and then stops the discussion there), I have explored how the show uses remix to create such a potent nostalgic lure. In attempting to deconstruct this process with the aid of classical rhetorical tropes *enthymeme*, *eudaimonia*, and *suasoria*, I conclude with the observation that if remix can be nostalgic, or, in other words, if remix can precipitate a profound revisiting of emotions related to the remixed source material, it can also amplify that nostalgia by further remixing it. In the case of *Stranger Things*, I have argued that the show uses the stylistic leanings of pastiche to quote past texts, but it downplays the irony and detachment inherent in pastiche in favor of a warmer reading of the mediated past. This reconstruction of the mediated past aims to be more authentic by focusing on human connection and an ethics of care. Therefore, the remixed text remixes pastiche to not only communicate nostalgia, but persuade the viewer to contemplate authentic human connection in a postmodern culture. In so doing, it primes the viewer to have an affective experience that leads to a eudaimonic state.

Conclusion

This book has been an inquiry into the contemporary practice of remix and the rhetorical tropes that can be used to both create and analyze remixed texts. Remix has helped me navigate thorny theoretical issues in that largely uncharted terrain at the intersection between rhetoric, music, digital media, streaming entertainment, and aesthetics. Like the interplay of layered samples in a mashup, this book offers scholarly contributions to any of the above fields of inquiry when they are examined concurrently.

An Analytic Lens for Rhetorical Tropes

More than a guide to these intersecting processes, remix has functioned here as a reflexive phenomenon, one that serves as an interpretive lens for these inquiries that can also turn the lens back on itself. The same reflexivity is equally true of rhetoric in this context. I have frequently discussed the parallels between remix and rhetoric throughout the book. This reflects one of its contributions to rhetorical theory. In using either remix or rhetoric to examine the other, both become mutually elucidated.

Earlier in the book, I posed questions about the rhetorical dimensions of remix and how this rhetorical perspective might reveal features of the practice. There are parallels between rhetoric and remix because remix is derivative of discursive practices. Accordingly, one of the unifying threads of this book relates to the parallels between remix and rhetoric. The rhetorical framing of remix helps us understand that the practice is not ahistorical but rather a post-parenthetical continuation of pre-parenthetical practices. Remix did not originate ex nihilo from the advent of the networked era. In fact, it has existed in different incarnations since the dawn of communication. The classical discursive innovations of Isocrates framed the contemporary practice of remix. The processes of collaborative creation, quoting others, and directing the audience's attention to one appropriate argument instead of another argument are all antecedents to the rhetorical dimensions of remix. This framework of remix as rhetoric elucidates features of the practice by making its connections with the rhetorical tradition explicit. Thus, an understanding of the contemporary phenomenon is augmented and clarified by a preliminary understanding of its classical rhetorical antecedents.

Remix is a rhetorical process, but more than that, remix *is* rhetoric and vice versa. This framework not only provides an impetus for a discussion on the role of remix in human communication, but it also challenges the notion that remix is facilitated solely by technology. Thus, this book challenges common perceptions of remix as ahistorical and strictly technological.

Another objective here was to investigate how a rhetorical perspective could demonstrate the broader cultural significance of remix. Insights relative to this question readily emerge when remix is situated within the copyright debate. Embedded in this discourse, we can see the rhetorical function of remix in public culture. Remix tries to determine the parameters of the debate. The aesthetically congruent relationships between the samples in Girl Talk's mashups create a sort of rhetorical potency by directing our attention away from the politics of digital sampling into a direct focus on the aesthetic success of the mashup. Kenneth Burke argued that relationships between terms had an innate power to create interpretations of reality among identifiable groups.[1] The same applies to Girl Talk's mashups; they *select* the reality of the discourse as being concerned with the musical interplay of samples, while they *deflect* the legal dimensions within which the practice had been hitherto embedded.[2] The auto-tunes of the Gregory

Brothers also direct attention to the beauty of the musical form away from the terrors of the persistent racial and classist attitudes manifested in the clips. As I have argued, this notion of musical form as argumentation is another example of how contemporary remix is inspired by avant-garde art. Minimalist composer Steve Reich once explained about the compositional process, "Focusing on the musical process makes possible that shift of attention away from *he* and *she* and *you* and *me* outward toward *it* [the process of composition]."[3] The process of remix shifting people's attitudes away from surrounding discourses to the music itself is rhetorical.[4]

I have also examined the rhetorical tropes embedded in remix across media—in music, on YouTube, in memes, and on Netflix. The wide-ranging spectrum of remixed texts analyzed in these pages reflects the prevalence of remix in multimodal cultural production.

Digital Invention and the Contemporary Enthymeme

Throughout this book, I have argued that remix-*qua*-rhetoric is a bridge between the classical rhetorical tradition and the contemporary practice of remix. This capacity is especially apparent in the application of remix to the classical rhetorical concepts of invention, imitatio, kairos, and the enthymeme. One essential component of the rhetorical canon that crosses over into the digital realm is invention. In the classical sense, invention is part of the process of crafting an argument. However, there is a specific variant of invention unique to digital media that particularly informs the practice of remix.

Both the contemporary remix artist and the traditional orator are engaged in the process of rhetorical invention. The remix artist, though, engages in a mode of invention that hybridizes the rhetorical tradition with digital technology, a phenomenon that I have so far been calling *digital invention.* This appellation is not simply the latest addition to the fashionable exercise of appending "digital" to concepts not previously considered as such. I chose to use the term because it describes not only an updated version of invention for the digital age, it is the branding of a practice uniquely possible because of digital technology.

Originally conceived as *inventio* in the Latin rhetoric primer *Rhetorica ad Herennium,* "invention" refers to the process of discovering and generating novel arguments. The process is both cognitive and collaborative. It is cognitive in the sense that the orator needs to mentally synthesize previously discovered arguments, and collaborative in the sense that the interaction of the orator and the audience may be crucial in formulating one's arguments. Invention is what makes the persuasive potential of remix possible.

Like the classical concept of invention, digital invention also uses classical rhetoric resources like imitatio and kairos. Recall that imitatio was a form of pedagogy in classical Greece, best exemplified by Isocrates. In this teachable concept, imitatio declared that students should find an orator whom they admired and essentially work to creatively imitate that orator's rhetorical strategies. This practice became stigmatized as theft and stripped of its inventional potential by Romantic thinkers—and the stigma still remains. However, remix artists use imitatio productively in their mashups as a variant of digital invention. They productively imitate the authors of the samples they use in their mashups, even while creatively modifying the samples for their use in a new context.

Kairos is another classical concept manifested anew in the contemporary era. Isocrates inculcated his students about kairos by telling them how the making of arguments had an appropriate place and time. In this way, the context determined the appropriateness of the content. Remix artists model this same philosophy in their mashups to an even greater degree. Kairos is a component of the logic that allows for a consonant mashup; a sample will likely be placed in a certain portion of a mashup because it "sounds good" or because it "fits" in that place. This primacy of appropriateness over legality defines much of the aesthetic structure (and controversies) of mashups.

The classical enthymeme still offers great heuristic potential in the hyper-participatory culture of the networked age. The remixed term "produser" hints at the contemporary utility of the enthymeme. While the classical definition of the term still holds true, the term needs to be broadened in scope to match its new context.[5] In the networked era, the enthymeme has shifted away from its classical conceptualization into a more hybridized classical-contemporary concept. In addition to the classical notion of a common set of experiences or ideas shared between the orator and the audience, the contemporary enthymeme also functions as a linkage between people and common artifacts of popular culture.[6] This is another contribution of the book: envisioning the commonplace between orator and audience much as the connection an audience makes with a remix artist, or with a mashup. The enthymeme, distanced from its exclusively civic context, has much to offer to rhetoricians interested in studying the post-parenthetical era.

The contemporary enthymeme functions as a resource for digital invention.

When Girl Talk creates a mashup, for example, it is the culmination of years of deejaying concerts and discovering what appeals to an audience. Remix is a musical impetus for cognitive linkages facilitated by the essential place of allegory within remix. Hearty responses from the audience indicate to Gillis (Girl Talk) that the audience considers the sample to be worthy for its inclusion in the mashup. Within that complicit approval is predicated a familiarity with the sample, which is subsequently layered in novel ways. This familiarity yields approval, but so does the common bond—the consubstantiality—between the remix artist and the audience. That shared participation leads to a digital brand of invention, wherein Gillis chooses the "approved" samples and their order in the mashup to be included in the official album version. He then uses novelty and surprise to layer the samples, thus defying the expectations of the audience while still retaining the allegorical power of the samples. This enthymematic process underlies much of the pleasure and intellectual satisfaction derived from listening to a mashup.

The participatory process is equally relevant to classical and contemporary cultures. In his treatise *On Rhetoric*, Aristotle wrote that the audience is essential to the cultivation of *pisteis*, or the means of persuading an audience: "It is necessary for *pisteis* and speeches [as a whole] to be formed on the basis of common [beliefs], as we said in the *Topics* about communication with a crowd."[7] This is a concept that remixers have practiced since the inception of digital remix; they understand the persuasive potential embedded in the idea of commonplaces between the remix artist and the audience. Remix artists exploit the allegorical function of remix and its enthymematic dimension. By inviting the audience to participate with the creation of the argument, the remixer is able to create a more palatable persuasive argument. Because of the role of the enthymeme in remix, when the remix artist surprises the audience with the mashup components, the co-construction of the argument entails that the audience participate more fully. Girl Talk systematically defies expectation in his remixing, thus evoking the pleasurable dimensions of a good mashup. On the other side, *Stranger Things* clearly draws from familiar repertoires of archetypes and characters—"the tried and true"—but still exploits the enthymematic power of remix every time its viewers recognize a reference.

The enthymeme is crucial in the construction of the mashup in other ways. First, the musico-rhetorical tropes *asyndeton* and *mimesis* are completely dependent on the enthymematic process. When a DJ layers the formerly disparate samples together, he or she creates an ostensibly continuous narrative out of a mélange of fragments. Remix exploits the cognitive possibilities of the enthymeme by creating mimetic mashups, songs that imitate the formula for other popular songs, thus covertly assuming the appearance and structure of a continuous song. Though the gaps still exist in the stutters of the mashup, ongoing musical elements stitch these fragments together, all of which are interstitially filled in by the listener's past musical experiences.

Second, the enthymeme is at the core of perspective by congruity. The unifying rhythms, pitches, and keys all function as cogs in the machine of the effective mashup. It is the musical connections chosen by the DJ that make a consonant mashup seem to "fit together." In this way, the mashup showcases the congruity of the contrasting samples and persuades by directing attention only to that component without acknowledging the division in the original material.

Third, the enthymeme is an essential homology for *epaesthetic* rhetoric. As I mentioned in an earlier case study, auto-tuned texts conflate the sensuousness of the aesthetic and the logical of the epistemic by evoking *jouissance* and commonplaces between remix artist and audience. Remix should be considered as similar to the pleasurable deconstructive effect of the enthymeme. It is something more than an agent only capable of transmitting affective pleasure—remix is also allegorical in a cognitive sense, which provides a different variety of pleasure for the audience. Recall that *jouissance* can be stimulated by the deciphering of difficult texts. This activity is highly oscillatory. For example, when DJs spin remixes on the dance floor, audiences may glean an enthymematic pleasure from connecting the meanings associated with the mashed-up samples. When DJs exploit these personal meanings, an audience not only *hears* and *feels* the music through its strategic use of a heavy beat, but it also *listens* to the choice of samples. In this capacity as oscillatio, remix can function as the textual equivalent of an empty white canvas. When the remix is performed, the members of the audience write upon the remix their associated feelings and memories and thus experience *jouissance* in a dual capacity. Considering remix as dependent on its affective dimension over its cognitive dimension is incomplete. This perspective considers the term as strictly musical, while stripping it of its rhetorical power. In other words, remix's utilization of *jouissance* helps demonstrate the *epaesthetic* rhetorical dimension of remix. This phenomenon is also representative of how rhetoric can work on both emotional and intellectual levels: "The hearer, easily swayed by pleasure and pain, may be persuaded without an appeal to his sympathies; instead, he may be moved by the pleasantness accompanying an elementary activity of intellect."[8] The oscillation from one to another makes this persuasion possible.

Digital invention, in sum, offers a bridge between classical rhetoric and contemporary remix. Uniquely facilitated by digital media, digital invention uses imitatio, kairos, and the enthymeme (albeit theoretically broader). The contemporary enthymeme is one that retains its function from its classical definition but continues into the networked era by examining the connections that the audience makes with popular-culture texts. A mashup, for example, manifests its appeal in profound ways that are only completely understood through the vehicle of the enthymeme.

Limitations to Studying Remix

No remix is ever finished. Correspondingly, no book about remix—regardless of the scope—can ever truly be comprehensive. Remix is a dynamic phenomenon that changes exponentially as technological innovations and cultural controversies continue. While a "golden age" of remix may emerge, which we may very well be experiencing right now given the enormous popularity of remixed content in music, online, and on Netflix, there is never any indication as to when those conditions will change. Despite these uncertainties, however, remix will never truly disappear. Much as it has exerted its potential to orators and musicians alike since the intellectual dawn of humankind, it continues as a dynamic component of the human experience.

Due to the scope and fluid nature of remix, there are several directions that remain unexplored here. Because the book presented, in part, an intellectual history of remix, more space could have been devoted to a more thorough discussion of the antecedents to remix. Thomas Pettitt's Gutenberg Parenthesis offered a succinct framing of technological progress and its corresponding historical epochs, and it provided a sufficient heuristic schema to demonstrate the influence of technology on the epochal creation of cultural texts. Still, the consultation of more media ecology literature could further explore other antecedents to remix not covered in detail by the parenthesis. Walter Ong's notion of "secondary orality" is a provocative concept, for example, that needs to be resituated from the electronic age to the networked age, perhaps using its place in remix culture to extend to a new "tertiary orality."[9] Digital remix is also situated in a longer tradition of African American storytelling that needs to be discussed in more depth; for this, I refer the reader to the excellent book *Digital Griots* by Adam J. Banks. There is also much literature dedicated to the artistic vanguard that I was unable to explore, specifically musical composers like Karlheinz Stockhausen, LeMonte Young, Terry Riley, Philip Glass, and Steve Reich. As artistic progenitors to remix, a thorough investigation of their influential works could shed more light on the oscillatory rhetorical and aesthetic dimensions of remix.

Because this book is situated within such a vast network of intersecting theoretical lines of inquiry, the argument precludes a more thorough and systematic discussion about the commonalities of aural and televisual media and rhetoric. This concept is rich in theoretical potential and sorely needed in the field of rhetorical studies. In the initial phases of this book, I examined each under the assumption that rhetoric and music in the post-parenthetical era are converging into a more hybridized entity reminiscent of the classical concept of *poetics*. Though this connection still colors my discussion, the full-fledged discussion of those points of convergence provides an idea that, though tantalizing, would require much more space to fully explore.

Given the notable similarities between rhetoric and remix, more exploration is needed into how remix challenges traditional rhetorical methods of analysis. Remix is highly rhetorical and yet still functions beyond the parameters of traditional methods. For example, generic criticism generally leads a critic to conduct a close and systematic reading of many different discourses, paying careful attention to similarities and deviations between those discourses and those of the past. Unlike this established use of genre as rhetorical method, the appeal of remix is how it subverts genre as opposed to how it follows it. It places value on its ability to make the incongruous seem congruous, irrespective of generic origin. Paradoxically, though it is subversive to genre, remix is also beholden to genre. Remix uses and challenges past genre in order to create its own meta-genre. Using remix as supplemental to generic criticism in this way presents possibilities that play with the previous method of examining similarities or deviations in genre.

There is another reason why remix offers a useful supplement to the canon of rhetorical methods: Remix is a return to the rhetorical tradition even while subverting many contemporary boilerplate analytic methods. In this application, remix functions like Burke's master trope of irony: it effectively throws a wrench into the cogs of the established methods, thus moving them to focus more on theoretical nuance than formulaic and uncritical application of "methods" to the text of analysis. Remix uses possession by misnomer to dislodge the *ēthē* of the rhetors once isolated by the dictates of neo-Aristotelian criticism, for example, or to demythologize particular narratives that serve as referents for mythic criticism.

Remix can be used to reframe an argument or subvert it completely by putting the opposing argument's words in the original rhetor's mouth, thus turning ideological criticism on its head. Much as the logic of remix is contingent on layering, perspective by congruity entails that rhetors layer contrasting perspectives together. By offering incongruent arguments in a congruent way, the rhetorical text is not only performing an aesthetic exercise, it is calling attention to the interplay of the arguments much like avant-garde artists would use oscillatio to invite the attention of the viewers and listeners. Each of these potential rhetorical techniques demonstrates the digital invention facilitated by remix.

Admittedly, the above applications of remix are incomplete and necessarily superficial. They are meant rather to demonstrate the heuristic potential of considering remix to be a challenge to established rhetorical methods of criticism. Regardless, though this book never systematically delineated how remix could function in these capacities on a grander scale, the critical vocabulary advanced here is immediately ready for use as a hopefully productive hermeneutic for remix and other post-parenthetical practices.

Future Scholarly Applications of Remix

As I mentioned earlier, it is inevitable that technologies and cultural practices will change. In a few years or less, the software used by remix artists to make mashups or auto-tunes may become obsolete. The debate surrounding the practice may change as well, because discourses are just as fluid as the people who use them. The argument I have advanced takes these points into account.

The concluding research question for this book asked if it is appropriate for the rhetorical tradition to be repurposed in order to investigate a networked phenomenon such as remix. My answer is yes, without reservation. The repurposing of rhetoric is not only appropriate, but *essential* for analyzing networked texts. Part of the utility of using classical terms and theories in new and remixed ways is its acknowledgement of the timelessness of epistemology. Like remix, rhetoric has evolved through the centuries. Although the classical roots of the discipline do remain sacred to purists, the purview of rhetoric continually evolves alongside new modes of rhetorical production. This is not to say that its foundation should be discarded. On the contrary—contemporary rhetorical theorists should use and derive benefit from rhetoric's classical foundation. Rhetoric does not need to be discarded, but rather used to examine the mediated artifacts of the post-parenthetical era. It is now incumbent upon rhetoricians to study more of the fragmented mosaics of discourse than the standard structure of discrete speeches.[10] Good theory is sufficiently malleable to be used in multiple contexts—even remix. The difference between the eulogistic "malleable" and the dyslogistic "thin" or "brittle" is key to determining how we approach rhetorical hermeneutics. Theory will be able to evolve and be mashed up in novel ways, just as theories of rhetoric were remixed for this book. The utility of the proposed tropological vocabulary expands beyond remix. My hope is that the vocabulary advanced in this book will equip scholars and students of rhetoric with a useful repertoire to address issues of the post-parenthetical era.

Appendix

A New Dictionary of Pivotal Terms

In his book *A Grammar of Motives*, Kenneth Burke developed a heuristically powerful concept called the "representative anecdote," which calls for the critic to choose especially representative portions of literature as texts of analysis in order to examine how the reader can use that literature as "equipment for living."[1] Importantly, however, the critic must ensure that the anecdote be truly representative of the whole and not reductive. Barry Brummett suggests that by substituting "discourse" for Burke's "literature," the critic can achieve an even broader circumference of communicative analysis, which includes mediated texts as well.[2] Brummett's modification does provide critical inroads in examining mediated texts, including remix, since remix is historically embedded in the continuing trajectory of communicative norms. But Burke's concept of the representative anecdote is especially useful for remix when we consider his injunction to "develop vocabularies."[3] Answering his call, I have focused in this book on a number of representative anecdotes in order to generate a new vocabulary that addresses the rhetorical dimensions of remix.

The texts analyzed in the chapters of this book serve as case studies of the power of remix. Broadly speaking, "Right Wing Radio Duck" functioned as representative of the political remix potential of online video. The mashups of Girl Talk represented the congruent form of musical remix, and "Bed Intruder Song" and "Double Rainbow Song" represented the *epaesthetic* rhetoric of the Gregory Brothers' auto-tunes. Swedemason's "Paul McCartney Rabbit Hole" video showed the prosōpopoetic potency of YouTube remix videos. The chapter on *Stranger Things* examined how the appropriation and mashing up of a vast amount of popular eighties archetypes can create a potent, nostalgic artifact that leads to a contemplative, eudaimonic state within the audience. Explored cumulatively, all of these case studies function as a representative anecdote for the post-parenthetical era. In striving to provide a theoretical resource for future scholars, I have generated a critical vocabulary rooted in classical and contemporary rhetorical theory. The following is a brief "dictionary of pivotal terms" or tropes for examining remix for its rhetorical and aesthetic function.[4]

Enthymeme

Translated from Greek, "enthymeme" means "something in the mind." The enthymeme is dependent on the interaction between the orator and the audience. This term relates to the text providing the requisite conditions for the audience to feel some degree of participation in interpreting the meaning of the text. That means the orator or remix artist might strategically withhold necessary information so that the listeners can provide it themselves. An enthymeme evokes a sense of pleasure from the reader (or viewer or listener) of the remix when that person makes connections that are not explicitly there, or when listeners recognize the original source material referenced in the remix.

Epaesthetic Rhetoric

This terminological mashup describes the type of rhetoric employed by remix. *Epaesthetic* rhetoric is a portmanteau of epistemic rhetoric and aesthetic rhetoric. The purpose of this term is to demonstrate that remix exhibits dimensions that are both cognitive and rational. Simultaneously, however, it embraces the pleasurable experience derived from its use of language equivalent to the primacy of the bodily senses. Remix performs the former when it ascribes meaning via its referentiality and enthymematic connection between the DJ and the audience, or the audience and the text. Remix performs the latter by deflecting attention away from the content of the message communicated to the aural sounds of the verbalized language. Remix both transmits affect from its heavy beats and invites cognition from its allegorical nature. By focusing on the rational emotionalism (or emotional rationalism) of remix, the concept of *epaesthetic* rhetoric demonstrates how opposing theoretical perspectives can exist simultaneously without requiring reconciliation. Avant-garde art, and its embrace of oscillatio, makes this concept possible.

Eudaimonia

Although eudaimonia originated in ancient Greece (it is roughly translated to mean happiness, fulfillment, or blessedness), it has become a term used in entertainment-psychology scholarship for the purpose of understanding reasons why people consume their entertainment. In the context of ethics or politics, eudaimonia refers to the "perfect happiness" that comes from living the good life in a just society. In the context of media content, eudaimonic media can lead to appreciation from the viewer, which might lead to contemplation and ambivalent affective responses. This trope relates to remix in that a text can be remixed as an attempt to facilitate the conditions that lead to a eudaimonic reception of that text.

Imitatio

In ancient Greece, Cicero used imitation to create. This rhetorical trope has been applied by today's remixers as well. Imitatio refers to imitation and learning from superior works; these works are well received because we are naturally drawn to this process of inspiration by imitation. Interpretation is an essential component of imitatio. Through a close viewing of an existing text, neophytes can focus on its weakness and limitations, which can inspire creativity. This process is especially evident in the work of remix artists who regularly imitate the works of others but create something distinct with their own personal insertion of creativity and skill.

Kairos

This rhetorical trope describes the relationship between the multiple texts that make up a remixed text. Kairos is an evaluative trope, alluding to appropriateness, good timing, and the "fit" of placing two works together. In sampling, the musical samples must fit with the other samples as well as the overall song; it must sound "right." Kairos also applies to *suasoria*—when a text draws from the allegorical power of other texts, it needs to take into account the historical and aesthetic contexts of the source material. Kairos, then, is a feature of the creative process of remix.

Oscillatio

The works of the avant-garde art movement have been particularly useful in understanding remix because remix is derivative of other art. Remix contains parallels to aesthetic notions of beauty, a highly sensuous process composed of an affect-transmitting beat, smooth transitions, congruent keys and pitch, and layers of samples, which, when mashed together, provide a novel song. In similar fashion to avant-garde art, remix uses oscillatio, a process of oscillation between opposing poles while each exists concurrently and without the need for reconciliation. It is oscillatio in avant-garde art that demands the attention of the people, as it does in remix. Oscillatio allows *epaesthetic* rhetoric to retain its dual character as both epistemic and aesthetic. It also is the process whereby the dichotomous sublime can function rhetorically.

Perspective by Congruity

This critical rhetorical trope is crucial for understanding the appeal of remix. Based on Kenneth Burke's seminal idea of perspective by incongruity, the remixed term *perspective by congruity* valorizes division and exclusion in the remix process when the remixer chooses starkly contrasting samples and mashes them up in congruent ways. In essence, the incongruity of the samples is so amplified that it disappears in the final product, as if it never existed. In contrast to the "atom cracking" of Burke's original term, perspective by congruity is a form of "atom fusion," exploiting the clashing origins of the samples while simultaneously transforming them into an explosive new mashup. Because of the oscillatory function of remix, the congruous process does not eradicate fragmentation but wrenches it free from its dyslogistic connotations and essentially redefines fragmentation and clash as no longer dissonant. In overcoming the unease of clash and fragmentation in favor of smooth transitions and ostensible unification, perspective by congruity impels order into the disquietudes of life, overcoming disorder and chaos and presenting aesthetic façades capable of soothing these anxieties. With perspective by congruity, the consonant relationships and overall interplay of the samples are more crucial than the samples themselves. Because the audience is able to oscillate between beauty and terror, the congruous pairing of incongruous ideas can both attract due attention to harmful ideologies or detract attention away from peripheral ones. A similar function is exhibited by a subset of perspective by congruity, possession by misnomer.

Possession by Misnomer

Possession by misnomer complicates the privileging of certain ideologies over others by extracting certain ideologies from texts and replacing them with others. Its capability to also extract and withdraw ēthē can be applied to scholarship, where the author's arguments can be manipulated and mashed up with contrasting arguments to debunk one while empowering the other. Regarding the conversion downward, from exalted to secularized, this method can certainly be useful for social protest. However, the process of conversion *upward* distinguishes the term from its Burkean progenitor. When one individual's credibility is challenged by removing it and replacing it with another individual's, the latter individual who has suddenly become exalted finds him- or herself the subject of much attention. As an example, Mighty Mike's mashup "Imagine a Jump" plays with the hagiographical portrayals of John Lennon by replacing his lyrics and voice with those of David Lee Roth, the singer of Van Halen. Of all the available samples to choose from, Mighty Mike's choice of Van Halen as musical proxies for Lennon certainly draws attention to the original song by Van Halen, thus earning them the all-important commodity of attention. This is a crucial characteristic of rhetoric in the digital age. Applied to social protest, the choices of candidate or policy by the dissenting group will likely receive attention and status by its perceived ubiquity and association with its remixed counterpart. Possession by misnomer, as subsidiary to perspective by congruity, grabs our attention.

Prosōpopoeia

The act of speaking in the first person as another historical figure. This trope can also be used to give voice to the deceased as if they were speaking from the dead—it's the (re)presentation of a once-absent voice. In an ancient Roman courtroom, for example, Cicero imitated the voice of a deceased dignitary in order to condemn the actions of the defendant. Prosōpopoeia is linked to a cluster of additional terms like *voice making*, *voice restoration*, and *voice projection*. Prosōpopoeia is one of the essential rhetorical tropes of remix because the act of remix entails projecting one's voice into another context, like a remixer interjecting his or her voice into the person who is being remixed, such as when Swedemason articulated his thoughts about remix and authority through the voice of Paul McCartney. Prosōpopoeia is also present when *Stranger Things* reimagines crucial events from *Poltergeist* in the context of an adolescent boy living in fictional Hawkins, Indiana.

Suasoria

In ancient Rome, *suasoria* was a type of rhetorical exercise that required students to speak in character on a topic related to a historical theme or dilemma. In giving hypothetical advice to past leaders in moral crises, as they would in these types of deliberative situations, students would need to be intimately aware of the historical context surrounding the dilemma. This trope, then, is closely related to other tropes, prosōpopoeia and kairos. Because *suasoria* is closely observant of historical context and audience expectations, this trope can be used to explain how remix can prepare the conditions whereby the audience can be receptive to the persuasion that is to follow.

Sublime

The sublime is a term adapted from the philosophy of art. It was originally coined and conceptually developed as a way of describing one's overwhelming experience with works of art or nature. Kant considered the sublime as the unrepresentable, an experience that defied material representation. An example of the sublime would be an individual traveling through a field and encountering a previously unseen, towering, snow-covered mountain. The grand and imposing scale of the mountain would be enough to inspire simultaneous feelings of intense awe and fear within the being of the traveler. These would be derived from the beauty of the spectacle and its interplay with the terror of the monolith exceeding human comprehension and thus ostensibly swallowing up the traveler by its starkly massive presence. Thanks to theorists like Jean-François Lyotard, these dual-pronged feelings of beauty and terror in the sublime have now been transferred to technology, and the fear that the unmitigated perfection of technology might consume the imperfect contributions of humans. The sublime proves to be an efficient lens when analyzing auto-tune; "Bed Intruder Song," for example, demonstrates the beauty of aesthetic consonance while exhibiting the triple terrors of poverty, violence, and racism. The opposing poles of the sublime are both manifested to the viewer by virtue of oscillatio.

Śūnyatā

Śūnyatā is a philosophical construct that offers a tentative explanation for the potential for remix to take place. An ancient Buddhist concept originating from the writings of Nāgārjuna, the trope simultaneously represents an emptiness and a fullness of essence. Nāgārjuna's invitation to understand śūnyatā demonstrates the tantalizing potential of the idea: "For whom emptiness is possible / For him all is possible."[5] To the remix artist, the possibilities for creative production are innumerable for the same reason.

Notes

PROLOGUE

1. Theodor W. Adorno, *Aesthetic Theory*, trans. Robert Hullot-Kentor (London: Continuum, 2004), 1.
2. Aram Sinnreich, *Mashed Up: Music, Technology, and the Rise of Configurable Culture* (Amherst: University of Massachusetts Press, 2010), 69.
3. Daphne Keller, "The Musician as Thief: Digital Culture and Copyright Law," in *Sound Unbound: Sampling Digital Music and Culture*, ed. Paul D. Miller (Cambridge, MA: MIT Press, 2008), 135.
4. Lawrence Lessig, *Remix: Making Art and Commerce Thrive in the Hybrid Economy* (New York: Penguin, 2008), 11.
5. Joanna Demers, *Listening through the Noise: The Aesthetics of Experimental Electronic Music* (New York: Oxford University Press, 2010), 58.
6. Eduardo Navas, *Remix Theory: The Aesthetics of Sampling* (New York: Springer Wien, 2012), 4.
7. David J. Gunkel, *Of Remixology: Ethics and Aesthetics after Remix* (Cambridge, MA: MIT Press, 2016), xvii.
8. Mark Katz, *Capturing Sound: How Technology Has Changed Music* (Berkeley:

University of California Press, 2004), 132.
9. Gunkel, *Of Remixology*, 83.
10. Katz, *Capturing Sound*, 132.
11. Kembrew McLeod, *Freedom of Expression: Resistance and Repression in the Age of Intellectual Property* (Minneapolis: University of Minnesota Press, 2007), 72.
12. Lessig, *Remix*, 82.
13. Navas, *Remix Theory*, 4, 3.
14. Isocrates, *Antidosis*, in *Isocrates, Volume II*, ed. and trans. George Norlin (Cambridge, MA: Harvard University Press, 1929), 217.
15. Navas, *Remix Theory*, 6.
16. Bruno Latour, quoted in Megan Foley, "Voicing Terri Schiavo: Prosopopeic Citizenship in the Democratic Aporia between Sovereignty and Biopower," *Communication and Critical/Cultural Studies* 7, no. 4 (2010): 395.
17. Kristine S. Bruss, "Persuasive Ethopoeia in Dionysius's Lysias," *Rhetorica: A Journal of the History of Rhetoric* 31, no. 1 (2013): 38.
18. Navas, *Remix Theory*, 67.
19. Ibid., 28.
20. Gunkel, *Of Remixology*, 132.
21. Quoting Jean Baudrillard in Gunkel, *Of Remixology*, 66.
22. Katz, *Capturing Sound*, 156.
23. Sinnreich, *Mashed Up*, 131–32.
24. Mark Hosler of the remix artists Negativland, quoted by Lessig, *Remix*, 75.
25. Katz, *Capturing Sound*, 140–41.
26. Laurel Westrup, "Thinking through Sampling, Literally," in *Sampling Media*, ed. David Laderman and Laurel Westrup (New York: Oxford University Press, 2014), 236.
27. Isocrates, *Antidosis*, 213.
28. Aristotle, *De Poetica* (*Poetics*), in *The Basic Works of Aristotle*, ed. Richard McKeon, trans. Ingram Bywater (New York: Random House, 1941), 1457.
29. Isocrates, *To Nicocles*, in *Isocrates, Volume I*, ed. and trans. George Norlin (Cambridge, MA: Harvard University Press, 1928), 63.
30. Gunkel, *Of Remixology*, 14.
31. Alicia D. Myers, "Prosopopoetics and Conflict: Speech and Expectations in John 8," *Biblica* 92, no. 4 (2011): 582.
32. Gunkel, *Of Remixology*, 137.
33. McLeod, *Freedom of Expression*, 72.
34. John Shiga, "Copy-and-Persist: The Logic of Mash-up Culture," *Critical Studies in*

Media Communication 24, no. 2 (2007): 105, 99.

35. Ragnhild Brøvig-Hanssen and Paul Harkins, "Contextual Incongruity and Musical Congruity: The Aesthetics and Humour of Mash-Ups," *Popular Music* 31, no. 1 (2012): 90.
36. Mashup artist Mark Vidler, quoted in David J. Gunkel, "Rethinking the Digital Remix: Mash-ups and the Metaphysics of Sound Recording," *Popular Music and Society* 31, no. 4 (2008): 497–98.
37. Sinnreich, *Mashed Up*, 127.
38. Ibid., 99; Mash-up artist Strictly Kev, quoted in ibid., 114.
39. Sinnreich, *Mashed Up*, 163, 143, 133.
40. Keller, "The Musician as Thief," 136.
41. Navas, *Remix Theory*, 3, 11.
42. Henry Jenkins, quoted by Lessig, *Remix*, 28.
43. Westrup, "Thinking through Sampling, Literally," 235–36.
44. McLeod, *Freedom of Expression*, 30.
45. Adrian Johns, *Piracy: The Intellectual Property Wars from Gutenberg to Gates* (Chicago: University of Chicago Press, 2009), 8.
46. McLeod, *Freedom of Expression*, 30.
47. Sinnreich, *Mashed Up*, 47.
48. McLeod, *Freedom of Expression*, 30.
49. Lewis Hyde, *Common as Air: Revolution, Art, and Ownership* (New York: Farrar, Straus and Giroux, 2010), 19.
50. Candice Breitz, quoted by Lessig, *Remix*, 7.
51. McLeod, *Freedom of Expression*, 75, 104.
52. Katz, *Capturing Sound*, 157.
53. Brøvig-Hanssen and Harkins, "Contextual Incongruity," 88.
54. Navas, *Remix Theory*, 6.
55. Sinnreich, *Mashed Up*, 99.
56. Marc Geiger, quoted in ibid., 98.
57. Brøvig-Hanssen and Harkins, "Contextual Incongruity," 87.
58. Gunkel, *Of Remixology*, 5, 6.
59. Keller, "Musician as Thief," 143.
60. David Shea, quoted in Christoph Cox and Daniel Warner, *Audio Culture: Readings in Modern Music* (New York: Continuum, 2004), 328.
61. Sinnreich, *Mashed Up*, 57, 161–62.
62. Brian Eno, quoted in Cox and Warner, *Audio Culture*, 328.

63. Sinnreich, *Mashed Up*, 122.
64. Peter Arcuni, quoted in Gunkel, *Of Remixology*, 4.
65. Navas, *Remix Theory*, 12.
66. John Seabrook, *The Song Machine: Inside the Hit Factory* (New York: Norton, 2015).
67. Jesse Stewart, "Articulating a Hip-Hop Sampling Aesthetic through Film," in *Sampling Media*, ed. David Laderman and Laurel Westrup (New York: Oxford University Press, 2014), 143.
68. DJ Spooky, quoted in Richard L. Edwards, "Remixing with Rules: Constraint and Potential in Restrictive Remixes," in *Sampling Media*, ed. David Laderman and Laurel Westrup (New York: Oxford University Press, 2014), 32.
69. Barry Mauer, "Rigorous Infidelity," in *Sampling Media*, ed. David Laderman and Laurel Westrup (New York: Oxford University Press, 2014), 66.
70. Ralph Waldo Emerson, remixed by DJ Spooky, quoted in Gunkel, *Of Remixology*, 136–37.
71. Greg Goodale, *Sonic Persuasion: Reading Sound in the Recorded Age* (Urbana: University of Illinois Press, 2011), ix–x.
72. Timothy D. Taylor, *Strange Sounds: Music, Technology and Culture* (New York: Routledge, 2001), 8–9.
73. Sinnreich, *Mashed Up*, 78.
74. Navas, *Remix Theory*, 7.
75. Isocrates, *Antidosis*, 191.
76. Marshall McLuhan, *Gutenberg Galaxy: The Making of Typographic Man* (Toronto: University of Toronto Press, 1962), vi.
77. Jonathan Lethem, "The Ecstasy of Influence: A Plagiarism Mosaic," in *Sound Unbound: Sampling Digital Music and Culture*, ed. Paul D. Miller (Cambridge, MA: MIT Press), 51.
78. Lessig, *Remix*, 51.
79. Walter Benjamin, *The Arcades Project*, trans. Howard Eiland and Kevin McLaughlin (Cambridge, MA: Belknap Press, 1999), 460. Also quoted in Keller, "The Musician as Thief," 142.

INTRODUCTION

1. Pop Culture Detective, "Donald Duck Meets Glenn Beck in Right Wing Radio Duck," YouTube video, 7:45, October 2, 2010, http://www.youtube.com/watch?v=HfuwNU0jsk0.

2. In an example of the congruity of the video of Donald Duck and the audio of Beck's radio program, the "fat cat" that Beck speaks of is portrayed by Pete, a Disney antagonist who is literally a fat cat.
3. This audio track of Glenn Beck is not an original soundtrack, but rather audio clips that have been synced together with the video clips.
4. The cartoon short "The Spirit of '43" is a cautionary video starring Donald Duck that teaches that he must be thrifty and pay his income taxes to support the U.S. war effort. One line repeated throughout is "Taxes . . . to Bury the Axis!"
5. xtine burrough and Frank Dufour, "Creativity," in *Keywords in Remix Studies*, ed. Eduardo Navas, Owen Gallagher, and xtine burrough (New York: Routledge, 2017), 95.
6. See Adrian Johns, *Piracy: The Intellectual Property Wars from Gutenberg to Gates* (Chicago: University of Chicago Press, 2009) as an exhaustive cultural history of the concept of piracy and how it is used in contemporary intellectual property debates.
7. The video also contains the creator's production name of self-proclaimed "Pop Culture Detective," Jonathan McIntosh's website "Rebellious Pixels." McIntosh's website can be located at http://popculturedetective.agency.
8. Quoted in Kembrew McLeod and Peter DiCola, *Creative License: The Law and Culture of Digital Sampling* (Durham, NC: Duke University Press, 2011), 145.
9. Lawrence Lessig, *Remix: Making Art and Commerce Thrive in the Hybrid Economy* (New York: Penguin, 2008), 76.
10. The idea of a closed system of intellectual property is one that is generated in the current discourse surrounding copyright law and the digital process of sampling music or, increasingly, text. I chose to frame this idea as such here using the language of the side of the debate that sees any creative output as finished and "closed" and therefore not open for further appropriations.
11. A music mashup occurs when one vocal track of a song is overlaid on the instrumental track of another. Its origins are in Jamaican reggae, dub, and dancehall music. Mashup typically deals with software manipulation of texts. See Nate Harrison and Eduardo Navas, "Mashup," in *Keywords in Remix Studies*, ed. Eduardo Navas, Owen Gallagher, and xtine burrough (New York: Routledge, 2017). The term, however, is not only applicable to music, as "the term mashup has been co-opted for the sake of the growth of an emerging 'productivist' culture, which itself is a hybrid of property interests and an open sharing of information"; ibid., 197.
12. Comment made on July 21, 2011, by a user named "Checkerholic" under the remix video ikat381, "Mickey Mouse Discovers the Government Cartoon Conspiracy

against Glenn Beck," YouTube video, 1:25, October 8, 2010, http://www.youtube.com/watch?v=dbjjTLVrkKA.

13. Lessig, *Remix*. See also arguments by James Boyle, *The Public Domain: Enclosing the Commons of the Mind* (New Haven, CT: Yale University Press, 2008); Kembrew McLeod, *Freedom of Expression: Resistance and Repression in the Age of Intellectual Property* (Minneapolis: University of Minnesota Press, 2007; McLeod and DiCola, *Creative License*; and Lewis Hyde, *Common as Air: Revolution, Art, and Ownership* (New York: Farrar, Straus and Giroux, 2010). Each of these books, in different ways, makes the case that copyright laws have not only grown outdated given the new digital landscape, but that they actually stifle creativity rather than facilitate it.
14. Quoted in McLeod and DiCola, *Creative License*, 5.
15. This portion of my definition of remix is conceptually based upon the work of Jenkins. We can consider the practice of remix as similar to the phenomena related to the "convergence culture" that has emerged in recent years. For further elaboration, see Henry Jenkins, *Convergence Culture* (New York: New York University Press, 2008). See also John Shiga, "Copy-and-Persist: The Logic of Mash-up Culture," *Critical Studies in Media Communication* 24, vol. 2 (June 2007): 96.
16. Seán Burke's reader on authorship is a compilation of the most influential works on the contended term. In addition to compiling these works, Burke includes commentary to historically situate each of these essays. See Seán Burke, *Authorship: From Plato to the Postmodern: A Reader* (Edinburgh: Edinburgh University Press, 1995). Likewise, Lawrence Lessig has produced several important works that all address the idea of authorship and creativity in an age of digital technology. A representative book addressing these issues is Lessig's *Remix*.
17. Swedemason, "Trump vs Talking Heads—Swedemason," https://www.youtube.com/watch?v=nSuregWhlWk.
18. Ragnhild Brøvig-Hanssen and Aram Sinnreich, "Do You Wanna Build a Wall? Remix Tactics in the Age of Trump," *Popular Music and Society* 43, no. 5 (2019): 539.
19. Ibid., 5.
20. Daniel Arkin, "Donald Trump Criticized after He Appears to Mock Reporter Serge Kovaleski," *NBC News*, November 26, 2015, https://www.nbcnews.com/politics/2016-election/donald-trump-criticized-after-he-appears-mock-reporter-serge-kovaleski-n470016.
21. Maestro Ziikos, "Queen—Bohemian Rhapsody (Donald Trump Cover)," https://www.youtube.com/watch?v=i05gKtHWjGY.
22. Sonali Nandi, "President Supervillain: Behind the Alarmingly Accurate

Trump-Marvel Mashup," *The Guardian*, October 23, 2019.

23. To adapt Richard Lanham's words from his *Economics of Attention: Style and Substance in the Age of Information* (Chicago: University of Chicago Press, 2006), 135.
24. Damien O'Brien and Brian Fitzgerald, "Mashups, Remixes, and Copyright Law," *Internet Law Bulletin* 9, no. 2 (2006): 17–19.
25. This portion of the definition is conceptually based upon the work of Henry Jenkins. For further elaboration, see Jenkins, *Convergence Culture*. Also see Henry Jenkins, "Multiculturalism, Appropriation, and the New Media Literacies: Remixing Moby Dick," in *Mashup Culture*, ed. Stefan Sonvilla-Weiss (New York: Springer Wien New York, 2010), 99–119. See Shiga, "Copy-and-Persist," 95.
26. Harold Adams Innis, an essential pioneer in the academic field of media ecology, argued that information varied on the media upon which it existed. The internet is an example of what Innis called "space-binding media," or media that is speedily exchanged and yet undergirded by temporality. In the digitally networked age, space and place is becoming increasingly detached from information. For Innis's original concepts, see Innis, *Empire and Communications* (Toronto: University of Toronto Press, 1972).
27. Lanham, *Economics of Attention*.
28. Manuel Castells, *The Rise of the Network Society*, 2nd ed. (Malden, MA: Wiley-Blackwell, 2010), 501. Castells defines "networked," in part, as a system of "interconnected nodes."
29. See Philip Sherburne, "How Streaming Is About to Reshape DJ Culture as We Know It," *Pitchfork*, July 17, 2019, https://pitchfork.com/thepitch/how-streaming-is-about-to-reshape-dj-culture-as-we-know-it/.
30. Remix has shifted to a cultural practice that encompasses music and videos among other texts. Eduardo Navas, "Remix," in *Keywords in Remix Studies*, ed. Eduardo Navas, Owen Gallagher, and xtine burrough (New York: Routledge, 2017).
31. David Hajdu, *Heroes and Villains: Essays on Music, Movies, Comics, and Culture* (Philadelphia: Da Capo Press, 2009). However, this essay claims that the apparent democratic nature of these bands releasing their tracks publicly and inviting the audience to creatively use the tracks is deceitful; ultimately, the tracks can be used only within the boundaries that the band sets. With the case of Radiohead, for instance, all remixes created by the public would eventually end up being the property of the band rather than the users that created them.
32. Simon Frith, *Popular Music: The Rock Era* (New York: Routledge, 2004).

33. Kaya Oakes, *Slanted and Enchanted: The Evolution of Indie Culture* (New York: Henry Holt and Co., 2009), 205. Radiohead gained a substantial amount of publicity for doing it for their album *In Rainbows*. Their 2011 album *The King of Limbs* was also released as a download *sans* standard record-company distribution, though they had set a fixed price.
34. Navas described remix as a "binder for the constant recycling and repurposing of material and immaterial things; it has helped develop an awareness of the constant exchange of ideas across specializations and cultural niches for different purposes." Navas, "Remix," 246.
35. Margie Borschke, *This Is Not a Remix: Piracy, Authenticity, and Popular Remix* (New York: Bloomsbury, 2017), 34.
36. Navas, *Remix Theory: The Aesthetics of Sampling* (New York: Springer Wien, 2012), 3.
37. Simon Frith argues that popular music is not only important to youth culture, but that it defines youth *in toto.* Frith, "Towards an Aesthetic of Popular Music," in *Music and Society: The Politics of Composition, Performance and Reception*, ed. Richard Leppert and Susan McClary (Cambridge: Cambridge University Press, 1989), 143.
38. Aram Sinnreich, *Mashed Up: Music, Technology, and the Rise of Configurable Culture* (Amherst: University of Massachusetts Press, 2010), 119. In his study of the phenomenon, which Sinnreich calls "configurability," he interviews a diverse group of participants about remix, ranging from the lay public to DJs, scholars, and attorneys. He reports that the trope of "some kid in his bedroom" has become commonplace in how the public often views the production process of remix.
39. Gregg Gillis—AKA Girl Talk—released his first album of mashups when he was only twenty-one, after all.
40. Baracksdubs, "Barack Obama Singing Born This Way by Lady Gaga," YouTube video, 1:49, http://www.youtube.com/watch?v=AijEQN6AuRs. The popularity of remixed videos to which I refer is evidenced by the sheer number of views that these clips receive and the speed at which they receive them.
41. This distinction was indisputable in early 2010, though many music videos have since surpassed it. Still, it remains the most-viewed video that is not an official music video. Richard MacManus, "Top 10 YouTube Videos of All Time," *Read Write*, January 9, 2012, https://readwrite.com/2008/09/29/top_10_youtube_videos_of_all_time_2008/.
42. Jean Baudrillard, *Simulacra and Simulation*, trans. Sheila Faria Glaser (Ann Arbor: University of Michigan Press, 1994).
43. Ryan Milner, *World Made Meme: Public Conversations and Participatory Media*

(Cambridge, MA: MIT Press, 2016), 2.

44. Elad Segev, Asaf Nissenbaum, Nathan Stolero, and Limor Shifman, "Families and Networks of Internet Memes: The Relationship between Cohesiveness, Uniqueness, and Quiddity Concreteness," *Journal of Computer-Mediated Communication* 20, no. 4 (2015): 417–33.
45. Asaf Nissenbaum and Limor Shifman, "Meme Templates as Expressive Repertoires in a Globalizing World: A Cross-Linguistic Study," *Journal of Computer-Mediated Communication* 23, no. 5 (2018): 294–310.
46. Limor Shifman, *Memes in Digital Culture* (Cambridge, MA: MIT Press, 2013), 22.
47. Quintilian, *Quintilian: The Orator's Education Books 6–8*, trans. Donald A. Russell (Cambridge, MA: Harvard University Press, 2002), 425.
48. Kenneth Burke, *A Grammar of Motives* (Berkeley: University of California Press, 1969), 503.
49. Kenneth Burke, *On Human Nature: A Gathering While Everything Flows, 1967–1984*, ed. William H. Rueckert and Angelo Bonadonna (Berkeley: University of California Press, 2003), 384.
50. Kermit Lansner, "Burke, Burke, the Lurk," *Kenyon Review* 13, no. 2 (1951): 264.
51. See also Roberto Franzosi, *Landmark Essays on Tropes and Figures* (New York: Routledge, 2017).
52. Borschke, *This Is Not a Remix*, 33.
53. For mashups and mashup communities, see Sinnreich, *Mashed Up*; Shiga, "Copy-and-Persist." For metaphysical properties of sound recording and mashups, see David Gunkel, "Rethinking the Digital Remix: Mash-ups and the Metaphysics of Sound Recording," *Popular Music and Society* 31, no. 4 (October 2008). For the implications of copying and imitation in remixing, see Marcus Boon, *In Praise of Copying* (Cambridge, MA: Harvard University Press, 2010).

CHAPTER 1. THE GUTENBERG PARENTHESIS: REMIX THROUGHOUT HISTORY

1. Margie Borschke assesses the dominant voice in the field of remix studies, Lawrence Lessig, as possessing a bias of cyber-utopianism when referring to remix culture. In performing this bias, Lessig sees the practice to be new and digital—both of which Borschke refutes. See Borschke, *This Is Not a Remix: Piracy, Authenticity, and Popular Remix* (New York: Bloomsbury, 2017).
2. This is an important definitional distinction to make, given that others have suggested that remix be analyzed wholly in the context of music and music

technologies, rather than as a synecdoche for digital culture (see Borschke, *This Is Not a Remix*).

3. Marshall McLuhan, *The Mechanical Bride: Folklore of Industrial Man* (New York: Vanguard Press, 1951), 40.
4. McLuhan's vocabulary provides somewhat of a disjunction between different concepts of the age of literacy when compared to other foundational works in media ecology. Walter J. Ong's *Orality and Literacy*, for example, describes the onset of writing as taking place during the "chirographic" age, which is perhaps more accurate than McLuhan's "typographic" culture, given the contemporary associations with print, typography, and mechanized type. See Walter J. Ong, *Orality and Literacy: The Technologizing of the Word* (New York: Routledge, 1999). However, some conflation between eras is appropriate given that an era did not become suddenly transformed into a purely chirographic or mechanical culture. Ong argues, in fact, that there was a residual element of orality even after the supposed onset of chirographic culture. Thus, one culture rarely (if ever) completely replaces another. It is this point that I continue to explore in this portion of the book, which is that even in the contemporary digital age, remnants from the discourse of the previous era initiated by the mechanical age of the printing press still exists and, in fact, frames the digitalized intellectual property debate.
5. Marshall McLuhan, *The Gutenberg Galaxy: The Making of Typographic Man* (Toronto: University of Toronto Press, 1962), 2.
6. To be sure, the complexity of the culture cannot be reduced to its manner of communication. However, it serves as a marked contrast to the changes that took place once writing became standard practice. It should also be noted that only in the last century have these distinctions become so absolute. In his landmark 1982 study, *Orality and Literacy*, Ong wrote that "Our understanding of the differences between orality and literacy developed only in the electronic age, not earlier." Ong, *Orality and Literacy*, 3.
7. Richard Lanham, *Economics of Attention: Style and Substance in the Age of Information* (Chicago: University of Chicago Press, 2006), 109.
8. I use Elizabeth Eisenstein's "scribal culture" here to describe the age where writing was invented rather than Ong's "chirographic" culture.
9. Elizabeth L. Eisenstein, *The Printing Press as an Agent of Change: Communications and Cultural Transformations in Early-Modern Europe* (Cambridge: Cambridge University Press, 1979), 33.
10. Thomas Pettitt, "Before the Gutenberg Parenthesis: Elizabethan-American

Compatibilities," paper presented at "Media in Transition 5: Creativity, Ownership and Collaboration in the Digital Age," Traverse City, MI, April 25, 2007, 2, http://web.mit.edu/comm-forum/legacy/mit5/papers/pettitt_plenary_gutenberg.pdf. Also see Pettitt, "Bracketing the Gutenberg Parenthesis," *Explorations in Media Ecology* 11, no. 2 (2012): 95–114.

11. Pettitt, "Before the Gutenberg Parenthesis," 3. It should be clarified here that the eras described by Pettitt do not exactly align with McLuhan's typographic-mechanical-electric classification. Whereas McLuhan was interested primarily in the invention of writing and onward, Pettitt expands back to a truly oral, bardic culture that took place before the invention of the alphabet.
12. Eisenstein, *The Printing Press*, 130. An interesting consideration here is the idea that the "exceptional literate villager" is actually not an individual genius, but rather a well-read individual who draws knowledge from other sources. Therefore, even their genius is derivative, suggesting a proto-remix culture even in the modern era. Thanks to Ed Carter for this insight.
13. Eisenstein, *The Printing Press*, 122.
14. Elizabeth L. Eisenstein, *The Printing Revolution in Early Modern Europe*, 2nd ed. (Cambridge: Cambridge University Press, 2005), 104. The point can also be made that this sullen silence in the salons and coffeehouses has made way for a type of "sullen staring," as the transition from reading printed text has begun shifting to staring at the screens of smartphones and electronic tablets.
15. Timothy D. Taylor, *Strange Sounds: Music, Technology and Culture* (New York: Routledge, 2001), 3.
16. This is an adaptation of Eisenstein's influential assertion that the Gutenberg printing press also created the concept of a genius; see Eisenstein, *The Printing Press*. See Taylor, *Strange Sounds*, 5, for mention of the masterpiece as a Western invention made possible by the music printing press.
17. Quoted in ibid., 4.
18. By this term, I mean *not* digital.
19. Taylor, *Strange Sounds*, 4, 5.
20. Lars Ole Sauerberg, "Preface: The Gutenberg Parenthesis—Print, Book and Cognition," *Orbis Litterarum* 64 (2009): 79.
21. Ronald C. Arnett, "A Conversation about Communication Ethics," in *Exploring Communication Ethics*, ed. Pat Arneson (New York: Peter Lang, 2007), 53–68.
22. Pettitt argues that both the premodern oral culture and postmodern internet technology thrive on "morphing," which continually takes place with cultural

products because they have a lack of finality. Pettitt, "Before the Gutenberg Parenthesis," 4.

23. Pop Culture Detective, "Donald Duck Meets Glenn Beck in Right Wing Radio Duck," YouTube video, 7:45, October 2, 2010, http://www.youtube.com/watch?v=HfuwNU0jsk0.
24. My application of Pettitt's vocabulary here to describe the video may raise the objections of some for semantic purposes. This is a potential problem rooted in the Gutenberg Parenthesis itself; how can one "borrow" video and audio clips from another person if the one that did the borrowing has no intention of returning them? This semantic distinction is important to my overall argument: the discourse we are accustomed to using may be inadequate to fully describe what is happening in the post-parenthetical age of cultural practices from using digital technology. In this case, I would hazard that McIntosh might be legally considered to be borrowing the texts because—as he states—he is protected under the clause of a creative commons license. Thus, he is protected from legal action reserved for those who are guilty of stealing.
25. This list is compiled by putting together the arguments of Alasdair MacIntyre, *After Virtue* (Notre Dame, IN: University of Notre Dame Press, 2007), and Ronald Beiner, *What's the Matter with Liberalism?* (Berkeley: University of California Press, 1992).
26. René Descartes, *Meditations on First Philosophy: With Selections from the Objections and Replies*, ed. John Cottingham (New York: Cambridge University Press, 1996), 68. This treatise was first published in 1637. Its familiar English translation is "I think, therefore I am." I included the Latin in this text because Descartes's notion of *cogito* is conspicuously present in scholarship by Derrida, Lacan, and Slovenian philosophers Slavoj Žižek and Alenka Zupančič. For more information on the *cogito*, see Alenka Zupančič, *Ethics of the Real* (New York: Verso Press, 2000).
27. Thomas M. Carr Jr., *Descartes and the Resilience of Rhetoric: Varieties of Cartesian Rhetoric* (Carbondale: Southern Illinois University Press, 1990). Similar to Bacon and Hume's empiricism, Descartes strongly favored scientific observation as a direct route to knowledge. Tellingly, he stated in his *Meditations*: "[If] it is not in my power to arrive at the knowledge of any truth, at the very least it is in my power to suspend my judgment"; quoted in John Durham Peters, *Courting the Abyss: Free Speech and the Liberal Tradition* (Chicago: University of Chicago Press, 2004), 181.
28. Daniel Gross, *The Secret History of Emotion: From Aristotle's Rhetoric to Modern Brain Science* (Chicago: University of Chicago Press, 2007).
29. Burke, *A Grammar of Motives* (Berkeley: University of California Press, 1969), 182.

30. Theodor Adorno, *The Stars Down to Earth, and Other Essays on the Irrational in Culture* (New York: Routledge, 1994), 157.
31. Peters, *Courting the Abyss*, 181.
32. This space for subjectivity is referring to Kant's primacy of "taste" in his philosophy, acknowledging that an individual may initiate a judgment that is different from another's. Of course, this idea is contrary to the absolutism that underlies Cartesian thought. For more on taste judgments and Kant's pronouncements on aesthetics, see John Poulakos, "From the Depths of Rhetoric: The Emergence of Aesthetics as a Discipline," *Philosophy and Rhetoric* 40, no. 4 (2007): 335–52. I would argue that this non-modernist perspective from Kant is actually harkening back to the pre-parenthetical era, when the Sophist Protagoras wrote about relativism. To illustrate Protagoras's position, Edward Schiappa wrote that the wind might feel cold to one and feel warm to another. For more on Protagorean thought, please refer to Edward Schiappa, *Protagoras and* Logos: *A Study in Greek Philosophy and Rhetoric* (Columbia: University of South Carolina Press, 1991).
33. Here, I speak of liberalism as synonymous with modernist thought; though each is distinct, they share some similarities that I will emphasize here, and for our (not comprehensive) purposes, they will serve the same function.
34. John Durham Peters states that it is difficult to give one uniform definition of liberalism, citing that the term means completely opposite things depending on which side of the Atlantic Ocean you are on. Still, germane to the discussion here, he acknowledges its debt to Enlightenment-era thinkers like Hobbes, Spinoza, Locke, Kant, and Mill. Peters, *Courting the Abyss*, 9–10.
35. David J. Gunkel, *Of Remixology: Ethics and Aesthetics after Remix* (Cambridge, MA: MIT Press, 2016).
36. See David J. Gunkel, "What Does It Matter Who Is Speaking? Authorship, Authority, and the Mashup," *Popular Music and Society* 35, no. 1 (2012): 71–91; and Aram Sinnreich, *Mashed Up: Music, Technology, and the Rise of Configurable Culture* (Amherst: University of Massachusetts Press, 2010).
37. Beiner, *What's the Matter with Liberalism?*, 39.
38. It should be noted here that the law is not uniformly opposed to the notion of creative sampling. The United States has a broad fair-use doctrine, for example, that allows for socially beneficial uses of content (for the purposes of education, parody, and other things) in ways that do not negatively impact the original work. Additionally, the idea-expression dichotomy doctrine protects the *manifestation* of an idea (its expression, in other words), meaning that ideas themselves cannot be

copyright protected. This flexibility in the law, in theory, can afford an artist-creator more opportunities for creativity without fear of legal issues. See Margreth Barrett, *Intellectual Property* (New York: Aspen Publishers, 2008).

39. Sinnreich, *Mashed Up*, 124–25.
40. In addition to the Lockean justification for intellectual property mentioned above, there is the Kantian/Hegelian "personhood" justification for copyright (i.e., creative works warrant copyright protection because they develop a person's self-actualization or personhood) as well as a social benefit/incentive rationale (copyright protects creative innovation because it is important for encouraging learning, which offers a "social benefit" to those who are enriched by consuming that creative output). See Christopher S. Yoo, "Rethinking Copyright and Personhood," *Faculty Scholarship at Penn Law* 423 (2019): 1039–78. See also Akhil Prasad and Aditi Agarwala, *Copyright Law Desk Book* (New Delhi, India: Universal Law Publishing, 2009), 135.
41. These metonymic terms are discussed in L. B. Bermingham, "Culture Jamming or a Culture Jammed? Rip!: A Remix Manifesto," *Screen Education* 54 (2009): 44–47. Both groups want to protect the same things: "originality, innovation, and the figure of the hardworking and talented artist"; David J. Gunkel, "Remixology: A Remix(ed) Rhetoric for the 21st Century," *Journal of Contemporary Rhetoric* 7, no. 2/3 (2017): 81. However, the Copy-Left sees remix as original work and the Copy-Right does not believe remix should be legal simply because of its creative merits.
42. McLuhan argued that Cartesian thought could not exist without the typological era; McLuhan, *Gutenberg Galaxy*, 7, 158.
43. Echoing McLuhan's prior argument that technology modifies human experience, Elizabeth Eisenstein argued that the invention of the printing press was part of a "communications revolution," a force that has shaped the modern mind. Eisenstein, *The Printing Press*, 44.
44. Eisenstein, *The Printing Press*.
45. Bermingham, "Culture Jamming."
46. Axel Bruns, "Distributed Creativity: Filesharing and Produsage," in *Mashup Cultures*, ed. Stefan Sonvilla-Weiss (New York: Springer Wien, 2010), 24–37.
47. Steven Weber, *The Success of Open Source* (Cambridge, MA: Harvard University Press, 2004).
48. Kembrew McLeod, *Freedom of Expression: Resistance and Repression in the Age of Intellectual Property* (Minneapolis: University of Minnesota Press, 2007), 153.
49. John Shiga, "Copy-and-Persist: The Logic of Mash-up Culture," *Critical Studies in*

Media Communication 24, vol. 2 (June 2007): 93–114. In this article, Shiga performs a sort of digital ethnography of mashup artists' online message boards. Much of what constituted a good mashup, to them, was the DJ's ability to rein in completely opposing musical styles into one coherent whole that actually sounded good.

50. Gunkel proposes that culture reframes how it looks at remix in order to accommodate Copy-Left ideas; remix should be viewed as simulation (i.e., as neither copy nor original), repetition (i.e., nothing can be created or destroyed, simply transformed), and unauthorized (i.e., authorship as a byproduct of creative genius). Gunkel, "Remixology."
51. James Boyle, *The Public Domain: Enclosing the Commons of the Mind* (New Haven, CT: Yale University Press, 2008), 181.
52. McLuhan, *The Gutenberg Galaxy*, 31.
53. Ibid., 38.
54. Incidentally, McLuhan demonstrated that remix can be used in different contexts than music alone. Notably, McLuhan used a "mosaic approach" for compiling his books *The Mechanical Bride* and *The Gutenberg Galaxy*. Written in a pseudo-fragmented style, these books provided for McLuhan a somewhat postmodern way for him to express a philosophy that his words should be able to be read and comprehended out of context. Eisenstein speculates that the arrangement may have been more out of convenience than innovation: "McLuhan's non-linear presentation at all events has not inspired confidence in his arguments." See Eisenstein, *The Printing Press*, 40.
55. Bruns, "Distributed Creativity," 24–37.
56. Nicholas Negroponte, *Being Digital* (New York: Random House, 1995), 84.
57. Tim O'Reilly, "What Is Web 2.0: Design Patterns and Business Models for the Next Generation of Software," *Communications & Strategies* 65, 1st quarter (March 2007), 19. Steven Johnson, "It's All about Us," *Time*, December 25, 2006.
58. Damien Smith Pfister, "Networked Expertise in the Era of Many-to-Many Communication: On Wikipedia and Invention," *Social Epistemology* 25 (July 2011): 218.
59. Ibid., 219.
60. Bruns, "Distributed Creativity," 35.
61. Johnson, "It's All about Us."
62. Glenn Reynolds, *An Army of Davids: How Markets and Technology Empower Ordinary People to Beat Big Media, Big Government and Other Goliaths* (Nashville: Thomas Nelson, 2006).

63. Brian Williams, "Enough about You," *Time*, December 25, 2006. .
64. Jean Burgess and Joshua Green, YouTube: Online Video and Participatory Culture (Malden, MA: Polity, 2009). See also Henry Jenkins, "What Happened before YouTube," in *YouTube*, ed. Jean Burgess and Joshua Green (Malden, MA: Polity, 2009), 109–25. See also Twinword, "6 Common Features of Top 250 YouTube Channels," *Twinword*, https://www.twinword.com/blog/features-of-top-250-youtube-channels. Incidentally, a similar participation gap appears with remix, though it follows gender lines more specifically. Though access to remixing tools is perpetually increasing, famous DJs are still overwhelmingly male. See Sinnreich, *Mashed Up*, 204–5.
65. For controversies regarding the corporate control of popular internet sites (especially MySpace), see Christine Harold, *OurSpace: Resisting the Corporate Control of Culture* (Minneapolis: University of Minnesota Press, 2007).
66. Jakob Nielsen, "Participation Inequality: Encouraging More Users to Contribute," *Jakob Nielsen's Alertbox* 9 (2006), http://www.useit.com/alertbox/participation_inequality.html.
67. Bruns, "Distributed Creativity," 24.
68. Sinnreich, *Mashed Up*, 75.
69. Axel Bruns, *Blogs, Wikipedia, Second Life, and Beyond: From Production to Produsage* (New York: Peter Lang, 2008).
70. Bruns, "Distributed Creativity," 26.
71. Ibid.
72. Shiga, "Copy-and-Persist," 94.
73. Fredric Jameson, *Postmodernism, or The Cultural Logic of Late Capitalism* (Durham, NC: Duke University Press, 1991), 17.
74. Barry Brummett, *Rhetorical Dimensions of Popular Culture* (Tuscaloosa: University of Alabama Press, 1991), 13. This point contrasts, of course, with those of other theorists. In Neil Postman's provocative condemnation of television, *Amusing Ourselves to Death*, Postman outlines how news broadcasters juxtapose horrifying tragedies and banal, overly precious news with a jarring "Now, this." See Postman, *Amusing Ourselves to Death* (New York: Penguin, 2006).
75. Henry Jenkins, *Convergence Culture* (New York: New York University Press, 2008), 3–4.
76. Brummett, *Rhetorical Dimensions*, 64. Though Brummett wrote of this concept years before the internet entered into the mainstream, his terminology is canny: the "bit" is now the recognized term for discrete units of information. Stefan Sonvilla-Weiss,

"Introduction: Mashups, Remix Practices and the Recombination of Existing Digital Content," in *Mashup Cultures*, ed. Stefan Sonvilla-Weiss (New York: Springer Wien, 2010), 9–10.

77. Brummett, *Rhetorical Dimensions*, 69.
78. Barry Brummett, "The Homology Hypothesis: Pornography on the VCR," *Critical Studies in Mass Communication* 5 (1988): 202–16. See also Brummett, "Electric Literature as Equipment for Living: Haunted House Films," *Critical Studies in Mass Communication* 2 (1985): 247–61. Brummett draws his argument of the use value of popular media from an adaptation of Kenneth Burke's famous argument that literature can serve as "equipment for living," thus offering the reader "strategies" to live his or her life. See Burke, *The Philosophy of Literary Form: Studies in Symbolic Action* (Berkeley: University of California Press, 1973), 293–304.
79. Simon Frith, "Towards an Aesthetic of Popular Music," in *Music and Society: The Politics of Composition, Performance and Reception*, ed. Richard Leppert and Susan McClary (Cambridge: Cambridge University Press, 1989).
80. Michael McGee, "Text, Context, and the Fragmentation of Contemporary Culture," *Western Journal of Speech Communication* 54 (Summer 1990): 281–82.
81. Ibid., 287.
82. Ibid., 283.
83. Ibid., 274.
84. Raymond Williams, *The Long Revolution* (Orchard Park, NY: Broadview Press, 2001), 57. He names three definitions of cultural analysis: ideal, documentary, and social. In outlining each of these aspects of criticism, Williams indicates that the critic can observe the cultural artifacts in order to better understand their shared cultural values.
85. Theodor W. Adorno, *Notes to Literature: Volume 2*, ed. Rolf Tiedemann, trans. Shierry Weber Nicholsen (New York: Columbia University Press, 1992), back cover.
86. Ross Wilson, *Theodor Adorno* (New York: Routledge, 2007), 2.
87. Theodor W. Adorno, "On Popular Music," in *Essays on Music*, ed. Richard Leppert (Berkeley: University of California Press, 2002).
88. Ibid., 439–40.
89. Kembrew McLeod, "Confessions of an Intellectual (Property): Danger Mouse, Mickey Mouse, Sonny Bono, and My Long and Winding Path as a Copyright Activist-Academic," *Popular Music and Society* 28, no. 1 (February 2005): 86.
90. OrbitalCafe, "It's Friday, Baby!," YouTube video, 3:32, April 4, 2011, https://www.youtube.com/watch?v=AamN773I2xg.

91. Daphne Keller, "The Musician as Thief: Digital Culture and Copyright Law," in *Sound Unbound: Sampling Digital Music and Culture*, ed. Paul D. Miller (Cambridge, MA: MIT Press, 2008), 135.
92. Shiga, "Copy-and-Persist," 103. Mito Hatori, from the band Cibo Matto, explains that the search can be tedious: "To find the right one or two seconds of sound . . . that's a lot of work." Quoted in Kembrew McLeod and Peter DiCola, *Creative License: The Law and Culture of Digital Sampling* (Durham, NC: Duke University Press, 2011), 22.
93. Gunkel, "Rethinking the Digital Remix: Mash-ups and the Metaphysics of Sound Recording," *Popular Music and Society* 31, no. 4 (October 2008): 500.
94. Theodor Adorno, *In Search of Wagner* (New York: Verso, 2009), 21.
95. Ibid., 22.
96. J. M. Bernstein, "Introduction," in Theodor W. Adorno, *The Culture Industry* (New York: Routledge, 1991).
97. Keith Tester, *Media, Culture and Morality* (New York: Routledge, 1994), 55.
98. Dennis Redmond, in *Facebook's "Adorno Changed My Life"*, film by Georg Boch (2011), 3:09–3:48.
99. Richard Lanham, *The Electronic Word: Democracy, Technology, and the Arts* (Chicago: University of Chicago Press, 1993), 227.
100. This statistic was discovered at the online results of an ambitious study by half a dozen researchers from Berkeley. Their objective was to estimate exactly how much new information is created every year. This particular number was gleaned from their analysis of "electronic flows," or the amount of information streamed or transmitted over electronic media such as the radio, television, telephone, and internet. Notably, the total number of terabytes transmitted through telephone surpassed the amount of information transmitted over the internet by 32 times. These numbers are certain to have become much closer together in the decade that has passed since the research was completed. See Peter Lyman and Hal R. Varian, "How Much Information? 2003," http://www2.sims.berkeley.edu/research/projects/how-much-info-2003/execsum.htm#summary.
101. Luciano Floridi, *The Logic of Information: A Theory of Philosophy as Conceptual Design* (New York: Oxford University Press, 2019).
102. Lanham, *Economics of Attention*, 5.
103. When I refer to classical Greece as the "pre-parenthetical era" often throughout this book, I conflate the entirely oral culture of pre-Homeric times discussed by Pettitt with the literate culture of classical Greece. This decision is based on Pettitt's schema, which does not offer an intermediate era between the purely oral

pre-parenthetical era and the print culture of the Gutenberg Parenthesis.

104. Plato, "Gorgias," in *The Rhetorical Tradition: Readings from Classical Times to the Present*, 2nd ed., ed. Patricia Bizzell and Bruce Herzberg (New York: Bedford/St. Martin's, 2001), 87–138. He considered it this way in contrast to the *techne*, or art, or philosophy.
105. Bradford Vivian, "Style, Rhetoric, and Postmodern Culture," *Philosophy and Rhetoric* 35, no. 3 (2002): 223–43.
106. W. Barnett Pearce and Karen A. Foss, "The Historical Context of Communication as a Science," in *Human Communication: Theory and Research*, ed. Gordon L. Dahnke and G. W. Clatterbuck (Belmont, CA: Wadsworth, 1990). For a representation of Aristotle's interest in the sciences, see Aristotle, *Physica*. Some have speculated that because Aristotle's father was a physician that he had an interest in empiricism. See Pierre Pellegrin, "The Aristotelian Way," in *A Companion to Ancient Philosophy*, ed. Mary-Louise Gill and Pierre Pellegrin (Malden, MA: Wiley-Blackwell, 2006), 237.
107. Cicero, quoted in Nathan Crick, "The Sophistical Attitude and the Invention of Rhetoric," *Quarterly Journal of Speech* 96, no. 1 (February 2010): 37.
108. Pearce and Foss, "Historical Context."
109. Edward P. J. Corbett, "The Cornell School of Rhetoric," *Rhetoric Review* 4, no. 1 (1985).
110. Lanham, *Economics of Attention*.
111. See Marshall McLuhan, *Understanding Media: The Extensions of Man* (Cambridge, MA: MIT Press, 1994).
112. Gordon Hull, "Digital Media and the Scope of 'Computer Ethics,'" in *Virtual Morality: Morals, Ethics and New Media*, ed. Mark J. P. Wolf (New York: Peter Lang, 2003).
113. Ibid., 18.
114. Ibid., 28.
115. Lanham, *Economics of Attention*, xi.
116. Incidentally, this need for a filter for human attention appears to guide the objectives of some of the most popular websites. For instance, Facebook has aggressively used the "like" button in recent years, which enables its users to isolate and declare what online information they find to be important to other users. Amazon, iTunes, Google, and Netflix use bots and algorithms to make suggestions for what to purchase or otherwise consume. In each of these websites, human attention is treated as the most valuable commodity.
117. Lanham, *Economics of Attention*, 25. Though this has not always been so implicit; in James A. Winans's 1915 textbook on public speaking, Winans was inspired by the psychology of William James in his definition of persuasion: "the process of

inducing others to give fair, favorable, or undivided attention to propositions." He also made the claim "What holds attention determines action." See William Norwood Brigance, "Can We Redefine the James-Winans Theory of Persuasion?" *Quarterly Journal of Speech* 21, no. 1 (February 1935): 20.

118. Herbert Wichelns, "The Literary Criticism of Oratory," in *Readings in Rhetorical Criticism*, 3rd ed., ed. Carl R. Burgchardt (State College, PA: Strata Publishing, 2005), 3–28.
119. Roderick P. Hart and Suzanne M. Daughton, *Modern Rhetorical Criticism*, 3rd ed. (Boston: Allyn & Bacon, 2005), 2.
120. Lanham, *Economics of Attention*, xii–xiii.
121. Shepard Fairey, interviewed in Banksy, dir., *Exit through the Gift Shop*, 2010; United Kingdom: Paranoid Pictures, 2011, DVD, 18:05–18:17.

CHAPTER 2. ISOCRATES AND KAIROS: REMIX IN ANCIENT GREECE

1. Pettitt, "Before the Gutenberg Parenthesis: Elizabethan-American Compatibilities," paper presented at "MIT5: Creativity, Ownership, and Collaboration in the Digital Age," Traverse City, MI, April 25, 2007, http://web.mit.edu/comm-forum/legacy/mit5/papers/pettitt_plenary_gutenberg.pdf, p. 2.
2. This definition comes from the ancient Roman rhetorician Quintilian. Summarized by Peter Ramus in his Rhetoricae. See Peter Ramus, *Arguments in Rhetoric against Quintilian: Translation and Text of Peter Ramus's* Rhetoricae Distinctiones in Quintilianum, ed. James J. Murphy, trans. Carole Newlands (Carbondale: Southern Illinois University Press, 2010), 109.
3. Michael Billig, *Arguing and Thinking: A Rhetorical Approach to Social Psychology* (Cambridge: Cambridge University Press, 1987), 64. Emphasis added.
4. Chaïm Perelman and Lucie Olbrechts-Tyteca, *The New Rhetoric: A Treatise on Argumentation* (Notre Dame, IN: University of Notre Dame Press, 1969). Also, Stephen Toulmin, *The Uses of Argument* (Cambridge: Cambridge University Press, 1958).
5. Wayne Brockriede, "Rhetorical Criticism as Argument," *Quarterly Journal of Speech* 60 (1974): 165–74. He also argued that rhetorical critics should consider their criticisms as performances. See Brockriede, "Arguers as Lovers," *Philosophy & Rhetoric* 5, no. 1 (1972): 1–11.
6. Regarding the influence of Isocrates, George Norlin wrote, "Few if any of the literary men of his [Isocrates's] age, whether or not they were members of his school, were

unaffected by his influence." George Norlin, "General Introduction," in *Isocrates, Volume I*, ed. and trans. George Norlin (Cambridge, MA: Harvard University Press, 1928), xxix.

7. Patricia Bizzell and Bruce Herzberg, "Isocrates," in *The Rhetorical Tradition: Readings from Classical Times to the Present*, 2nd ed., ed. Patricia Bizzell and Bruce Herzberg (New York: Bedford/St. Martin's, 2001), 67–71.
8. Kathleen Welch calls Isocrates both a literate sophist and an "anti-Sophist" because he would not speak publicly, and, in fact, held a negative attitude toward public speech. See Kathleen E. Welch, *Electric Rhetoric: Classical Rhetoric, Oralism, and a New Legacy* (Cambridge, MA: MIT Press, 1999), 31. It is notable, also, to consider his dissatisfaction with the objectives of the sophists in light of his allegiance to his *philosophia*, essentially a hybrid of philosophy and rhetoric that was markedly different from the sophistic practices of the era. A propos of my argument, Isocrates recognized the broad utility of philosophy, and yet tried to emphasize its situatedness—all of which would suggest that Isocrates, to some extent, took both sophistic and philosophical tenets, and mashed them up to become uniquely his own.
9. Isocrates, *Against the Sophists*, in *Isocrates, Volume II*, ed. and trans. George Norlin (Cambridge, MA: Harvard University Press, 1929), 163.
10. Isocrates, *Antidosis*, in *Isocrates, Volume II*, ed. and trans. George Norlin (Cambridge, MA: Harvard University Press, 1929), 269.
11. Though the self-defense crafted by Isocrates was prompted by real-life events, the trial has been considered by some to be fictional (see Bizzell and Herzberg, "Isocrates," 69). Whether it was real or fictional, however, is uncertain; the historical record remains unclear. It could have been a defense he crafted to defend his pedagogy, or it could have been, as Robert Bonner suggests, essentially a reworking of Plato's *Apology*. See Bonner, "The Legal Setting of Isocrates' *Antidosis*," *Classical Philology* 15 (April 1920): 193–97. For my purposes, however, it is compelling to consider it as an enactment of Isocrates's pedagogy: a creative imitation of an influential discourse.
12. Isocrates, *Antidosis*, 203, 219.
13. Norlin, "General Introduction," xxx.
14. David D. Perlmutter, *Blogwars: The New Political Battleground* (New York: Oxford University Press, 2008).
15. Welch, *Electric Rhetoric*.
16. Ibid., 33. Notably, Welch also bridges some of the theoretical issues that we have

discussed, arguing that Isocrates is crucial for our digital times: "His writing fluctuates between eye dominance and ear dominance. He relies, in fact, on what we now regard as sampling, a musical construction defined by recording one musical text onto another. Isocrates samples extensively in *Antidosis*, where he quotes previous writing he had circulated;" ibid., 37. Recall our earlier discussion that remix exhibits properties of both the pre-parenthetical and the post-parenthetical eras. Welch's invocation of Isocratic writing as oscillating between eye dominance and ear dominance argues (anticipating media ecology theory) that Isocrates kept one foot in the age of orality and the other in the age of literacy. We could consider Isocrates, then, to be the patron saint of secondary orality, a revisiting of the communicative norms of orality in our new digital age. See Walter J. Ong, *Orality and Literacy: The Technologizing of the Word* (New York: Routledge, 1999).

17. Isocrates, *Antidosis*, 191.
18. Gregg Gillis (Girl Talk), quoted in All Things Considered, "Girl Talk: Cataloguing Samples 'All Day,'" *NPR*, December 4, 2010, http://www.npr.org/2010/12/04/131791011/girl-talk-cataloging-samples-all-day..
19. Isocrates, *Antidosis*, 191.
20. Classical scholar Edward Schiappa has cautioned rhetorical scholars against mixing "neo-sophistic theorizing," and historical reconstructions of sophistic doctrine. While he does acknowledge that there should be an appreciation of the contemporary applications of the heuristic theories of the sophists, he argues that there should be a distinction between historically re-creating how the sophists argued about texts and adapting those arguments and theories to contemporary times. Neo-sophistic critiques contribute by emphasizing the creative adaptations of sophistic doctrines to contemporary rhetorical theory over historical accuracy. On the other hand, historical reconstructions, as evidenced in the works of George A. Kennedy, for example, aim at interpreting sophists in a historical context. Schiappa prefers, instead, to capture the contribution of the sophists in their own time and as much as possible in their own language. See Edward Schiappa, "Neo-Sophistic Rhetorical Criticism or the Historical Reconstruction of Sophistic Doctrines?" *Philosophy and Rhetoric* 23, no. 3 (1990): 192–217; Schiappa, Skype conversation, June 7, 2010. While this portion of the book likely aligns itself closer with neo-sophistic theorizing than historical reconstruction, I do not believe that each camp needs to be discrete in this situation. Regarding the work of Isocrates, the very fact that his discourses did not fit easily within the context of his historical

milieu is what makes his work so intriguing and useful when analyzing today's understanding of remix. By judging the incongruity of his *philosophia* and that of Plato, for example, we can see how remix does, indeed, have rhetorical antecedents. I agree that there is a danger of sensationalizing Isocrates by recklessly imposing upon him the label of postmodernist. However, by comparing his discourses with post-parenthetical practices like remix, we not only better understand the rhetorical foundation of remix, we gain a greater appreciation of the innovation of Isocrates and his pedagogy.

21. Isocrates, *Against the Sophists*, 171. Though my discussion only focuses on Isocrates's use of kairos, he was greatly influenced by his teacher Gorgias, who is credited as the progenitor of the concept.
22. Ronald C. Arnett, "A Conversation about Communication Ethics with Ronald C. Arnett," in *Exploring Communication Ethics: Interviews with Influential Scholars in the Field*, ed. Pat Arneson (New York: Peter Lang, 2007), 62.
23. John Shiga, "Copy-and-Persist: The Logic of Mash-up Culture," *Critical Studies in Media Communication* 24, vol. 2 (June 2007): 103. Mito Hatori, from the band Cibo Matto, explains that the search can be tedious: "To find the right one or two seconds of sound . . . that's a lot of work," quoted in Kembrew McLeod and Peter DiCola, *Creative License: The Law and Culture of Digital Sampling* (Durham, NC: Duke University Press, 2011), 22.
24. Tara Rodgers, *Pink Noises: Women on Electronic Music and Sound* (Durham, NC: Duke University Press, 2010), 68.
25. He does so throughout *Antidosis*. See also David Depew, "The Inscription of Isocrates into Aristotle's Practical Philosophy," in *Isocrates and Civic Education*, ed. Takis Poulakos and David Depew (Austin: University of Texas Press, 2004), 160.
26. In her discussion of the implications of *philosophia*, Welch argues that the term is important because it clearly differentiates the philosophy of Isocrates from that of Plato. Through her explication of the term, Welch paints Isocrates more as a cultural theorist than a philosopher in the traditional classical sense. Whereas Plato was interested in knowing about "the good," Isocrates focused on interacting in culture and making corollary judgments. Incidentally, this same argument was supported roughly a few years before Welch's book in an unpublished manuscript by McGee, who argues that Isocrates was crucial to both rhetoric and cultural studies. See Michael McGee, "Isocrates: A Parent of Rhetoric and Culture Studies" (unpublished manuscript, 1986).
27. David M. Timmerman and Edward Schiappa, *Classical Greek Rhetorical Theory and*

the Disciplining of Discourse (Cambridge: Cambridge University Press, 2010), 52, 54.

28. Takis Poulakos, "Isocrates's Use of Narrative in the Evagoras: Epideictic Rhetoric and Moral Action," *Quarterly Journal of Speech* 73 (August 1987): 326.
29. Ragnhild Brøvig-Hanssen, "Humor's Role in Mashups and Remixes: Similarities between Humor Structure and Remix Structure," in *On Popular Music in Its Unruly Entanglements: Pop Music, Culture and Identity*, ed. Nick Braae and Kai Arne Hansen (London: Palgrave Macmillan, 2019), 194.
30. Bizzell and Herzberg, "Isocrates," 71.
31. Michael McGee, "Choosing a Poros: Reflections on How to Implicate Isocrates in Liberal Theory" (unpublished manuscript, 1998).
32. McGee, "Isocrates," 2. Emphasis added.
33. Isocrates, quoted in McGee, "Isocrates," 3. Also David Depew and Takis Poulakos, "Introduction," in *Isocrates and Civic Education*, ed. Takis Poulakos and David Depew (Austin: University of Texas Press, 2004), 118.
34. Bizzell and Herzberg, "Isocrates," 71. Though Isocrates was certainly a loyal citizen—his writings indicate that he was relentlessly patriotic—Norlin argues that Isocrates was not necessarily inclined to exclusively stay within the community. Rather, Isocrates preferred peace and tranquility and thus was particularly withdrawn and aloof. He certainly did not enjoy speaking to a public audience and frequently eschewed opportunities to do so, preferring instead to transmit his ideas through writing. See Norlin, "General Introduction," xix.
35. Shiga, "Copy-and-Persist."
36. Norlin, "General Introduction," xxiv. Depew and Poulakos add that Isocrates taught through moral argumentation and reiterating the values of the *polis* that good speaking and good action were connected. Depew and Poulakos, "Introduction." Also, see Isocrates's *Against the Sophists* for his pedagogical dissociation from ethical imperatives.
37. Norlin, "General Introduction," xxii.
38. Isocrates, *Antidosis*. See Norlin, "General Introduction," xxvii.
39. Shiga, "Copy-and-Persist," 99.
40. McGee, "Isocrates."
41. Aristotle, *De Poetica* (*Poetics*), in *The Basic Works of Aristotle*, ed. Richard McKeon, trans. Ingram Bywater (New York: Random House, 1941).
42. John Muckelbauer, "Imitation and Invention in Antiquity: An Historical-Theoretical Revision," *Rhetorica: A Journal of the History of Rhetoric* 21, no. 2 (Spring 2003): 65.
43. Isocrates, To Nicocles, in *Isocrates, Volume I*, ed. and trans. George Norlin

(Cambridge, MA: Harvard University Press, 1928), 47, 49.

44. Aristotle, *Poetics*, 1455.
45. Ibid., 1457. Emphasis added.
46. Quoted in McLeod and DiCola, *Creative License*, 41.
47. Michael Leff, "The Idea of Rhetoric as Interpretive Practice: A Humanist's Response to Gaonkar" in *Rhetorical Hermeneutics: Invention and Interpretation in the Age of Science*, ed. Alan G. Gross and William M. Keith (Albany, NY: SUNY Press, 1997), 97.
48. Muckelbauer, "Imitation and Invention," 62.
49. DJ Adrian, quoted in Aram Sinnreich, *Mashed Up: Music, Technology, and the Rise of Configurable Culture* (Amherst: University of Massachusetts Press, 2010), 133.
50. Muckelbauer, "Imitation and Invention," 74.
51. Leff, "Idea of Rhetoric as Interpretive," 97–98.
52. Muckelbauer, "Imitation and Invention," 67.
53. Quintilian, quoted in Muckelbauer, "Imitation and Invention," 69.
54. Isocrates, quoted in Muckelbauer, "Imitation and Invention," 70.
55. Poulakos, "Isocrates's Use of Narrative in the *Evagoras*," 323. See also Robert Hariman, "Civic Education, Classical Imitation, and Democratic Polity," in *Isocrates and Civic Education*, ed. Takis Poulakos and David Depew (Austin: University of Texas Press, 2004).
56. Ibid., 229.
57. Muckelbauer, "Imitation and Invention," 77.
58. Aristotle, *Poetics*, 1463. See also Muckelbauer, "Imitation and Invention," 78.
59. Hariman, "Civic Education," 222–23.
60. Ibid.
61. Muckelbauer, "Imitation and Invention," 76.
62. Hariman, "Civic Education," 230.
63. Adam J. Banks, *Digital Griots: African American Rhetoric in a Multimedia Age* (Carbondale: Southern Illinois University Press, 2010), 28.
64. Quoted in McLeod and DiCola, *Creative License*, 194. DJs may hide or manipulate the recognizable qualities of samples for reasons that may be more pragmatic than aesthetic: "Hiding samples saves money." Ibid., 196.
65. Muckelbauer, "Imitation and Invention," 75.
66. DJs like to imprint their own aesthetic style upon their mashups. This can be communicated in their choice of samples or in their use of transitions and beats. T. S. Monk explains that the appeal of this practice may be to demonstrate their creative abilities: Aram Sinnreich, quoting digital media professional and

DJ Tony Zeoli, wrote that "a remix producer can have a 'signature sound' that's so identifiable it's 'like their handwriting.'" Further, says DJ Eric Kleptone, "you can recognize [the style of a mashup artist the same way you would] recognize someone's style on a saxophone or on a piano." Sinnreich, *Mashed Up*, 126.

67. DJs frequently use the music from artists and songs that they admire and, in sampling it, want to pay tribute to the "greatness" of that particular song. Eduardo Navas, "Regressive and Reflexive Mashups in Sampling Culture," in *Mashup Cultures*, ed. Stefan Sonvilla-Weiss (New York: Springer Wien, 2010), 166.
68. This is an important point in the delineation of remix culture. DJs are usually portrayed in the discourse as thieves, stealing music from artists without their consent. This is core to the arguments of prosecuting attorneys in cases about intellectual property that have been tried in court. In the 1991 case between rapper Biz Markie and artist Gilbert O'Sullivan's recording label Grand Upright Music, for example, Biz Markie was reprimanded by the judge for sampling O'Sullivan's song "Alone Again (Naturally)." Notably, the judge stated "Thou Shalt Not Steal" as rationale for finding Biz Markie guilty of copyright infringement. See McLeod and DiCola, *Creative License*, 132–39, for a description of the case.
69. Takis Poulakos, "Isocrates's Use of Narrative in the *Evagoras*," 324. Poulakos's quotation marks indicate a cited passage from Aristotle, *The Poetics*, ix.
70. Joanna Demers, *Listening through the Noise: The Aesthetics of Experimental Electronic Music* (New York: Oxford University Press, 2010), 57.
71. Quoted in Sinnreich, *Mashed Up*, 114.
72. Isocrates, "To Nicocles," 63.
73. Welch, Electric *Rhetoric*, 32. It would seem appropriate that the logic of arrangement permeated sophistic rhetoric. It has been claimed that the sophist Protagoras invented syntax. See Billig, *Arguing and Thinking*, 70.
74. Welch, *Electric Rhetoric*. See also Isocrates, *Antidosis*, 191.
75. Isocrates quotes from Homer and Socrates in *Against the Sophists* and echoed some of Thucydides's work in *Antidosis*. In one of his criticisms of the sophists, he even echoes Plato's arguments from "Gorgias": "But men who inculcate virtue and sobriety—is it not absurd if they do not trust in their own students before all others?" For further examples of his sampling Socrates, see Isocrates, *Antidosis*, 215, 237, 365. For the argument that Isocrates remixed Plato, see Bonner, "The Legal Setting." Also see Yun Lee Too, *The Rhetoric of Identity in Isocrates: Text, Power,* Pedagogy (Cambridge: Cambridge University Press, 1995), 108.
76. Isocrates, *Antidosis*, 215, 217.

77. A particular type of remix, which Eduardo Navas calls the "megamix," has the objective of sampling songs that are particularly representative: "Its purpose is to present a musical composition riding on a uniting groove to create a type of pastiche that allows the listener to recall a whole time period and not necessarily one single artist or composition." Navas, "Regressive and Reflexive," 166.
78. McLeod and DiCola, *Creative License*, 101.
79. Theodor Adorno, "On Popular Music," in *Essays on Music*, ed. Richard Leppert (Berkeley: University of California Press, 2002).
80. Welch, *Electric Rhetoric*, 38.
81. Yun Lee Too, *The Rhetoric of Identity in Isocrates*, 53. Too, citing another study, gives citations from six of Isocrates's works that demonstrate his affinity for repetition.
82. Isocrates, *To Philip*, in *Isocrates, Volume I*, ed. and trans. George Norlin (Cambridge, MA: Harvard University Press, 1928), 303. In the 1894 translation by J. H. Freese, Isocrates states his point a bit more succinctly: "Some of my statements are repetitions of previous ones. For, when I came to consider the same subject, I preferred not to weary myself in the endeavour to express differently what has been already set forth satisfactorily." See Isocrates, *The Phillipus*, in *The Orations of Isocrates*, vol. 1, trans. J. H. Freese (London: George Bell & Sons, 1894), 140.
83. Too, *The Rhetoric of Identity*, 54.
84. Eric A. Havelock explains that in the classical era, "the task of the poetic education [was] to memorise and recall." Havelock, *Preface to Plato* (Cambridge, MA: Harvard University Press, 1963), 207.
85. Sinnreich, *Mashed Up*, 87.
86. As David J. Gunkel states, "mash-ups are exceedingly and unapologetically redundant." In Gunkel, "Rethinking the Digital Remix: Mash-ups and the Metaphysics of Sound Recording," *Popular Music and Society* 31, no. 4 (October 2008): 499.
87. Welch, *Electric Rhetoric*, 37–38.
88. Isocrates, *Against the Sophists*, 162. This was cited from the first footnote in George Norlin's translation of *Against the Sophists*.
89. Norlin, "General Introduction," xv.
90. Ibid., xvi.
91. Poulakos, "Isocrates's Use of Narrative in the Evagoras," 319.
92. Norlin, "General Introduction," xxiv.
93. Ibid., xv.
94. Mashups can grow wearisome as well. Despite the abilities of DJs to connect

otherwise disparate samples of music together, it can bewilder the audience as much as avant-garde art. After playing a mashup by Girl Talk to my class once, a student responded that it was aesthetically "irritating" to listen to. Indeed, it can be taxing to listen to some mashups, and they might require multiple listens to appreciate what was the DJ's purpose in making the remix.

CHAPTER 3. GIVE ME A BEAT: GIRL TALK, KENNETH BURKE, AND REMIX AESTHETICS

1. There are various places online that discuss these mashup breakdowns, including Mashup Breakdown on Reddit (https://www.reddit.com/domain/mashupbreakdown.com), as well as visual representations of the sampled material, like "GirlTalk—AllDay—Video Mash Up—Tracks 1–7" (41:00, "fishinabirdcage the editor," November 7, 2017), https://www.youtube.com/watch?v=dgGMUhM2KdM.
2. Matthew Rimmer, "The Grey Album: Copyright Law and Digital Sampling," *Media International Australia* 114, no. 1 (2005): 40–53.
3. Ibid.
4. Ibid., 44. See also Charles Fairchild, *The Grey Album* (New York: Bloomsbury, 2014).
5. Kembrew McLeod and Peter DiCola, *Creative License: The Law and Culture of Digital Sampling* (Durham, NC: Duke University Press, 2011). See also David Toop, "Replicant: On Dub," in *Audio Culture: Readings in Modern Music*, ed. Christoph Cox and Daniel Warner (New York: Continuum, 2004).
6. Toop, "Replicant," 357.
7. Adam Banks, *Digital Griots: African American Rhetoric in a Multimedia Age* (Carbondale: Southern Illinois University Press, 2010), 90.
8. Bruce Gerrish, *Remix: The Electronic Music Explosion* (Vallejo, CA: EM Books, 2001), 13.
9. DJ Kool Herc, quoted in McLeod and DiCola, *Creative License*, 54.
10. Gerrish, *Remix*, 15.
11. Ferguson et al., "The Recombinant DNA of the Mash-Up," *New York Times*, January 6, 2011.
12. McLeod and DiCola, *Creative License*, 39.
13. Attorney David Kelley, personal interview, December 24, 2011.
14. McLeod and DiCola, *Creative License*, 19. Others have called it the "Wild West era" of hip hop. See Greg Kot, *Ripped: How the Wired Generation Revolutionized Music* (New York: Scribner, 2009), 162.

15. Dr. Dre's rap release *The Chronic* sold over 3 million copies, for example. Nelson George, *Hip Hop America* (New York: Penguin, 2005).
16. United States Copyright Office, Library of Congress, Copyright Law of the United States and Related Laws Contained in Title 17 of the United States Code, 8.
17. Ibid. Most songs are by default, unless the artist opts to release his or her music under the Creative Commons license.
18. McLeod and DiCola, *Creative License*, 76–77.
19. Ibid.
20. Ibid., 193.
21. Though this creative response to sampling regulations was innovative, other artists would likely disapprove, given that its practice violated the archival appeal of real sampling in hip hop. For example, sampling artists often laud their ability to find old and obscure samples to integrate into their music. In that way, their ability to find old sounds and use them in a new way in their recordings is part of their ethos. By sampling one's own samples, it could be said that Portishead violated this standard.
22. Aram Sinnreich, *Mashed Up: Music, Technology, and the Rise of Configurable Culture* (Amherst: University of Massachusetts Press, 2010), 30.
23. Brett Gaylor, *Rip: A Remix Manifesto*, http://vimeo.com/8040182; James Boyle, *The Public Domain: Enclosing the Commons of the Mind* (New Haven, CT: Yale University Press, 2008), 184.
24. Kot, *Ripped*, 170.
25. This event even prompted MTV News to post a story with the headline "Girl Talk Apologizes for Breaking the Internet." For this story, see Zachary Lazar, "The 373-Hit Wonder," *New York Times*, January 6, 2011.
26. Bonnie Stiernberg, "Pittsburgh Celebrates 'Gregg Gillis Day,'" *Paste* magazine, December 7, 2010, http://www.pastemagazine.com/articles/2010/12/pittsburgh-celebrates-gregg-gillis-day.html.
27. McLeod and DiCola, *Creative License*, 2.
28. Daphne Keller, "The Musician as Thief: Digital Culture and Copyright Law," in *Sound Unbound: Sampling Digital Music and Culture*, ed. Paul D. Miller (Cambridge, MA: MIT Press, 2008), 136.
29. Joanna Demers, *Listening through the Noise: The Aesthetics of Experimental Electronic Music* (New York: Oxford University Press, 2010), 58. See David Shea, quoted in Cox and Warner, *Audio Culture*, 328. The full quote reads, "The work of composing is not one of invention but one of arrangement. All materials being both

unique and fundamentally connected, the strategy and art of connecting forms creative work."

30. Kot, *Ripped*, 163; McLeod and DiCola, *Creative License*, 2.
31. These figures were calculated by Kembrew McLeod and Peter DiCola after creating a cost matrix and applying it to numerous aspects of each recording, including the number of identifiable samples, sound-recording royalties, musical-composition shares, artists' share of revenue per CD, sample licensing fees per CD, estimated transaction costs, and estimated sales. See McLeod and DiCola, *Creative License*, 204–12.
32. Debra Hawhee, *Moving Bodies: Kenneth Burke at the Edges of Language* (Columbia: University of South Carolina Press, 2009), 27.
33. Kenneth Burke, *Attitudes toward History*, 3rd ed. (Berkeley: University of California Press, 1984), 99.
34. Gregory Clark, "Aesthetic Power and Rhetorical Experience," in *Kenneth Burke and His Circles*, ed. Jack Selzer and Robert Wess (Anderson, SC: Parlor Press, 2008), 96–109.
35. Barry Brummett, *Rhetorical Dimensions of Popular Culture* (Tuscaloosa: University of Alabama Press, 1991), 95.
36. Nathan Crick argues that one of the primary forms of sophistic invention, *dissoi logoi*, was generated through the novelty of competing perspectives clashing. See Crick, "The Sophistical Attitude and the Invention of Rhetoric," *Quarterly Journal of Speech* 96, no. 1 (February 2010): 36. When discussing modern aesthetics, Umberto Eco speaks about "novelty" and "innovation" synonymously, arguing that aesthetic value is assessed in a work of art, in part, by the amount of novelty the artist exhibited. Eco, "Innovation and Repetition: Between Modern and Postmodern Aesthetics," *Daedalus* 134 (2005): 191, 200.
37. From George Campbell, *The Philosophy of Rhetoric, in The Rhetoric of Blair, Campbell, and Whately*, ed. James L. Golden and Edward P. J. Corbett (New York: Holt, Rinehart and Winston, 1968), 145.
38. Ibid., 150. Emphasis added.
39. Ragnhild Brøvig-Hanssen and Paul Harkins, "Contextual Incongruity and Musical Congruity: The Aesthetics and Humour of Mash-Ups," *Popular Music* 31, no. 1 (2012): 87.
40. John D. Schaeffer, *Sensus Communis: Vico, Rhetoric, and the Limits of Relativism* (Durham, NC: Duke University Press, 1990), 63.
41. Ibid., 63.

42. Ibid.
43. McLeod, "Confessions of an Intellectual (Property): Danger Mouse, Mickey Mouse, Sonny Bono, and My Long and Winding Path as a Copyright Activist-Academic," *Popular Music and Society* 28, no. 1 (February 2005): 86.
44. Bill Brewster and Frank Broughton, *Last Night a DJ Saved My Life: The History of the Disc Jockey* (New York: Grove Press, 2000), 275.
45. Kenneth Burke, *Counter-Statement*, 2nd ed. (Berkeley: University of California Press, 1968), 36–37, 145.
46. Leonard B. Meyer, *Emotion and Meaning in Music* (Chicago: University of Chicago Press, 1956).
47. Kenneth Burke, *Permanence and Change: An Anatomy of Purpose*, 3rd ed. (Berkeley: University of California Press, 1984), 5.
48. A good example of the ease of remixing is the website The Gendered Advertising Remixer: A Media Literacy Web Application, created by Jonathan McIntosh, the same person who made "Right Wing Radio Duck," which I will discuss further in this chapter. This site allows users to juxtapose the audio and video of different children's commercials, thus amplifying the gendered conventions of advertising. See Jonathan McIntosh, *The Gendered Advertising Remixer*, http://www.genderremixer.com.
49. Margie Borschke, "Rethinking the Rhetoric of Remix," *Media International Australia* 141 (November 2011): 17–25.
50. Ian Hill, "'The Human Barnyard' and Kenneth Burke's Philosophy of Technology," *KB Journal* 5, no. 2 (Spring 2009), http://www.kbjournal.org/ian_hill.
51. William H. Rueckert, *Encounters with Kenneth Burke* (Urbana: University of Illinois Press, 1994).
52. Hill, "The Human Barnyard."
53. James L. Kastely, "Kenneth Burke's Comic Rejoinder to the Culture of Empire," *College English* 58 (1996): 307–26. It should be noted that often when Burke was writing about technology, it was specifically about devices like the atomic bomb, rather than how we perceive digital media today.
54. Burke, *Counter-Statement*, 114. His quote is made in the context of paralleling technology to government. In this work, Burke equated government and technology as dangerous forces in need of control.
55. Though it may be more accurate to say "cautious." Hill argues that to consider Burke as a Luddite is an overly reductive perspective. See Hill, "The Human Barnyard"; Dale S. Keller, "A Rhetorician Ponders Technology; or, Why Kenneth Burke Never

Owned a 'Personal' Computer," *Electronic Journal of Communication* 6, no. 1 (1996).

56. Brøvig-Hanssen and Harkins, "Contextual Incongruity."
57. "The doctrine of perspective would suggest that perspective is heuristic insofar as we see close at hand the things we had formerly seen from afar, and vice versa." Burke, *Permanence and Change*, 124.
58. Ibid., 117. Perspective by incongruity is a process by which an audience sees one angle from the perspective of another angle. Burke argued that perspective by incongruity "refers to the methodic merger of particles that had [previously] been considered mutually exclusive"; ibid., lv. Burke later discusses this idea further, an idea that is central to many of his arguments, that "In its origins, language is an implement of action"; ibid., 173. Key to his argument is the fact that sociological misfortunes happen because of misunderstandings in language. Thus, there is a value in shifting one's perception to see something in a new light. By using an apparently paradoxical pairing of words, perspective by incongruity entails that the terms may be rethought, given new meaning, and transformed. As an example of perspective by incongruity, Burke cites T. S. Eliot's oxymoron "decadent athleticism"; see ibid., 91. See also Burke, *Attitudes toward History*, 269.
59. Burke, *Permanence and Change*, 10.
60. Ibid., 35.
61. See Herbert Wichelns, "The Literary Criticism of Oratory," in *Readings in Rhetorical Criticism*, 3rd ed., ed. Carl R. Burgchardt (State College, PA: Strata Publishing, 2005).
62. Brøvig-Hanssen and Harkins, "Contextual Incongruity."
63. Burke, *Permanence and Change*, 49.
64. Kenneth Burke, *A Rhetoric of Motives* (Berkeley: University of California Press, 1969).
65. For more on the "atom cracking" potential of perspectives by incongruity, see Burke, *Permanence and Change*, 308.
66. DJ Earworm, quoted in Sinnreich, *Mashed Up*, 127.
67. Ibid.
68. https://girltalk.fandom.com/wiki/Feed_the_Animals.
69. The following description may be located at https://girltalk.fandom.com/wiki/All_Day; or https://adereth.github.io/oneoff/girltalk-v2/.
70. Burke, *Permanence and Change*, 133.
71. Burke, *Attitudes toward History*, 4–5.
72. Quoted in Gaylor, *Rip: A Remix Manifesto*, 3:56–4:17.
73. To be clear, I am not arguing that rap or hip hop is less worthy of prestige than the rock 'n' roll bands listed here. There is a hierarchy that has been codified into

contemporary rap as well, with rap artists like Jay-Z or Kendrick Lamar situated at the top, while Drama is less visible (and prolific) in best-of hip hop lists. Though Salt-N-Pepa are nostalgically regarded for their visible presence in the nascent hip hop of the early nineties, their music still straddles the boundary between influential music and kitsch.

74. This particular mashup can be found at "(Mighty Mike) Van Lennon—Imagine Jump (Gordie Edit)," Vimeo video, 2:16, 2010, https://vimeo.com/20120196.
75. When I say that each element is "congruent," I mean that each component of the mashup functions together in harmony. Each constituent part of the mashup seems as if it were created to complement the others. I am aware that this sort of serendipitous pairing is rare and generally doesn't happen ex nihilo. The skill of the DJ plays a large role in selecting each sample and manipulating at least one of these musical elements to make the mashup work.
76. The list in *Rolling Stone* was compiled and posted online. "500 Greatest Songs of All Time," *Rolling Stone*, http://www.rollingstone.com/music/lists/the-500-greatest-songs-of-all-time-20110407/john-lennon-imagine-20110516.
77. Debby Elliott, "Carter Helps Monitor Nicaragua Presidential Election," *NPR News*, November 5, 2006, http://www.npr.org/templates/story/story.php?storyId=6439233.
78. Recall street artist (and originator of the famous Barack Obama "Hope" poster) Shepard Fairey's equation of perceived importance with ubiquity: "the more stickers that are out there, the more important it seems, [and] the more important it seems, the more people want to know what it is, the more they ask each other, and *it gains real power from perceived power*." (Emphases are added. From the Banksy film *Exit through the Gift Shop*, 2010; United Kingdom: Paranoid Pictures, 2011, DVD, 18:05–18:17.)
79. Jonathan McIntosh, "About the Project," *The Gendered Advertising Remixer*, http://www.genderremixer.com/about/.
80. Burke, *Permanence and Change*, 35.
81. His suggestion sounds like an a priori endorsement of the method used in this chapter of remixing terms from his lexicon.
82. This is George Campbell's Enlightenment-era idea of what constitutes novelty.
83. Kenneth Burke, *Language as Symbolic Action* (Berkeley: University of California Press, 1966), 45.
84. Edwin Black, *Rhetorical Criticism: A Study in Method* (Madison: University of Wisconsin Press, 1978).
85. This quotation is a remixed version of Isocrates's justification of his kairotic

philosophy in *Antidosis*, 191 (in *Isocrates, Volume II*, ed. and trans. George Norlin [Cambridge, MA: Harvard University Press, 1929]). The original word that has been bracketed out and replaced by "mashup" is "subject." The following quote delivers what I believe to be Girl Talk's explanation of his kairotic philosophy: "I have many folders detailing the music [samples], whether it's a melody or a beat or percussion. I kind of have a running list of things where they fit in by tempo, so if I have that bit of Drake or that bit of Willow Smith vocals, and it's at a particular tempo, I can go into this text document and look at it and say, 'Oh, here's the list of melodies that go well here." Gregg Gillis, quoted in *All Things Considered*, "Girl Talk: Cataloguing Samples 'All Day,'" 2010.

CHAPTER 4. *EPAESTHETIC* RHETORIC: REMIX AND AUTO-TUNE ON YOUTUBE

1. Andy Carvin, "'Bed Intruder Meme': A Perfect Storm of Race, Music, Comedy and Celebrity," *NPR All Tech Considered—Technology News and Culture*, para. 2, August 5, 2010, http://www.npr.org/blogs/alltechconsidered/2010/08/05/129005122/youtube-bed-intruder-meme.
2. CrazyLaughAction, "Antoine Dodson 'Hide Yo Kids, Hide Yo Wife' Interview (Original)," YouTube video, 2:02, April 11, 2012, http://www.youtube.com/watch?v=EzNhaLUT520. Quote occurs 1:01–1:15.
3. Ibid., 1:21–1:26, 1:39–1:48.
4. "The Gregory Brothers" is a misnomer, given the presence of Sarah in the mix. But this chapter will continue to refer to them in that way because most of the press on the group refers to them as such.
5. YouTube, "Double Rainbows, Annoying Oranges and Bed Intruders: The Year on YouTube," *YouTube Official Blog*, December 12, 2010, http://youtube-global.blogspot.com/2010/12/double-rainbows-annoying-oranges-and.html?utm_source= feedburner&utm_medium=feed&utm_campaign=Feed%3A+youtube%2FPKJx+%28YouTube+Blog%29.
6. Jenna Wortham, "From Viral Video to Billboard 100," *New York Times*, September 5, 2010; Ki Mae Heussner, "From Sex Assault Fury to Internet-Fueled Fortune," *ABC News*, August 17, 2010, https://abcnews.go.com/Technology/sex-assault-fury-internet-fueled-fortune/story?id=11413687; Robert Mackey, "'Bed Intruder' Rant Earns Family a New Home," *New York Times*, August 19, 2010, https://thelede.blogs.nytimes.com/2010/08/19/bed-intruder-rant-buys-family-a-new-home.
7. "Behind the Gregory Brothers' Viral Videos," *CBS News Sunday Morning*, January 8,

2012, https://www.cbsnews.com/video/behind-the-gregory-brothers-viral-videos.

8. Mackey, "'Bed Intruder' Rant."
9. Ibid.
10. Philip Kennicott, "Auto-Tune Turns the Operatic Ideal into a Shoddy Joke," *Washington Post*, August 29, 2010, http://www.washingtonpost.com/wp-dyn/content/article/2010/08/27/AR2010082702197.html/, para. 3.
11. Richard Lanham, *Economics of Attention: Style and Substance in the Age of Information* (Chicago: University of Chicago Press, 2006), 144.
12. Axel Bruns, "Distributed Creativity: Filesharing and Produsage," in *Mashup Cultures*, ed. Stefan Sonvilla-Weiss (New York: Springer Wien, 2010), 26.
13. Aristotle, *Poetics*, in *The Basic Works of Aristotle*, ed. Richard McKeon, trans. Ingram Bywater (New York: Random House, 1941), 1455–87; Bruce Markgraf, "John Cage: Ideas and Practices of a Contemporary Speaker," *Quarterly Journal of Speech* 48, no. 2 (1962): 128–35.
14. Steven B. Katz considers the human voice as sensuous and musical. Katz, *The Epistemic Music of Rhetoric: Toward the Temporal Dimension of Affect in Reader Response and Writing* (Carbondale: Southern Illinois University Press, 1996). Aristotle addresses the meter and rhythm of the spoken voice in his *Poetics*. The Gregory Brothers describe the work of auto-tune as a tool to "songify" the human voice.
15. Kennicott, "Auto-Tune Turns the Operatic Ideal into a Shoddy Joke." A similar sentiment was shared by Brian Eno: "When people speak passionately they speak in melodies." Quoted in Simon Reynolds, *Rip It Up and Start Again: Postpunk 1978–1984* (London: Faber and Faber, 2005), 137.
16. Wortham, "From Viral Video to Billboard 100," para. 20.
17. CBS News, "Behind the Gregory Brothers."
18. Amber Johnson, "Antoine Dodson and the (Mis)Appropriation of the Homo Coon," *Critical Studies in Media Communication* 30, no. 2 (2013): 156.
19. Johnson, "Antoine Dodson," 154.
20. Safiya Umoja Noble, *Algorithms of Oppression: How Search Engines Reinforce Racism* (New York: NYU Press, 2018), 9.
21. See Johnson, "Antoine Dodson." See also Jonathan Nichols-Pethick, "Going with the Flow: On the Value of Randomness, Flexibility, and Getting Students in on the Conversation, or What I Learned from Antoine Dodson," *Cinema Journal* 50, no. 4 (2011): 182–87; Riché Richardson, "The Bed Intruder—News Video Goes Viral: Antoine Dodson as Internet Celebrity and Commodity," *Technoculture: An*

Online Journal of Technology in Society 4 (2014): 1–18; and Lyndsay Michalik, "How Antoine Dodson and the Bed Intruder Keep Climbin' in Our Windows: Viral Video Appropriation as Performance," *Liminalities: A Journal of Performance Studies* 10, no. 3/4 (2014): 1–19.

22. Schmoyoho, "Backin Up Song!!," YouTube video, 1:34, September 3, 2010, http://www.youtube.com/watch?v=qIoG4PlEPtY.
23. Schmoyoho, "Songify This—SunnyD and Rum—The Pop Single!," YouTube video, 1:41, September 27, 2010, http://www.youtube.com/watch?v=IdRo2NJJcUU.
24. Lanham, *Economics of Attention*, 117. Note that each of these binaries essentially explain the aesthetic process of remixing.
25. Ibid., 80.
26. Ibid., 144.
27. "Dadaism . . . revealed an organized hatred of good taste, courted a deliberate flouting of the appropriate, and thus is squarely in the movement toward planned incongruity." Kenneth Burke, *Permanence and Change: An Anatomy of Purpose*, 3rd ed. (Berkeley: University of California Press, 1984), 115.
28. Lanham, *Economics of Attention*, 50.
29. Audio examples of these sound collages can be found at William Ferguson et al., "The Recombinant DNA of the Mash-Up," *New York Times*, January 6, 2011.
30. Composer Pierre Schaeffer wrote "Railroad Study," which incorporates railroad whistles, trains chugging, and other related elements of noise into a sound collage that resembles the repetition and phrasing of a song. Ferguson et al., "The Recombinant DNA." Perhaps the most (in)famous and commercial example of *Musique concrète* is the song "Revolution #9," which was included on the fourth side of the Beatles' album *The Beatles* ("The White Album") in 1969. In this eight-minute composition, John Lennon and Yoko Ono included samples of noises and recordings to create a sound collage. Ironically, note McLeod and DiCola in *Creative License*, the Beatles' record label EMI is among the most stringent enforcers of copyright, as evidenced by their cease-and-desist order for DJ Danger Mouse's *Gray Album*, which heavily sampled the Beatles. And yet, it is very unlikely that Lennon and Ono asked for permission to use the samples in "Revolution #9." Kembrew McLeod and Peter DiCola, *Creative License: The Law and Culture of Digital Sampling* (Durham, NC: Duke University Press, 2011).
31. Mel Gordon, quoted in Christoph Cox and Daniel Warner, eds., *Audio Culture: Readings in Modern Music* (New York: Continuum, 2004), 5.
32. Aldous Huxley, in ibid., 5.

33. Jacques Attali, *Noise: The Political Economy of Music*, trans. Brian Massumi (Minneapolis: University of Minnesota Press, 1985), 27.
34. Greg Goodale, *Sonic Persuasion: Reading Sound in the Recorded Age* (Urbana: University of Illinois Press, 2011), 60.
35. Ibid., 62. To illustrate this point, he reminds the reader that the infamous propaganda of the Nazi film *Triumph of the Will* was saturated with noise; voices enter the film only after nearly twenty-three minutes of music, crowd noise, and bells.
36. Ken Jordan and Paul D. Miller, "Freeze Frame: Audio, Aesthetics, Sampling, and Contemporary Multimedia," in *Sound Unbound: Sampling Digital Music and Culture*, ed. Paul D. Miller (Cambridge, MA: MIT Press, 2008), 98.
37. It might be beneficial to upgrade "phonographs" to "turntables" in order to see how this free-form compositional style could be influential for the digital era of remix.
38. Lanham, *Economics of Attention*, 74.
39. Jordan and Miller, "Freeze Frame," 102.
40. For a depiction of this reaction, see John Cage's *Water Walk* piece. Nave for Eva, "John Cage 'Water walk,'" YouTube video, 3:58, October 2, 2014, https://www.youtube.com/watch?v=gXOIkT1-QWY.
41. Lanham, *Economics of Attention*, 66.
42. Quoted in Stephen Davies, *Themes in the Philosophy of Music* (New York: Oxford University Press, 2003), 12. Cage did not believe in the concept of perfect silence. A famous anecdote reveals that Cage once tried an anechoic chamber at Harvard to attain a perfect silence. He was disconcerted to find, however, that it didn't work, and told the technicians that he could hear two noises the entire time he was in there, one high and one low: "'Oh,' they said, 'everyone hears those—the low hum is your circulating blood, the high whine is your nervous system.'" From Lewis Hyde, *Common as Air: Revolution, Art, and Ownership* (New York: Farrar, Straus and Giroux, 2010), 72.
43. Lanham, *Economics of Attention*, 71.
44. Ibid., 15.
45. Aram Sinnreich, *Mashed Up: Music, Technology, and the Rise of Configurable Culture* (Amherst: University of Massachusetts Press, 2010), 86.
46. John Zorn, "The Game Pieces," in *Audio Culture: Readings in Modern Music*, ed. Christoph Cox and Daniel Warner (New York: Continuum, 2004), 198.
47. This connection perhaps is more understandable since John Cage acknowledged an admiration and kinship to McLuhan in 1967: "Not a moment passes without my

being influenced by [McLuhan] and grateful to him." Cage, "McLuhan's Influence," in *John Cage*, ed. Richard Kostelanetz (New York: Praeger Publishers, 1970), 171. Cage and McLuhan's mutual admiration can be also attributed to the fact that McLuhan was intellectually attuned to avant-garde art. McLuhan's poetic writing style merely mirrored the pop art of his day. His writing had the same function as Duchamp's *Fountain*, which was to problematize notions of communication technologies to move them away from being perceived as self-evident. His inspiration in avant-garde art also presented an opportunity to inject aesthetic theories into his conceptualizing about media; I find this fact fascinating because it demonstrates that McLuhan remixed aesthetics and transformed them into media hermeneutics. Donald Theall, "The Role of Aesthetic Theory in (Mass) Communication Theory," *Quarterly Journal of Speech* 61 (October 1975): 274. McLuhan remixed the idea of information transmission away from its previously articulated genesis in sound engineering into a more communicative one of symbolic language exchange.

48. Quoted in Markgraf, "John Cage," 128.
49. As demonstrated by his most famous composition, *4'33"*.
50. Markgraf, "John Cage," 129–32.
51. Edgard Varèse and Chou Wen-chung, "The Liberation of Sound," *Perspectives of New Music* 5, no. 1 (1966): 18.
52. As evidenced by their inclusion in virtually every book about the music of the twentieth century. Martin Heidegger's words can be applied to music's incorporation of the digital: "Everywhere, we remain unfree and chained to technology whether we passionately affirm or deny it. But we are delivered over to it in the worst possible way when we regard it as something neutral." Martin Heidegger, *The Question Concerning Technology*, in *Basic Writings*, ed. David Farrell Krell (New York: HarperCollins, 2008), 311–12.
53. While this particular call is my own, it is inspired by the words of Kenneth Burke, who used "both/and" more often than "either/or." See Burke, *Attitudes Toward History*, 3rd ed. (Berkeley: University of California Press, 1984), 402. See also Charles Ess, *Digital Media Ethics* (Malden, MA: Polity Press, 2009). He argued that in a postmodern age of digital media, pluralism permeates older notions of absolutism, and thus "both/and" is a consequence of the dialogic properties of the era.
54. Ann Clark, quoted in Cynthia M. Grund, "Kierkegaard: Metaphor and the Musical Erotic," *Danish Yearbook of Philosophy* 31 (1996): 74.
55. This definition is adapted from anthropologist Steven Mithen. See Mithen, *The Singing Neanderthal* (Cambridge, MA: Harvard University Press, 2007), 11.

56. Academics much more frequently turn to other disciplines to examine music. Not surprisingly, the lion's share of literature on music comes from within the discipline of music itself. Musicologists, for example, focus their efforts on the specific elements of music, such as melody, tone, chords, rhythm, meter, intervals, cadences, and timbre. As evidence, in musicology, a technical vocabulary of musical terms is essential. Further, a taste for classical music is helpful because much of the studies address this specific musical genre. There has been somewhat of a turn toward popular music in the last several decades, perhaps because of the influx of popular music studies taking place in cultural studies and sociology. Other approaches to music come from psychology, philosophy, and sociology.
57. George Buelow, "Rhetoric and Music," in *New Grove Dictionary of Music and Musicians*, ed. Stanley E. Sadie (London: Macmillan, 1980), 793.
58. Patrick McCreless, "Music and Rhetoric," in *The Cambridge History of Western Music Theory*, ed. Thomas Christensen (Cambridge: Cambridge University Press, 2002).
59. Francis Bacon in *Sylva Sylvarum* (1627) stated, "There be in music certain figures and tropes almost agreeing with the figures of rhetoric." Quoted in Gerard G. LeCoat, "Music and the Three Appeals of Classical Rhetoric," *Quarterly Journal of Speech* 62 (1976): 159.
60. James R. Irvine and Walter G. Kirkpatrick, "The Musical Form in Rhetorical Exchange: Theoretical Considerations," *Quarterly Journal of Speech* 58, no. 3 (1972): 272.
61. LeCoat, "Music and the Three Appeals," 161–62.
62. Quoted in ibid., 162.
63. Ibid.
64. Irvine and Kirkpatrick, "The Musical Form," 275.
65. LeCoat, "Music and the Three Appeals," 160.
66. Irvine and Kirkpatrick, "The Musical Form," 276.
67. McCreless, "Music and Rhetoric," 856.
68. The most productive era for theorizing music via rhetorical figures began in the early seventeenth century and lasted for nearly two centuries. However, the influence of rhetoric waned after that. In some ways, the emphasis on rationality and logic in the Enlightenment could be culpable for this decline; however, despite the prevailing trends of his time, one German music theorist worked against the decline of rhetoric and music. His name was Johann Mattheson and he produced works making rhetoric more credible even as the musico-rhetorical decline continued around him. Even while Peter Ramus was condemning rhetoric as being

too fixated on the canon of style, Mattheson shifted focus away from style to put invention and arrangement in the forefront of musico-rhetorical pedagogy. He did so by focusing on the rhetorical invention of melody in music. In other words, Mattheson bucked the trend of what was happening to rhetoric-*qua*-rhetoric during the eighteenth century. It is Mattheson's admirable rethinking of rhetoric and music that inspires me in the subsequent discussion of how contemporary music can function rhetorically.

69. Aristotle, *On Rhetoric: A Theory of Civic Discourse, 2nd ed., trans. George A. Kennedy* (New York: Oxford University Press, 2007), 227. *Asyndeta* is the plural form of asyndeton.
70. Ibid., 250. Words in brackets were provided by the translator, George A. Kennedy.
71. Ibid., 228.
72. Elizabeth Blettner, "One Made Many and Many Made One: The Role of Asyndeton in Aristotle's Rhetoric," *Philosophy and Rhetoric* 16, no. 1 (1983): 51. Blettner also considers the asyndeton as the stylistic equivalent of the period, providing a "readily perceivable whole" in oral delivery, much as the period does in written arguments. This is a structural component of the "periodic style" of speech, important in Aristotle's rhetoric because of its utility as a pleasurable learning technique. For our purposes, it is notable that the asyndeton's role in a periodic style of speech mirrors Isocratic rhetoric as an aesthetic and rhetorical antecedent of remix.
73. Ibid., 53.
74. Michel de Certeau, *The Practice of Everyday Life*, trans. Steven Rendall (Berkeley: University of California Press, 1984), 101.
75. Flow is crucial to remix as well. The "basic guiding principle" of hip hop (remix) is that "the flow and juxtaposition are everything." Peter Shapiro, "Deck Wreckers: The Turntable as Instrument," in *Undercurrents: The Hidden Wiring of Modern Music*, ed. Rob Young (New York: Continuum, 2002), 174.
76. Incidentally, if we play with this representative allegory enough, we can learn of some of the true tensions in remix culture today. The government-created sidewalk is music officially recorded and released from the music publishing industries. Stepping off of that sidewalk puts the child in danger of getting injured by the truck of copyright regulation.
77. For a summary of Langer's arguments and their rhetorical application, see Deanna Sellnow and Timothy Sellnow, "The 'Illusion of Life' Rhetorical Perspective: An Integrated Approach to the Study of Music as Communication," *Critical Studies in*

Media Communication 18, no. 4 (December 2001): 395–415.

78. See Roderick P. Hart and Suzanne M. Daughton, *Modern Rhetorical Criticism*, 3rd ed. (Boston: Allyn & Bacon, 2005).
79. Irvine and Kirkpatrick, "The Musical Form," 273.
80. Ibid., 277.
81. Ibid.
82. Ibid. Though Irvine and Kirkpatrick neglect to offer further explanation, I read it to mean that listeners are apt to "dance away their objections" if there are, indeed, controversial meanings laden throughout the music.
83. Simon Frith argues that one of the four social functions of music is to organize and control time. In this way, it can calm listener anxieties regarding the past or uncertainties regarding the future. See Frith, "Towards an Aesthetic of Popular Music," in *Music and Society: The Politics of Composition, Performance and Reception*, ed. Richard Leppert and Susan McClary (Cambridge: Cambridge University Press, 1989). Incidentally, this perspective echoes Nietzsche's, that music has the ability to save us from the terrifying chaos of life.
84. I am aware in my report of their theorizing that my discussion somewhat crosses out of the realm of rhetoric and into the realm of aesthetic and music theory. In rhetoric, because of exigencies, contingencies (and all manner of other -ies), it is outside of the purview of rhetoric to speculate as to what effect a rhetorical text will have on the audience. Throughout this book, I have made every effort to avoid theorizing to this end. However, a complex issue cannot be avoided here when theorizing music theory and aesthetics, because they are much less averse to discussing effects upon the audience. Indeed, the principal thread unifying John Dewey's famous aesthetic theories is aesthetics as consummatory experiences within the auditor of the art. See John Dewey, *Art as Experience* (New York: Minton, Balch & Co., 1934).

    Adorno's *Aesthetic Theory* is another example of discussing aesthetics only in its sociological context, that its understanding is only possible in its direct relationship (and effect) upon its audience. See Theodor W. Adorno, *Aesthetic Theory*, trans. Robert Hullot-Kentor (London: Continuum, 2004).
85. Irvine and Kirkpatrick, "The Musical Form," 280.
86. For a more detailed description of the controversy, see Steve Whitson and John Poulakos, "Nietzsche and the Aesthetics of Rhetoric," *Quarterly Journal of Speech* 79 (May 1993): 131–45.
87. Ibid., 132.

88. Ibid., 143.
89. John Poulakos and Steve Whitson, "Rhetoric Denuded and Redressed: Figs and Figures," *Quarterly Journal of Speech* 81 (August 1995): 385.
90. Whitson and Poulakos, "Nietzsche and the Aesthetics," 136.
91. Ibid., 141.
92. John Poulakos, "From the Depths of Rhetoric: The Emergence of Aesthetics as a Discipline," *Philosophy and Rhetoric* 40, no. 4 (2007): 340.
93. Ibid., 350.
94. See Roland Barthes, *The Pleasure of the Text*, trans. Richard Miller (New York: Hill & Wang, 1975).
95. John Fiske, *Understanding Popular Culture*, 2nd ed. (New York: Routledge, 2010), 41. More discussion of *jouissance* and the enthymeme will take place in a later chapter.
96. Whitson and Poulakos, "Nietzsche and the Aesthetics," 141.
97. Ibid.
98. Ibid.
99. This type of remix has been called *songification*, wherein a pitch manipulation tool is employed to make someone's speaking voice sound like a melody. Ragnhild Brøvig-Hanssen, "Humor's Role in Mashups and Remixes: Similarities between Humor Structure and Remix Structure," in *On Popular Music in Its Unruly Entanglements: Pop Music, Culture and Identity*, ed. Nick Braae and Kai Arne Hansen (London: Palgrave Macmillan, 2019).
100. Wortham, "From Viral Video to Billboard 100."
101. Sinnreich, *Mashed Up*, 105–6. Zachary Lazar, "The 373-Hit Wonder," *New York Times*, January 6, 2011, para. 22.
102. Daniel Herwitz, *Aesthetics: Key Concepts in Philosophy* (New York: Continuum, 2008), 71.
103. Thomas Weiskel, "The Logic of Terror," in *The Sublime*, ed. Simon Morley (Cambridge, MA: MIT Press, 2010), 157.
104. Simon Morley, "Introduction: The Contemporary Sublime," in *The Sublime*, ed. Simon Morley (Cambridge, MA: MIT Press, 2010), 14.
105. Morley, "Introduction," 15.
106. These are not Kant's words, but rather his argument summarized succinctly by philosopher Jacques Rancière. Rancière, "The Aesthetic Revolution and Its Outcomes," in *The Sublime*, ed. Simon Morley (Cambridge, MA: MIT Press, 2010), 68.
107. It should be noted that the contemporary sublime of which Lyotard writes is conceptually related to technology and its omnipresence. Jean-François Lyotard,

"The Sublime and the Avant-Garde," in *The Sublime*, ed. Simon Morley, trans. Geoffrey Bennington and Rachel Bowlby (Cambridge, MA: MIT Press, 2010), 30.

108. Herwitz, *Aesthetics*, 117–18.
109. There are strong religious connotations in the concept, and it is reflected in many religious artifacts, naturally. Cathedrals are exemplars of the sublime in architecture. When I traveled to the cathedral La Sagrada Familia in Barcelona, the scale of the artifice stunned and humbled me. This evinces another potential rhetorical dimension of the sublime—the clandestine or occluded insertion of religious themes or narratives into an otherwise secular postmodern culture. See Morley, "Introduction," 18.
110. Though he was not a de facto member of the Frankfurt School, Jacques Rancière's words on the sublime are notable because he uses the language of rhetoric to frame the sublime in the shared terms of logos and pathos. He sees *logos* and *pathos* as "the aesthetic identification of consciousness and unconsciousness" respectively. "Art inscribes on the surface of the work the immanence of *pathos* in the *logos*, of the unthinkable in thought." Rancière, "The Aesthetic Revolution," 67. This element of the sublime is also present in the rhetorical dimensions of music, most clearly illustrated by its invoking of emotion: "Baroque music in general aimed for a musical expression of words comparable to impassioned rhetoric or a *musica pathetica* . . . each musical idea must express an inherent or sometimes an imposed affective element of the text to which it was joined." Buelow, "Rhetoric and Music," 793–94.
111. Jean-François Lyotard, "Presenting the Unpresentable: The Sublime," in *The Sublime*, ed. Simon Morley, trans. Lisa Liebmann (Cambridge, MA: MIT Press, 2010), 134.
112. "Double Rainbow Song!!" https://www.youtube.com/watch?v=MX0D4oZwCsA.
113. Michael Martinez, "Double Rainbow Guy of YouTube Fame: Where Is He Now, Man?" *CNN*, https://www.cnn.com/2015/11/05/us/double-rainbow-guy/index.html.
114. Jimmy Kimmel, Twitter, July 3, 2010, https://twitter.com/jimmykimmel/status/17665533038.
115. It was coined the "sensitive female chord progression" on December 31, 2008, by Marc Hirsh, a *Boston Globe* correspondent. Clearly, this popular chord progression isn't exclusive to female artists, but Hirsh coined it after he noticed it appearing frequently in late-nineties songs by female artists such as Sarah McLachlan's "Building a Mystery" and Joan Osborne's "One of Us." http://archive.boston.com/ae/music/articles/2008/12/31/striking_a_chord/.
116. Mark Katz, *Capturing Sound: How Technology Has Changed Music* (Berkeley:

University of California Press, 2004), 148.

117. Quoted in ibid.
118. Ibid., 149.
119. Ibid., 150. This is the general opinion of a class of Katz's undergraduate students once they had been apprised of the case study.
120. Heussner, "From Sex Assault Fury," para. 15.
121. RAGECRY, "Antoine Dodson Performs—The Bed Intruder Song—At the 2010 BET Hip Hop Awards," YouTube video, 1:27, October 15, 2010, http://www.youtube.com/watch?v=vvzZExUSwTw. .
122. Katz, *Capturing Sound*, 151.
123. Aristotle, *Poetics*, 1455.
124. Quoted in Poulakos, "From the Depths of Rhetoric," 341.
125. Isocrates, *Antidosis*, in *Isocrates, Volume II*, ed. and trans. George Norlin (Cambridge, MA: Harvard University Press, 1929), 189.
126. W. B. Stanford, quoted in Katz, *Epistemic Music*, 87.
127. Ibid., 84–85.

CHAPTER 5. PROJECTING VOICE IN THE DIGITAL AGE: REMIX, ŚŪNYATĀ, AND PROSŌPOPOEIA

1. Horace, *The Art of Poetry*, trans. James Hynd (Albany: State University of New York, 1974), 59. In writing about the ephemerality of voice, Horace also pronounced, "Dead words shall live / and live words shall die / and only the mouths of men can decide / only what's said is said / and therefore alive. And therefore correct." Ibid., 12.
2. *Rhetorica ad Herennium*, in *The Rhetorical Tradition: Readings from Classical Times to the Present*, 2nd ed., ed. Patricia Bizzell and Bruce Herzberg (New York: Bedford/St. Martin's, 2001), 4.53.66, 399.
3. Quintilian's works offer examples of Roman literature that conflate both terms. See Quintilian, *The Orator's Education, Books 9–10*, trans. Donald A. Russell (Cambridge, MA: Harvard University Press, 2002), 51.
4. For example, Megan Foley addresses prosōpopoeia, "the trope of giving voice to a voiceless body," in a democratic context by arguing that it represents the citizens by projecting their voice. More specifically, it described how the trope of "voice" was materially projected to bodies incapable of speaking, like the incapacitated Terri Schiavo. See Foley, "Voicing Terri Schiavo: Prosopopeic Citizenship in the

Democratic Aporia between Sovereignty and Biopower," *Communication and Critical/Cultural Studies* 7, no. 4 (2010): 381–400.

5. Cicero, *Brutus*, trans. G. L. Hendrickson and H. M. Hubbell (Cambridge, MA: Harvard University Press, 1939), 369. Quintilian, *The Orator's Education, Books 9–10*, 9.2.29, 51.
6. According to the writings of the progymnasmatists, there are other types of speech for the absent as well, like *eidōlopoeia* (image, idol, or ghost making) and ēthopoeia (character making). See George A. Kennedy, *Progymnasmata: Greek Textbooks of Prose Composition and Rhetoric* (Atlanta: Society of Biblical Literature, 2003).
7. Eduardo Navas, *Remix Theory: The Aesthetics of Sampling* (New York: Springer Wien, 2012), 66.
8. Kembrew McLeod and Peter DiCola, *Creative License: The Law and Culture of Digital Sampling* (Durham, NC: Duke University Press, 2011), 66. This process here, however, is not exactly congruent to strategies of argumentation. While it is similar in the way that argumentation uses portions of arguments that directly complement those being posed by the rhetor, the relative obscurity of crate digging seems counterintuitive to the ethos that needs to be transmitted in argumentation—namely, that it is beneficial to one's credibility if he or she is able to successfully draw from arguments from reputable sources. Regarding our discussion here about the allegorical properties of remix, DJs generally sample from well-known popular hits in order to stoke the excitement of the audience. But "crate digging" is different, in that the rare or obscure songs are being rediscovered and deployed. Still, this creates a perverse sense of ethos that permeates internet culture. In order to be deemed worthy to be circulated, internet memes need to be sufficiently funny, fascinating, or shocking—despite their source. In the same way, according to the doctrine of crate digging, if a song is too good to leave untouched, despite its obscurity, it can provide the sampling DJ with a measure of respect for finding it in the dusty confines of retail bins.
9. See Marcus Boon, *In Praise of Copying* (Cambridge, MA: Harvard University Press, 2010), 27.
10. Jeffrey Hopkins, *Meditation on Emptiness* (Boston: Wisdom Publications, 1996), 404.
11. Gay Watson, *A Philosophy of Emptiness* (London: Reaktion Books, 2014), 15.
12. David Ross Komito, *Nagarjuna's Seventy Stanzas: A Buddhist Psychology of Emptiness* (Ithaca, NY: Snow Lion, 1987), 68.
13. "If we examine causes, conditions, and their aggregations we discover that their individual existence is unfindable because they can not be separated and still retain

their own natures in dependence on each other"; Komito, *Nagarjuna's Seventy*, 102.

14. Michael G. Barnhart, "*Śūnyatā*, Textualism, and Incommensurability," *Philosophy East & West* 44, no. 4 (1994): 649–58.
15. Komito, *Nagarjuna's Seventy*, 102.
16. Watson, *A Philosophy of Emptiness*, 10, 14.
17. Martin Irvine, "Remix and the Dialogic Engine of Culture," in *The Routledge Companion to Remix Studies*, ed. Eduardo Navas, Owen Gallagher, and xtine burrough (New York: Routledge, 2015), 30.
18. Ibid., 30.
19. Colin Davis, "Can the Dead Speak to Us? De Man, Levinas and Agamben," *Culture, Theory & Critique* 45, no. 1 (2004): 79.
20. Diana Fuss, "Corpse Poem," *Critical Inquiry* 30, no. 1 (2003): 1–30, 1.
21. Giorgio Agamben, *Remnants of Auschwitz: The Witness and the Archive* (New York: Zone Books, 1999), 34. For further discussion on the controversy of imposing one's voice over another's, see Linda Alcoff, "The Problem of Speaking for Others," *Cultural Critique* 20 (1991–92): 5–32.
22. Adam Banks, *Digital Griots: African American Rhetoric in a Multimedia Age* (Carbondale: Southern Illinois University Press, 2010), 103.
23. Ibid., 103–4.
24. *Rhetorica ad Herennium*, 4.53.66, 401.
25. Kristine S. Bruss, "Persuasive *Ethopoeia* in Dionysius's Lysias," *Rhetorica: A Journal of the History of Rhetoric* 31, no. 1 (2013): 35. In the writers of the *Progymnasmata*, Hermogenes is explicit about the difference between the variants: "The difference is clear: in [ēthopoeia] we imagine words for a real person, in *prosōpopoeia* we imagine a non-existing person." Kennedy, *Progymnasmata*, 84. George Kennedy, however, opts to follow Theon's path and not distinguish between both, nor do other recent expert commentaries. The parlance of this chapter will also follow this well-trodden path, despite the potential taxonomic differences introduced by these ancient writers. Though clear differences between these terms will emerge in this discussion, the definitional distinction offered by Hermogenes is not so distinct when applied to remix; remix not only "speaks" the absent recording artists' songs, including artists who have long passed on, it also breathes life into previously closed songs or videos, thereby vivifying them. See also Kennedy, *Progymnasmata*, 47; Alicia Myers, "Prosopopoetics and Conflict: Speech and Expectations in John 8," *Biblica* 92, no. 4 (2011): 580–96.

26. R. G. Austin, trans., *M. Tulli Ciceronis' Pro M. Caelio Oratio*, 3rd ed. (London: Oxford Press, 1960), 90.
27. So distinguished was Appius that the Appian Way in Rome would be named for him.
28. Cicero, *Pro Caelio*, in *Cicero XIII*, trans. R. Gardner (Cambridge, MA: Harvard University Press, 1970), 14:33, 445, 447.
29. See Cicero, *Pro Marco Caelio*, ed. Andrew R. Dyck (New York: Cambridge Press, 2013), 20–21. Also Ciceronis, *Pro M. Caelio*. Later, Quintilian approves of Cicero's stratagem to change his tone to fit the character: "Publius Clodius and Appius Caecus are imagined very differently" (11.1.39).
30. Cicero, *Pro Caelio*, trans. Gardner, 15.36, 451. Considering the historical context, this statement is particularly cutting because it was doubly defamatory toward Clodia and her brother. Cicero certainly did not consider Clodius, his political enemy, to be perfect. Nor did Cicero mean that Clodius loved his sister in the familial sense; rather, this statement was scandalous, a euphemism for the rumored incestuous relationship between the two siblings. Indeed, Cicero wittily hinted at the gross impropriety earlier: "were I not hindered by my personal enmity to that woman's husband—I meant to say brother; I always make that slip" (13.32). Cicero, *Pro Caelio*, 445. If even her brother, the "petty gangster," considered Clodia's actions inappropriate, as Cicero's masked statement makes clear, her transgressions must have been quite egregious. W. M. F. Rundell, "Cicero and Clodius: The Question of Credibility," *Historia* 28, no. 3 (1979): 301, 318.
31. Quintilian, *The Orator's Education*, 12.10.61, 313.
32. Austin, *Pro M. Caelio*, 91.
33. "Tiger Woods Commercial: Earl and Tiger," https://www.youtube.com/watch?v=czNR8S-OUpc.
34. Portions of the audio were taken from a 2004 interview with Earl Woods, as displayed in "Tiger: The Authorized DVD Collection." Russell Goldman, "Tiger Woods Ad Ripped Audio from 2004 Documentary," *ABC News*, January 22, 2020, http://abcnews.go.com/Business/tiger-woods-ad-ripped-audio-2004-documentary/story?id=10323878/.
35. Bruss, "Persuasive *Ethopoeia*," 38, 50.
36. Ibid., 51.
37. Austin, *Pro M. Caelio*, 90; Quintilian, *Orator's Education, Books 11–12*, 29–31: "The same differentiation must be observed. This is because we use imaginary persons

and speak as it were with other men's lips, and so have to provide the appropriate personalities for those to whom we lend our voice . . . in Prosopopoeia we simulate the emotions of children, women, nations, and even things which cannot speak, and they are all entitled to their appropriate character" (11.1.39–41).

38. Bruss, "Persuasive *Ethopoeia*," 44.
39. "Different styles of eloquence too are appropriate to different people . . . It is the same too with clothes: old age does not go well with the brilliance of purple and scarlet" (11.1.31); Quintilian, *Orator's Education, Books 11–12*, 25.
40. "Paul McCartney Rabbit Hole—Swedemason," YouTube video, 2:58, "Swedemason," August 23, 2017, https://www.youtube.com/watch?v=G4EcRPlaXoQ.
41. Eduardo Navas argues that remixes are necessarily allegorical because "their effectiveness depends on the recognition of pre-existing recordings"; Navas, *Remix Theory*, 96. This allegorical potential of remixes offers dual readings characterized by the tension between the sampled materials and the mashup; ibid., 43.
42. This album changed the way people thought about music production and distribution. "Danger Mouse created a broad, inventive commentary on forms of musical creativity that have defined all kinds of music for centuries: borrowing, appropriation, homage, derivation, allusion, recomposition, collage, pastiche and quotation . . . He unwittingly drew a sharp line between those exploring the capabilities of new tools for making music and those trying to contain them." Charles Fairchild, *The Grey Album* (New York: Bloomsbury, 2014), 6.
43. Regardless of its reading, this is also an example of "possession by misnomer."
44. John Shiga, "Copy-and-Persist: The Logic of Mash-up Culture," *Critical Studies in Media Communication* 24, vol. 2 (June 2007): 96.
45. For one of the most musically talented remix artists on the internet, please see Andy Rehfeldt's YouTube channel, which showcases such videos as "Judy Garland Sings Death Metal" and "Metallica-Enter Sandman (Smooth Jazz version)." Though he does not collect and mash up samples of recorded music like other remix artists, he dedicates his considerable musical talent to performing the incongruous generic musical background while retaining the original vocals. In other videos, he retains only the video and title, while recording a new death-metal backing track and employing the guttural death-metal growl as the new vocal.
46. Watson, *A Philosophy of Emptiness*, 170.
47. Fernando Tola and Carmen Dragonetti, "Nagarjuna's Conception of 'Voidness' (Sunyata)," *Journal of Indian Philosophy* 9, no. 3 (1981): 273–82.
48. Diané Collinson, Kathryn Plant, and Robert Wilkinson, *Fifty Eastern Thinkers* (New

York: Routledge, 2000), 95.

49. Tola and Dragonetti, "Nagarjuna's Conception," 276–77.
50. Ibid., 275; Hopkins, *Meditation on Emptiness*, 494.
51. Tola and Dragonetti, "Nagarjuna's Conception," 276; Hopkins, *Meditation on Emptiness*, 401. This notion of a "destructive dialectic" contains provocative parallels with a classical sophistic practice called *dissoi logoi*. Though both the sophists and the Mādhyamaka School addressed a similar deliberative phenomenon, they conflicted in how they conceptualized the purpose of countervailing arguments. An ancient Greek fragment, *dissoi logoi* presupposes that argumentation is made more robust when the rhetor addresses both sides of the debate, often with the pedagogical objective of making the weaker argument appear stronger. However, the Mādhyamaka School considers opposition to be less ontologically defined. To the followers of Nāgārjuna, the opposition, rather, is the perspective of "concealment reality" held by the interlocutor instead of one that can be discursively articulated. Though each school holds a similar objective, the goal of *dissoi logoi* is perhaps more easily obtainable because the task is more discursive than ontological. Hence, *dissoi logoi* aims for persuasion through perspective-taking engagement; the more difficult perspective-shattering process that leads to śūnyatā can be fructified only through a sustained process of dialectical "abolishment" and "destruction." I offer my thanks to Damien Smith Pfister for calling my attention to these parallels.
52. These clips have showcased Williams "rapping" to songs such as Sir Mix-a-Lot's "Baby Got Back," Snoop Dogg's "Gin and Juice," and Sugarhill Gang's "Rappers Delight."
53. GK BackwardInduction, "'Rapper's Delight Brian Williams feat Lester Holt," YouTube video, 1:12, November 4, 2019, https://www.youtube.com/watch?v=v--znY7yk84.
54. This claim refers to remix in all of its iterations. Science fiction writer William Gibson explains, "The remix is the very nature of the digital . . . The recombinant (the bootleg, the remix, the mash-up) has become the characteristic pivot at the turn of our two centuries." Quoted in David Gunkel, *Of Remixology: Ethics and Aesthetics after Remix* (Cambridge, MA: MIT Press, 2016), xvii.
55. Quoted in Fuss, "Corpse Poem," 28.
56. Christian Marclay, quoted in Christoph Cox and Daniel Warner, eds., *Audio Culture: Readings in Modern Music* (New York: Continuum, 2004), 327.
57. For more on the trope's potential for empowerment, see Foley, "Voicing Terry Schiavo."

CHAPTER 6. FROM ALLEGORY TO ANTHOLOGY: *STRANGER THINGS* AND NOSTALGIA

1. Jason Landrum, "Nostalgia, Fantasy, and Loss: *Stranger Things* and the Digital Gothic." *Intertexts* 21, no. 1–2 (2017): 138.
2. Kayla McCarthy, "Remember Things: Consumerism, Nostalgia, and Geek Culture in *Stranger Things*," *Journal of Popular Culture* 52, no. 3 (2019): 663–77.
3. John Koblin, "New Netflix Ratings Confirm 'Stranger Things' Is a Hit," *New York Times*, November 2, 2017. The real numbers are likely higher; these reported totals from Netflix do not take into account the number of viewers who watched the show on devices like phones, tablets, and computers.
4. Patrick Hipes, "'Stranger Things' Season 3 Series' Most Viewed Ever as Netflix Reveals More Data," *Deadline*, October 16, 2019, https://deadline.com/2019/10/stranger-things-season-3-viewers-netflix-statistics-1202761915/.
5. Eduardo Navas, *Remix Theory: The Aesthetics of Sampling* (New York: Springer Wien, 2012). Umberto Eco, "*Casablanca*, or, the Clichés Are Having a Ball," in *On Signs*, ed. Marshall Blonsky (Baltimore, MD: Johns Hopkins University Press, 1985).
6. Myke Bartlett, "Rose-Coloured Rear-View: *Stranger Things* and the Lure of a False Past," *Screen Education* 85 (2017): 20.
7. Eco, "*Casablanca*, or, the Clichés Are Having a Ball"; Umberto Eco, "*Casablanca*: Cult Movies and Intertextual Collage," *SubStance* 14, no. 2 (1985): 3–12.
8. Roger Ebert, "Charlie Kaufman and Spike Jonze: Twin Pleasures," December 17, 2002, https://www.rogerebert.com/interviews/charlie-kaufman-and-spike-jonze-twin-pleasures.
9. Eco, "*Casablanca*, or, The Clichés Are Having a Ball," 35–36.
10. Eco, "*Casablanca*: Cult Movies and Intertextual Collage," 5.
11. Eco, "*Casablanca*, or, The Clichés Are Having a Ball," 36, 38. I should be clear here that Eco is not valorizing the use of recycled tropes as a creative device. He considers *Casablanca* overrated, melodramatic, and creatively impoverished. These two essays reflect his attempt to understand how a mediocre film can be elevated into the status of a classic when it clearly draws from a repertoire of the "tried and true" more than other, more traditionally considered original films. In framing this chapter with Eco's words, I am not endorsing or applying any value judgment about *Casablanca* to *Stranger Things*. Rather, this chapter is meant to explore how this phenomenon of nostalgia and perceived value from recycled archetypes works in the current text of analysis.
12. Eco, "*Casablanca*: Cult Movies and Intertextual Collage," 3.
13. Ibid., 5. Music educator Bennett Reimer has discussed this connection between

aesthetics and emotion. From the standpoint of referentialism, the viewer of the show would not be moved merely because of the text's aesthetic coherence, but rather because of the value of the text external to the text itself. See Bennett Reimer, *A Philosophy of Music Education*, 2nd ed. (Englewood Cliffs, NJ: Prentice Hall, 1989). In other words, rather than referencing other texts, Reimer's definition of referentialism alludes to extradiegetic emotions and feelings conjured up by the text. In the case of remix and *Stranger Things*, I believe that this referential power for emotion can function both on a diegetic and extradiegetic level. The references to popular culture made within the narrative of the show trigger emotions within the fictional characters. For example, Mike, Dustin, Will, and Lucas all identify as geeks due to their enjoyment of pastimes like *Dungeons and Dragons*. The reference is meaningful to them within the fictional context of eighties Hawkins, Indiana. However, the reference also appeals to an audience that perhaps remembers being geeky as well at some point in their lives, feeling nostalgia for the eighties and the popularity of *Dungeons and Dragons* that they remember from living during that time. But they also might feel nostalgia for other texts that reference and celebrate geek culture, like *Freaks and Geeks*, for example. For more on the geek culture and nostalgia of *Stranger Things*, see McCarthy, "Remember Things."

14. Eco, "*Casablanca*: Cult Movies and Intertextual Collage," 12.
15. Noël Carroll, "The Future of Allusion: Hollywood in the Seventies (and Beyond)," *October* 20 (1982): 61.
16. Ibid., 56.
17. The films Carroll refers to here as examples of this type of deathly sincere film is *Kramer vs. Kramer, Ordinary People, and The Four Seasons.*
18. I acknowledge that the latter objective of this chapter—to address the potential reception of the text by the audience—is a departure from the rest of the book, which focuses on the text, not its effects. However, given that the impact of the text on the audience can be addressed through a tropological lens, I trust that this deviation from the book's usual approach will offer another perspective through which rhetorical tropes can be addressed.
19. "I call a rhetorical syllogism an enthymeme, a rhetorical induction a paradigm . . . Speeches using paradigms are not less persuasive, but those with enthymemes excite more favorable audience reaction." Aristotle, *On Rhetoric: A Theory of Civic Discourse*, 2nd ed., trans. George A. Kennedy (New York: Oxford University Press, 2007), 40.
20. Aristotle, *On Rhetoric*, 40.

21. Ibid., 34. The explanation of enthymeme is derived from the translator's footnotes. In context, Isocrates uses the term in this way: "But to choose from these elements those which should be employed for each subject, to join them together, to arrange them properly, and also, not to miss what the occasion demands but appropriately to adorn the whole speech with striking thoughts and to clothe it in flowing and melodious phrase—these things, I hold, require much study and are the task of a vigorous and imaginative mind." Isocrates, *Against the Sophists*, in *Isocrates, Volume II*, ed. and trans. George Norlin (Cambridge, MA: Harvard University Press, 1929), 173, 175.
22. Jeffrey Walker, *Rhetoric and Poetics in Antiquity* (New York: Oxford University Press, 2000), 179.
23. Kenneth Burke, *Counter-Statement*, 2nd ed. (Berkeley: University of California Press, 1968), 145, emphasis added.
24. Scott McCloud, *Understanding Comics: The Invisible Art* (New York: William Morrow, 1994).
25. John Fiske, *Understanding Popular Culture*, 2nd ed. (New York: Routledge, 2010), 42.
26. David B. Levy, *Directing Animation* (New York: Allworth, 2010): 167–68.
27. Tracey Mollet, "Looking through the Upside Down: Hyper-postmodernism and Trans-mediality in the Duffer Brothers' *Stranger Things*," *Journal of Popular Television* 7, no. 1 (2019): 72.
28. Mike Watson, *Can the Left Learn to Meme? Adorno, Video Gaming, and* Stranger Things (Dexter, MI: Zero Books, 2019).
29. Linda Hutcheon and Mario J. Valdés, "Irony, Nostalgia, and the Postmodern: A Dialogue," *Poligrafías: Revista de teoría literaria y literatura comparada* 3 (1998): 20. William C. Kurlinkus, *Nostalgic Design: Rhetoric, Memory, and Democratizing Technology* (Pittsburgh: University of Pittsburgh Press, 2018).
30. Landrum, "Nostalgia, Fantasy," 156. Bartlett, "Rose-Coloured," 23.
31. Megan Fariello, ""Mediating the 'Upside Down': The Techno-Historical Acoustic in Netflix's *Stranger Things* and *The Black Tapes* Podcast," *Sound Studies* 5, no. 2 (2019): 123.
32. Mary Beth Oliver and Anne Bartsch, "Appreciation as Audience Response," *Human Communication Research* 36 (2010): 54.
33. Ibid., 76.
34. Mary Beth Oliver, "Exploring the Paradox of the Enjoyment of Sad Films," *Human Communication Research* 19, no. 3 (1993): 315–42.
35. Mary Beth Oliver, "Tender Affective States," *Journal of Communication* 58 (2008): 44.

36. Ibid., 42.
37. William C. Kurlinkus, *Nostalgic Design: Rhetoric, Memory, and Democratizing Technology* (Pittsburgh: University of Pittsburgh Press, 2018). Although Kurlinkus does not explicitly theorize the term *eudaimonia* in his book, he often refers to nostalgia as a means for achieving eudaimonia.
38. Hutcheon and Valdés, "Irony, Nostalgia," 19.
39. Ibid., 19–20.
40. Andrew Higson, "Re Presenting the National Past: Nostalgia and Pastiche in the Heritage Film," in *Fires Were Started: British Cinema and Thatcherism*, ed. Lester Friedman (Minneapolis: University of Minnesota Press, 1993), 113.
41. Hutcheon and Valdés, "Irony, Nostalgia," 22.
42. Eco, "*Casablanca*: Clichés Are Having a Ball," 36.
43. Paul Grainge, "Nostalgia and Style in Retro America: Moods, Modes, and Media Recycling," *Journal of American & Comparative Cultures* 23, no. 1 (2000): 27–34.
44. Chuck Klosterman, *Chuck Klosterman X* (New York: Blue Rider Press, 2017): 32.
45. Carol Lynne Krumhansl and Justin Adam Zupnick, "Cascading Reminiscence Bumps in Popular Music," *Psychological Science* 24, no. 10 (2013): 2057–68.
46. Ibid., 2065–66.
47. McCarthy, "Remember Things," 674.
48. Emily Nussbaum, quoted in McCarthy, "Remember Things," 668.
49. Richard Lanham, *Economics of Attention: Style and Substance in the Age of Information* (Chicago: University of Chicago Press, 2006).
50. Fredric Jameson, *Postmodernism, or The Cultural Logic of Late Capitalism* (Durham, NC: Duke University Press, 1991), 17.
51. Ibid., 18, 25.
52. Margaret A. Rose, "Post-Modern Pastiche," *British Journal of Aesthetics* 31, no. 1 (1991): 29.
53. Jameson, *Postmodernism*, 19.
54. Hutcheon and Valdés, "Irony, Nostalgia," 22–23.
55. Ibid., 23.
56. Sandra Annett, "The Nostalgic Remediation of Cinema in *Hugo* and *Paprika*," *Journal of Adaptation in Film & Performance* 7, no. 2 (2014): 169–80.
57. Ibid., 170.
58. Stephanie Lambert, "'The Real Dark Side, Baby': New Sincerity and Neoliberal Aesthetics in David Foster Wallace and Jennifer Egan," *Critique: Studies in Contemporary Fiction* 61, no. 4 (2020): 394–411.

59. Quoted in Sunyoung Ahn, "New Sincerity, New Worldliness: The Post-9/11 Fiction of Don DeLillo and David Foster Wallace," *Critique: Studies in Contemporary Fiction* 60, no. 2 (2019): 248.
60. Ibid., 248.
61. Warren Buckland, "Wes Anderson: A 'Smart' Director of the New Sincerity?" *New Review of Film and Television Studies* 10, no. 1 (2012): 4.
62. Ahn, "New Sincerity," 236. It should be noted that not all critics agree with this assertion; indeed, others have argued the exact opposite, that the dread associated with the catastrophe made the unease of postmodernism feel especially relevant. See Jennie Yabroff, "The Corrections," *Newsweek*, December 12, 2008, https://www.newsweek.com/corrections-82825.
63. My thanks to Kerry Soper for alerting me to this phenomenon and sharing some of these examples with me.
64. Mollet, "Looking through the Upside Down," 71.
65. Bartlett, "Rose-Coloured Rear-View," 22.
66. Aristotle, *Aristotle's Nicomachean Ethics*, trans. Robert C. Bartlett and Susan D. Collins (Chicago: University of Chicago Press, 2011).
67. Werner Jaeger, *Paidaia: The Ideals of Greek Culture*, vol. 2, *In Search of the Divine Center* (New York: Oxford University Press, 1943).
68. Jaeger, *Paideia*, vol. 3, 90.
69. Ibid., 90.
70. Isocrates, *On the Peace*, in *Isocrates, Volume II*, ed. and trans. George Norlin (Cambridge, MA: Harvard University Press, 1929), 19.
71. Jaeger, *Paideia*, vol. 3, 90–91.
72. Robert Hariman, "Civic Education, Classical Imitation, and Democratic Polity," in *Isocrates and Civic Education*, ed. Takis Poulakos and David Depew (Austin: University of Texas Press, 2004).
73. See Oliver, "Tender Affective States."
74. Richard Lanham, *A Handlist of Rhetorical Terms*, 2nd ed. (Berkeley: University of California Press, 1991), 144. These *suasoriae* also permeated the writings of Virgil and Ovid. George Kennedy, *The Art of Rhetoric in the Roman World* (Princeton, NJ: Princeton University Press, 1972), 316.
75. "I do not understand why one has to shout so furiously at the outset." Quintilian, *The Orator's Education, Books 3–5* (3.8.59), trans. Donald A. Russell (Cambridge, MA: Harvard University Press, 2002), 145.
76. Michael Mendelson, "Declamation, Context, and Controversiality," *Rhetoric Review*

13, no. 1 (1994): 93.

77. Kennedy, *Art of Rhetoric in the Roman World*, 317.
78. Quintilian explains how these practice speeches were rhetorical: "Thus Deliberative—also called the *suasoria*—debates the future, but also asks questions about the past. It has two functions: to persuade and to dissuade." Quintilian, *The Orator's Education* (3.8.6), 119. Quintilian described his students who engaged in *suasoriae* as assuming as many roles on stage as did the comic actors of the time. Mendelson, "Quintilian and the Pedagogy of Argument," *Argumentation* 15 (2001): 285.
79. Kennedy, *Art of Rhetoric in the Roman World*, 316. Michael Mendelson calls them outright "impersonations of historical figures." Mendelson, "Quintilian," 285.
80. Mendelson, "Declamation," 94.
81. Ibid., 94.
82. Mendelson, "Quintilian," 285.
83. Scott Haden Church, "Against the Tyranny of Musical Form: Glitch Music, Affect, and the Sound of Digital Malfunction," *Critical Studies in Media Communication* 34, no. 4 (2017): 315–28.

CONCLUSION

1. Kenneth Burke, *Permanence and Change: An Anatomy of Purpose*, 3rd ed. (Berkeley: University of California Press, 1984), 35.
2. Adapting Kenneth Burke, *Language as Symbolic Action* (Berkeley: University of California Press, 1966), 45.
3. Steve Reich, "Music as a Gradual Process," in *Audio Culture: Readings in Modern Music*, ed. Christoph Cox and Daniel Warner (New York: Continuum, 2004), 306.
4. In an earlier chapter, I discussed how the mimesis of musical form to argumentation could make music persuasive. James Irvine and Walter Kirkpatrick described the process, in part, as happening because musical form strategically occludes its embedded messages: "When listening to a message couched in music, one is less prepared to argue in opposition to the projected message." Irvine and Kirkpatrick, "The Musical Form in Rhetorical Exchange: Theoretical Considerations," *Quarterly Journal of Speech* 58, no. 3 (1972): 273.
5. I do not advocate a radical reenvisioning or disposal of the classical enthymeme in the networked age. However, my argument that it needs to be definitionally broadened is analogous to the evolution of "rhetoric" between classical and

contemporary eras. For example, though rhetoric used to be strictly focused on speech as persuasive, now the definition is generally broadened to accept signs and symbols into its purview. Likewise, I argue that the scope of enthymeme should be broadened as well to reflect the richer repertoire of rhetorical resources from which we have to draw.

6. "So, a good appropriated sample has those two qualities. It has a good quality of its own, and it has a strong reference that evokes cultural resonance as well"; quoted in Kembrew McLeod and Peter DiCola, *Creative License: The Law and Culture of Digital Sampling* (Durham, NC: Duke University Press, 2011), 99.
7. Aristotle, *On Rhetoric: A Theory of Civic Discourse*, 2nd ed., trans. George A. Kennedy (New York: Oxford University Press, 2007), 35. The bracketed insertions are added by the translator.
8. Elizabeth Blettner, "One Made Many and Many Made One: The Role of Asyndeton in Aristotle's Rhetoric," *Philosophy and Rhetoric* 16, no. 1 (1983): 52–53.
9. Walter J. Ong, *Orality and Literacy: The Technologizing of the Word* (New York: Routledge, 1999).
10. Barry Brummett, *Rhetorical Dimensions of Popular Culture* (Tuscaloosa: University of Alabama Press, 1991).

APPENDIX: A NEW DICTIONARY OF PIVOTAL TERMS

1. "The representative anecdote is a critical tool especially well-suited to analysis of the media." Barry Brummett, "Burke's Representative Anecdote as a Method of Media Criticism," *Critical Studies in Mass Communication* 1 (1984): 165.
2. Ibid., 162.
3. Kenneth Burke, *A Grammar of Motives* (Berkeley: University of California Press, 1969), 59. Robert Wess points out that Burke's definition of language carries over into his use of representative anecdote as rhetorical method. Robert Wess, "Representative Anecdotes in General, with Notes toward a Representative Anecdote for Burkean Ecocriticism in Particular," *K. B. Journal* 1, no. 1 (2004), http://www.kbjournal.org/node/54.4. This phrase is taken from the terminology section in Kenneth Burke's *Attitudes toward History*, 3rd ed. (Berkeley: University of California Press, 1984).
5. Jeffrey Hopkins, *Meditation on Emptiness* (Boston: Wisdom Publications, 1996), 404.

Selected Bibliography

Adorno, Theodor W. *Aesthetic Theory*. Translated by Robert Hullot-Kentor. London: Continuum, 2004.

———. *The Culture Industry*. New York: Routledge, 1991.

———. *In Search of Wagner*. New York: Verso, 2009.

———. *Notes to Literature: Volume 2*. Edited by Rolf Tiedemann. Translated by Shierry Weber Nicholsen. New York: Columbia University Press, 1992.

———. "On Popular Music." In *Essays on Music*, edited by Richard Leppert, 437–69. Berkeley: University of California Press, 2002.

———. *The Stars Down to Earth, and Other Essays on the Irrational in Culture*. New York: Routledge, 1994.

Agamben, Giorgio. *Remnants of Auschwitz: The Witness and the Archive*. New York: Zone Books, 1999.

Ahn, Sunyoung. "New Sincerity, New Worldliness: The Post-9/11 Fiction of Don DeLillo and David Foster Wallace." *Critique: Studies in Contemporary Fiction* 60, no. 2 (2019): 236–50.

Alcoff, Linda. "The Problem of Speaking for Others." *Cultural Critique* 20 (1991–92): 5–32.

Annett, Sandra. "The Nostalgic Remediation of Cinema in *Hugo* and *Paprika*." *Journal of Adaptation in Film & Performance* 7, no. 2 (2014): 169–80.

Aristotle. *Aristotle's Nicomachean Ethics*. Translated by Robert C. Bartlett and Susan D. Collins. Chicago: University of Chicago Press, 2011.

———. *De Poetica* (*Poetics*). In *The Basic Works of Aristotle*, edited by Richard McKeon, translated by Ingram Bywater, 1455–87. New York: Random House, 1941.

———. *On Rhetoric: A Theory of Civic Discourse*. 2nd ed. Translated by George A. Kennedy. New York: Oxford University Press, 2007.

———. *Physica*. In *The Basic Works of Aristotle*, edited by Richard McKeon, translated by R. P. Hardie and R. K. Gaye, 218–394. New York: Random House, 1941.

Arnett, Ronald C. "A Conversation about Communication Ethics with Ronald C. Arnett." In *Exploring Communication Ethics: Interviews with Influential Scholars in the Field*, edited by Pat Arneson, 53–68. New York: Peter Lang, 2007.

Attali, Jacques. *Noise: The Political Economy of Music*. Translated by Brian Massumi. Minneapolis: University of Minnesota Press, 1985.

Austin, R. G., trans. *M. Tulli Ciceronis' Pro M. Caelio Oratio*. 3rd ed. London: Oxford Press, 1960.

Banks, Adam J. *Digital Griots: African American Rhetoric in a Multimedia Age*. Carbondale: Southern Illinois University Press, 2010.

Banksy, dir. *Exit through the Gift Shop*. 2010; United Kingdom: Paranoid Pictures, 2011. DVD.

Barnhart, Michael G. "Śūnyatā, Textualism, and Incommensurability." *Philosophy East & West* 44, no. 4 (1994): 649–58.

Barrett, Margreth. *Intellectual Property*. New York: Aspen Publishers, 2008.

Barthes, Roland. *The Pleasure of the Text*. Translated by Richard Miller. New York: Hill & Wang, 1975.

Bartlett, Myke. "Rose-Coloured Rear-View: *Stranger Things* and the Lure of a False Past." *Screen Education* 85 (2017): 16–25.

Baudrillard, Jean. *Simulacra and Simulation*. Translated by Sheila Faria Glaser. Ann Arbor: University of Michigan Press, 1994.

Beiner, Ronald. *What's the Matter with Liberalism?* Berkeley: University of California Press, 1992.

Bermingham, L. B. "Culture Jamming or a Culture Jammed? Rip!: A Remix Manifesto." *Screen Education* 54 (2009): 44–47.

Bernstein, J. M. "Introduction." In Theodor W. Adorno, *The Culture Industry: Selected Essays on Mass Culture*, 1–28. New York: Routledge, 1991.

Benjamin, Walter. *The Arcades Project*. Translated by Howard Eiland and Kevin McLaughlin. Cambridge, MA: Belknap Press, 1999.

Billig, Michael. *Arguing and Thinking: A Rhetorical Approach to Social Psychology*. Cambridge: Cambridge University Press, 1987.

Bizzell, Patricia, and Bruce Herzberg. "Isocrates." In *The Rhetorical Tradition: Readings from Classical Times to the Present*, 2nd ed., edited by Patricia Bizzell and Bruce Herzberg, 67–71. New York: Bedford/St. Martin's, 2001.

Black, Edwin. *Rhetorical Criticism: A Study in Method*. Madison: University of Wisconsin Press, 1978.

Blettner, Elizabeth. "One Made Many and Many Made One: The Role of Asyndeton in Aristotle's Rhetoric." *Philosophy and Rhetoric* 16, no. 1 (1983): 49–53.

Boch, Georg. *Facebook's "Adorno Changed My Life."* Directed and written by Georg Boch. ZeLIG Film, 2011. DVD.

Bonner, Robert J. "The Legal Setting of Isocrates' *Antidosis*." *Classical Philology* 15 (April 1920): 193–97.

Boon, Marcus. *In Praise of Copying*. Cambridge, MA: Harvard University Press, 2010.

Borschke, Margie. "Rethinking the Rhetoric of Remix." *Media International Australia* 141 (November 2011): 17–25.

———. *This Is Not a Remix: Piracy, Authenticity, and Popular Remix*. New York: Bloomsbury, 2017.

Boyle, James. *The Public Domain: Enclosing the Commons of the Mind*. New Haven, CT: Yale University Press, 2008.

Brewster, Bill, and Frank Broughton. *Last Night a DJ Saved My Life: The History of the Disc Jockey*. New York: Grove Press, 2000.

Brigance, William Norwood. "Can We Redefine the James-Winans Theory of Persuasion?" *Quarterly Journal of Speech* 21, no. 1 (February 1935): 19–26.

Brockriede, Wayne. "Arguers as Lovers." *Philosophy & Rhetoric* 5, no. 1 (1972): 1–11.

———. "Rhetorical Criticism as Argument." *Quarterly Journal of Speech* 60 (1974): 165–74.

Brøvig-Hanssen, Ragnhild. "Humor's Role in Mashups and Remixes: Similarities between Humor Structure and Remix Structure." In *On Popular Music in Its Unruly Entanglements: Pop Music, Culture and Identity*, edited by Nick Braae and Kai Arne Hansen, 189–207. London: Palgrave Macmillan, 2019.

Brøvig-Hanssen, Ragnhild, and Aram Sinnreich. "Do You Wanna Build a Wall? Remix Tactics in the Age of Trump." *Popular Music and Society* 43, no. 5 (2019): 535–49.

Brøvig-Hanssen, Ragnhild, and Paul Harkins. "Contextual Incongruity and Musical Congruity: The Aesthetics and Humour of Mash-Ups." *Popular Music* 31, no. 1 (2012): 87–104.

Brummett, Barry. "Burke's Representative Anecdote as a Method of Media Criticism." *Critical Studies in Mass Communication* 1 (1984): 161–76.

———. "Electric Literature as Equipment for Living: Haunted House Films." *Critical Studies in Mass Communication* 2 (1985): 247–61.

———. "The Homology Hypothesis: Pornography on the VCR." *Critical Studies in Mass Communication* 5 (1988): 202–16.

———. *Rhetorical Dimensions of Popular Culture.* Tuscaloosa: University of Alabama Press, 1991.

Bruns, Axel. *Blogs, Wikipedia, Second Life, and Beyond: From Production to Produsage.* New York: Peter Lang, 2008.

———. "Distributed Creativity: Filesharing and Produsage." In *Mashup Cultures*, edited by Stefan Sonvilla-Weiss, 24–37. New York: Springer Wien, 2010.

Bruss, Kristine S. "Persuasive *Ethopoeia* in Dionysius's Lysias." *Rhetorica: A Journal of the History of Rhetoric* 31, no. 1 (2013): 34–57.

Buckland, Warren. "Wes Anderson: A 'Smart' Director of the New Sincerity?" *New Review of Film and Television Studies* 10, no. 1 (2012): 1–5.

Buelow, George J. "Rhetoric and Music." In *New Grove Dictionary of Music and Musicians*, edited by Stanley E. Sadie, 793–802. London: Macmillan, 1980.

Burgess, Jean, and Joshua Green. *YouTube: Online Video and Participatory Culture.* Malden, MA: Polity, 2009.

Burke, Kenneth. *Attitudes toward History.* 3rd ed. Berkeley: University of California Press, 1984.

———. *Counter-Statement.* 2nd ed. Berkeley: University of California Press, 1968.

———. *A Grammar of Motives.* Berkeley: University of California Press, 1969.

———. *Language as Symbolic Action.* Berkeley: University of California Press, 1966.

———. *On Human Nature: A Gathering While Everything Flows, 1967–1984.* Edited by William H. Rueckert and Angelo Bonadonna. Berkeley: University of California Press, 2003.

———. *Permanence and Change: An Anatomy of Purpose.* 3rd ed. Berkeley: University of California Press, 1984.

———. *The Philosophy of Literary Form: Studies in Symbolic Action.* 3rd ed. Berkeley: University of California Press, 1973.

———. *A Rhetoric of Motives.* Berkeley: University of California Press, 1969.

Burke, Seán, ed. *Authorship: From Plato to the Postmodern: A Reader.* Edinburgh: Edinburgh University Press, 1995.

burrough, xtine, and Frank Dufour. "Creativity." In *Keywords in Remix Studies*, edited by Eduardo Navas, Owen Gallagher, and xtine burrough, 92–103. New York: Routledge, 2017.

Cage, John. "McLuhan's Influence." In *John Cage*, edited by Richard Kostelanetz, 170–71. New York: Praeger Publishers, 1970.

Campbell, George. *The Philosophy of Rhetoric.* In *The Rhetoric of Blair, Campbell, and Whately*, edited by James L. Golden and Edward P. J. Corbett, 145–271. New York: Holt, Rinehart and Winston, 1968.

Carr, Thomas M., Jr. *Descartes and the Resilience of Rhetoric: Varieties of Cartesian Rhetoric.* Carbondale: Southern Illinois University Press, 1990.

Carroll, Noël. "The Future of Allusion: Hollywood in the Seventies (and Beyond)." *October* 20 (1982): 51–81.

Castells, Manuel. *The Rise of the Network Society.* 2nd ed. Malden, MA: Wiley-Blackwell, 2010.

Certeau, Michel de. *The Practice of Everyday Life.* Translated by Steven Rendall. Berkeley: University of California Press, 1984.

Church, Scott Haden. "Against the Tyranny of Musical Form: Glitch Music, Affect, and the Sound of Digital Malfunction." *Critical Studies in Media Communication* 34, no. 4, (2017): 315–28.

Cicero. *Brutus. Orator.* Translated by G. L. Hendrickson and H. M. Hubbell. Cambridge, MA: Harvard University Press, 1939.

Clark, Gregory. "Aesthetic Power and Rhetorical Experience." In *Kenneth Burke and His Circles*, edited by Jack Selzer and Robert Wess, 96–109. Anderson, SC: Parlor Press, 2008.

Collinson, Diané, Kathryn Plant, and Robert Wilkinson. *Fifty Eastern Thinkers.* New York: Routledge, 2000.

Corbett, Edward P. J. "The Cornell School of Rhetoric." *Rhetoric Review* 4, no. 1 (1985): 4–14.

Cox, Christoph, and Daniel Warner, eds. *Audio Culture: Readings in Modern Music.* New York: Continuum, 2004.

Crick, Nathan. "The Sophistical Attitude and the Invention of Rhetoric." *Quarterly Journal of Speech* 96, no. 1 (February 2010): 25–45.

Davies, Stephen. *Themes in the Philosophy of Music.* New York: Oxford University Press, 2003.

Davis, Colin. "Can the Dead Speak to Us? De Man, Levinas and Agamben." *Culture, Theory & Critique* 45, no. 1 (2004): 77–89.

Demers, Joanna. *Listening through the Noise: The Aesthetics of Experimental Electronic Music.* New York: Oxford University Press, 2010.

Depew, David. "The Inscription of Isocrates into Aristotle's Practical Philosophy." In *Isocrates and Civic Education*, edited by Takis Poulakos and David Depew, 157–85. Austin: University of Texas Press, 2004.

Depew, David, and Takis Poulakos. "Introduction." In *Isocrates and Civic Education*, edited by Takis Poulakos and David Depew, 118. Austin: University of Texas Press, 2004.

Descartes, René. *Meditations on First Philosophy: With Selections from the Objections and Replies.* Edited by John Cottingham. New York: Cambridge University Press, 1996.

Dewey, John. *Art as Experience.* New York: Minton, Balch & Company, 1934.

Eco, Umberto. "*Casablanca*: Cult Movies and Intertextual Collage." *SubStance* 14, no. 2 (1985): 3–12.

———. "*Casablanca*, or, the Clichés Are Having a Ball." In *On Signs*, edited by Marshall Blonsky. Baltimore, MD: Johns Hopkins University Press, 1985.

———. "Innovation and Repetition: Between Modern and Postmodern Aesthetics." *Daedalus* 134 (2005): 191–207.

Edwards, Richard L. "Remixing with Rules: Constraint and Potential in Restrictive Remixes." In *Sampling Media*, edited by David Laderman and Laurel Westrup, 31–42. New York: Oxford University Press, 2014.

Eisenstein, Elizabeth L. *The Printing Press as an Agent of Change: Communications and Cultural Transformations in Early-Modern Europe*. 2 vols. Cambridge: Cambridge University Press, 1979.

———. *The Printing Revolution in Early Modern Europe*. 2nd ed. Cambridge: Cambridge University Press, 2005.

Ess, Charles. *Digital Media Ethics*. Malden, MA: Polity Press, 2009.

Fairchild, Charles. *The Grey Album*. New York: Bloomsbury, 2014.

Fariello, Megan. "Mediating the 'Upside Down': The Techno-Historical Acoustic in Netflix's *Stranger Things* and *The Black Tapes* Podcast." *Sound Studies* 5, no. 2 (2019): 122–39.

Fiske, John. *Understanding Popular Culture*. 2nd ed. New York: Routledge, 2010.

Foley, Megan. "Voicing Terri Schiavo: Prosopopeic Citizenship in the Democratic Aporia between Sovereignty and Biopower." *Communication and Critical/Cultural Studies* 7, no. 4 (2010): 381–400.

Floridi, Luciano. *The Logic of Information: A Theory of Philosophy as Conceptual Design*. New York: Oxford University Press, 2019.

Franzosi, Roberto, ed. *Landmark Essays on Tropes and Figures*. New York: Routledge, 2017.

Frith, Simon. *Popular Music: The Rock Era*. New York: Routledge, 2004.

———. "Towards an Aesthetic of Popular Music." In *Music and Society: The Politics of Composition, Performance and Reception*, edited by Richard Leppert and Susan McClary, 133–49. Cambridge: Cambridge University Press, 1989.

Fuss, Diana. "Corpse Poem." *Critical Inquiry* 30, no. 1 (2003): 1–30.

Gaylor, Brett, dir. *Rip: A Remix Manifesto*. 2008; National Film Board of Canada, EyeSteelFilm. DVD.

George, Nelson. *Hip Hop America*. New York: Penguin, 2005.

Gerrish, Bruce. *Remix: The Electronic Music Explosion*. Vallejo, CA: EM Books, 2001.

Goodale, Greg. *Sonic Persuasion: Reading Sound in the Recorded Age*. Urbana: University of Illinois Press, 2011.

Grainge, Paul. "Nostalgia and Style in Retro America: Moods, Modes, and Media Recycling." *Journal of American & Comparative Cultures* 23, no. 1 (2000): 27–34.

Gross, Daniel. *The Secret History of Emotion: From Aristotle's Rhetoric to Modern Brain Science.* Chicago: University of Chicago Press, 2007.

Grund, Cynthia M. "Kierkegaard: Metaphor and the Musical Erotic." *Danish Yearbook of Philosophy* 31 (1996): 65–88.

Gunkel, David J. *Of Remixology: Ethics and Aesthetics after Remix.* Cambridge, MA: MIT Press, 2016.

———. "Remixology: A Remix(ed) Rhetoric for the 21st Century." *Journal of Contemporary Rhetoric* 7, no. 2/3 (2017): 79–86.

———. "Rethinking the Digital Remix: Mash-ups and the Metaphysics of Sound Recording." *Popular Music and Society* 31, no. 4 (October 2008): 489–510.

———. "What Does It Matter Who Is Speaking? Authorship, Authority, and the Mashup." *Popular Music and Society* 35, no. 1 (2012): 71–91.

Hajdu, David. *Heroes and Villains: Essays on Music, Movies, Comics, and Culture.* Philadelphia: Da Capo Press, 2009.

Hariman, Robert. "Civic Education, Classical Imitation, and Democratic Polity." In *Isocrates and Civic Education*, edited by Takis Poulakos and David Depew, 217–34. Austin: University of Texas Press, 2004.

Harold, Christine. *OurSpace: Resisting the Corporate Control of Culture.* Minneapolis: University of Minnesota Press, 2007.

Harrison, Nate, and Eduardo Navas. "Mashup." In *Keywords in Remix Studies*, edited by Eduardo Navas, Owen Gallagher, and xtine burrough, 188–201. New York: Routledge, 2017.

Hart, Roderick P., and Suzanne M. Daughton. *Modern Rhetorical Criticism.* 3rd ed. Boston: Allyn & Bacon, 2005.

Havelock, Eric A. *Preface to Plato.* Cambridge, MA: Harvard University Press, 1963.

Hawhee, Debra. *Moving Bodies: Kenneth Burke at the Edges of Language.* Columbia: University of South Carolina Press, 2009.

Heidegger, Martin. *The Question Concerning Technology.* In *Basic Writings*, edited by David Farrell Krell, 307–41. New York: HarperCollins, 2008.

Herwitz, Daniel. *Aesthetics: Key Concepts in Philosophy.* New York: Continuum, 2008.

Higson, Andrew. "Re Presenting the National Past: Nostalgia and Pastiche in the Heritage Film." In *Fires Were Started: British Cinema and Thatcherism*, edited by Lester Friedman, 109–29. Minneapolis: University of Minnesota Press, 1993.

Hill, Ian. "'The Human Barnyard' and Kenneth Burke's Philosophy of Technology." *KB Journal* 5, no. 2 (Spring 2009). http://www.kbjournal.org/ian_hill.

Hopkins, Jeffrey. *Meditation on Emptiness.* Boston: Wisdom Publications, 1996.

Horace. *The Art of Poetry.* Translated by James Hynd. Albany: State University of New York, 1974.

Hull, Gordon. "Digital Media and the Scope of 'Computer Ethics.'" In *Virtual Morality: Morals, Ethics and New Media*, edited by Mark J. P. Wolf, 17–38. New York: Peter Lang, 2003.

Hutcheon, Linda, and Mario J. Valdés. "Irony, Nostalgia, and the Postmodern: A Dialogue." *Poligrafías: Revista de Teoría Literaria y Literatura Comparada* 3 (1998): 18–41.

Hyde, Lewis. *Common as Air: Revolution, Art, and Ownership.* New York: Farrar, Straus and Giroux, 2010.

Innis, Harold. *Empire and Communications*. Toronto: University of Toronto Press, 1972.

Irvine, James R., and Walter G. Kirkpatrick. "The Musical Form in Rhetorical Exchange: Theoretical Considerations." *Quarterly Journal of Speech* 58, no. 3 (1972): 272–84.

Irvine, Martin. "Remix and the Dialogic Engine of Culture: A Model for Generative Combinatoriality." In *The Routledge Companion to Remix Studies*, edited by Eduardo Navas, Owen Gallagher, and xtine burrough, 15–42. New York: Routledge, 2015.

Isocrates. *Against the Sophists*. In *Isocrates, Volume II*, edited and translated by George Norlin, 159–77. Cambridge, MA: Harvard University Press, 1929.

———. *Antidosis*. In *Isocrates, Volume II*, edited and translated by George Norlin, 179–365. Cambridge, MA: Harvard University Press, 1929.

———. *On the Peace*. In *Isocrates, Volume II*, edited and translated by George Norlin, 1–98. Cambridge, MA: Harvard University Press, 1929.

———. *The Phillipus*. In *The Orations of Isocrates, Volume I*, translated by J. H. Freese, 115–58. London: George Bell & Sons, 1894.

———. "To Nicocles." In *Isocrates, Volume I*, edited and translated by George Norlin, 37–71. Cambridge, MA: Harvard University Press, 1928.

———. "To Philip." In *Isocrates, Volume I*, edited and translated by George Norlin, 243–339. Cambridge, MA: Harvard University Press, 1928.

Jaeger, Werner. *Paideia: The Ideals of Greek Culture*. Vol. 2, *In Search of the Divine Center*. New York: Oxford University Press, 1943.

———. *Paideia: The Ideals of Greek Culture*. Vol. 3, *The Conflict of Cultural Ideals in the Age of Plato*. New York: Oxford University Press, 1944.

Jameson, Fredric. *Postmodernism, or The Cultural Logic of Late Capitalism.* Durham, NC: Duke University Press, 1991.

Jenkins, Henry. *Convergence Culture*. New York: New York University Press, 2008.

———. "Multiculturalism, Appropriation, and the New Media Literacies: Remixing Moby Dick." In *Mashup Cultures*, edited by Stefan Sonvilla-Weiss, 99–119. New York: Springer Wien, 2010.

———. "What Happened before YouTube." In *YouTube: Online Video and Participatory Culture*, edited by Jean Burgess and Joshua Green, 109–25. Malden, MA: Polity, 2009.

Johns, Adrian. *Piracy: The Intellectual Property Wars from Gutenberg to Gates*. Chicago: University of Chicago Press, 2009.

Johnson, Amber. "Antoine Dodson and the (Mis)Appropriation of the Homo Coon: An Intersectional Approach to the Performative Possibilities of Social Media." *Critical Studies in Media Communication* 30, no. 2 (2013): 152–70.

Jordan, Ken, and Paul D. Miller. "Freeze Frame: Audio, Aesthetics, Sampling, and Contemporary Multimedia." In *Sound Unbound: Sampling Digital Music and Culture*, edited by Paul D. Miller, 97–108. Cambridge, MA: MIT Press, 2008.

Kastely, James L. "Kenneth Burke's Comic Rejoinder to the Culture of Empire." *College English* 58 (1996): 307–26.

Katz, Mark. *Capturing Sound: How Technology Has Changed Music*. Berkeley: University of California Press, 2004.

Katz, Steven B. *The Epistemic Music of Rhetoric: Toward the Temporal Dimension of Affect in Reader Response and Writing*. Carbondale: Southern Illinois University Press, 1996.

Keller, Dale S. "A Rhetorician Ponders Technology; or, Why Kenneth Burke Never Owned a 'Personal' Computer." *Electronic Journal of Communication* 6, no. 1 (1996).

Keller, Daphne. "The Musician as Thief: Digital Culture and Copyright Law." In *Sound Unbound: Sampling Digital Music and Culture*, edited by Paul D. Miller, 135–50. Cambridge, MA: MIT Press, 2008.

Kennedy, George. *The Art of Rhetoric in the Roman World*. Princeton, NJ: Princeton University Press, 1972.

———, trans. *Progymnasmata: Greek Textbooks of Prose Composition and Rhetoric*. Atlanta: Society of Biblical Literature, 2003.

Klosterman, Chuck. *Chuck Klosterman X*. New York: Blue Rider Press, 2017.

Komito, David Ross. *Nagarjuna's Seventy Stanzas: A Buddhist Psychology of Emptiness*. Ithaca, NY: Snow Lion, 1987.

Kot, Greg. *Ripped: How the Wired Generation Revolutionized Music*. New York: Scribner, 2009.

Krumhansl, Carol Lynne, and Justin Adam Zupnick. "Cascading Reminiscence Bumps in Popular Music." *Psychological Science* 24, no. 10 (2013): 2057–68.

Kurlinkus, William C. *Nostalgic Design: Rhetoric, Memory, and Democratizing Technology*. Pittsburgh: University of Pittsburgh Press, 2018.

Lambert, Stephanie. "'The Real Dark Side, Baby': New Sincerity and Neoliberal Aesthetics in David Foster Wallace and Jennifer Egan." *Critique: Studies in Contemporary Fiction* 61, no. 4 (2020): 394–411.

Landrum, Jason. "Nostalgia, Fantasy, and Loss: *Stranger Things* and the Digital Gothic." *Intertexts* 21, no. 1–2 (2017): 136–58.

Lanham, Richard. *A Handlist of Rhetorical Terms*. 2nd ed. Berkeley: University of California Press, 1991.

———. *Economics of Attention: Style and Substance in the Age of Information*. Chicago: University of Chicago Press, 2006.

———. *The Electronic Word: Democracy, Technology, and the Arts*. Chicago: University of Chicago Press, 1993.

Lansner, Kermit. "Burke, Burke, the Lurk." *Kenyon Review* 13, no. 2 (Spring 1951): 324–28, 330–32, 334–35.

LeCoat, Gerard G. "Music and the Three Appeals of Classical Rhetoric." *Quarterly Journal of Speech* 62 (1976): 157–66.

Leff, Michael. "The Idea of Rhetoric as Interpretive Practice: A Humanist's Response to Gaonkar." In *Rhetorical Hermeneutics: Invention and Interpretation in the Age of Science*, edited by Alan G. Gross and William M. Keith, 89–100. Albany, NY: SUNY Press, 1997.

Lessig, Lawrence. *Remix: Making Art and Commerce Thrive in the Hybrid Economy*. New York: Penguin, 2008.

Lethem, Jonathan. "The Ecstasy of Influence: A Plagiarism Mosaic." In *Sound Unbound: Sampling Digital Music and Culture*, edited by Paul D. Miller, 25–51. Cambridge, MA: MIT Press, 2008.

Levy, David B. *Directing Animation*. New York: Allworth, 2010.

Low, Sor-Ching. "Romancing Emptiness." *Contemporary Buddhism* 7, no. 2 (2006): 129–47.

Lyotard, Jean-François. "Presenting the Unpresentable: The Sublime." In *The Sublime*, edited by Simon Morley, translated by Lisa Liebmann, 130–36. Cambridge, MA: MIT Press, 2010.

———. "The Sublime and the Avant-Garde." In *The Sublime*, edited by Simon Morley, translated by Geoffrey Bennington and Rachel Bowlby, 27–41. Cambridge, MA: MIT Press, 2010.

MacIntyre, Alasdair. *After Virtue*. 3rd ed. Notre Dame, IN: University of Notre Dame Press, 2007.

Markgraf, Bruce. "John Cage: Ideas and Practices of a Contemporary Speaker." *Quarterly Journal of Speech* 48, no. 2 (1962): 128–35.

Mauer, Barry. "Rigorous Infidelity." In *Sampling Media*, edited by David Laderman and Laurel Westrup, 60–72. New York: Oxford University Press, 2014.

McCarthy, Kayla. "Remember Things: Consumerism, Nostalgia, and Geek Culture in *Stranger Things*." *Journal of Popular Culture* 52, no. 3 (2019): 663–77.

McCloud, Scott. *Understanding Comics: The Invisible Art*. New York: William Morrow, 1994.

McCreless, Patrick. "Music and Rhetoric." In *The Cambridge History of Western Music Theory*, edited by Thomas Christensen, 847–77. Cambridge: Cambridge University Press, 2002.

McGee, Michael Calvin. "Choosing a Poros: Reflections on How to Implicate Isocrates in Liberal Theory." Unpublished manuscript, 1998.

———. "Isocrates: A Parent of Rhetoric and Culture Studies." Unpublished manuscript, 1986.

———. "Text, Context, and the Fragmentation of Contemporary Culture." *Western Journal of Speech Communication* 54 (Summer 1990): 274–89.

McLeod, Kembrew. "Confessions of an Intellectual (Property): Danger Mouse, Mickey Mouse, Sonny Bono, and My Long and Winding Path as a Copyright Activist-Academic." *Popular Music and Society* 28, no. 1 (February 2005): 79–93.

———. *Freedom of Expression: Resistance and Repression in the Age of Intellectual Property.* Minneapolis: University of Minnesota Press, 2007.

McLeod, Kembrew, and Peter DiCola. *Creative License: The Law and Culture of Digital Sampling.* Durham, NC: Duke University Press, 2011.

McLuhan, Marshall. *The Gutenberg Galaxy: The Making of Typographic Man.* Toronto: University of Toronto Press, 1962.

———. *The Mechanical Bride: Folklore of Industrial Man.* New York: Vanguard Press, 1951.

———. *Understanding Media: The Extensions of Man.* Cambridge, MA: MIT Press, 1994.

Mendelson, Michael. "Declamation, Context, and Controversiality." *Rhetoric Review* 13, no. 1 (1994): 92–107.

———. "Quintilian and the Pedagogy of Argument." *Argumentation* 15 (2001): 277–93.

Meyer, Leonard B. *Emotion and Meaning in Music.* Chicago: University of Chicago Press, 1956.

Michalik, Lyndsay. "How Antoine Dodson and the Bed Intruder Keep Climbin' in Our Windows: Viral Video Appropriation as Performance." *Liminalities: A Journal of Performance Studies* 10, no. 3/4 (2014): 1–19.

Milner, Ryan M. *The World Made Meme: Public Conversations and Participatory Media.* Cambridge, MA: MIT Press, 2016.

Mithen, Steven. *The Singing Neanderthal.* Cambridge, MA: Harvard University Press, 2007.

Mollet, Tracey. "Looking through the Upside Down: Hyper-postmodernism and Transmediality in the Duffer Brothers' *Stranger Things*." *Journal of Popular Television* 7, no. 1 (2019): 57–77.

Morgan, Robert P. "Schenker and the Theoretical Tradition: The Concept of Musical Reduction." *College Music Symposium* 18, no. 1 (Spring 1978): 72–96.

Morley, Simon. "Introduction: The Contemporary Sublime." In *The Sublime*, edited by Simon Morley, 12–21. Cambridge, MA: MIT Press, 2010.

Muckelbauer, John. "Imitation and Invention in Antiquity: An Historical-Theoretical Revision." *Rhetorica: A Journal of the History of Rhetoric* 21, no. 2 (Spring 2003): 61–88.

Myers, Alicia D. "Prosopopoetics and Conflict: Speech and Expectations in John 8." *Biblica* 92, no. 4 (2011): 580–96.

Navas, Eduardo. "Regressive and Reflexive Mashups in Sampling Culture." In *Mashup Cultures*, edited by Stefan Sonvilla-Weiss, 157–77. New York: Springer Wien, 2010.

———. "Remix." In *Keywords in Remix Studies*, edited by Eduardo Navas, Owen Gallagher, and xtine burrough, 256–58. New York: Routledge, 2017.

———. *Remix Theory: The Aesthetics of Sampling*. New York: Springer Wien, 2012.

Negroponte, Nicholas. *Being Digital*. New York: Random House, 1995.

Nichols-Pethick, Jonathan. "Going with the Flow: On the Value of Randomness, Flexibility, and Getting Students in on the Conversation, or What I Learned from Antoine Dodson." *Cinema Journal* 50, no. 4 (2011): 182–87.

Nielsen, Jakob. "Participation Inequality: Encouraging More Users to Contribute." *Jakob Nielsen's Alertbox* 9 (2006). http://www.useit.com/alertbox/participation_inequality.html.

Nissenbaum, Asaf, and Limor Shifman. "Meme Templates as Expressive Repertoires in a Globalizing World: A Cross-Linguistic Study." *Journal of Computer-Mediated Communication* 23, no. 5 (2018): 294–310.

Noble, Safiya Umoja. *Algorithms of Oppression: How Search Engines Reinforce Racism*. New York: New York University Press, 2018.

Norlin, George. "General Introduction." In *Isocrates, Volume I*, edited and translated by George Norlin, ix–li. Cambridge, MA: Harvard University Press, 1928.

O'Brien, Damien, and Brian Fitzgerald. "Mashups, Remixes, and Copyright Law." *Internet Law Bulletin* 9, no. 2 (2006): 17–19.

O'Reilly, Tim. "What Is Web 2.0: Design Patterns and Business Models for the Next Generation of Software." *Communications & Strategies* 65, 1st quarter (March 2007): 17–37. http://mpra.ub.uni-muenchen.de/4578/1/MPRA_paper_4578.pdf.

Oakes, Kaya. *Slanted and Enchanted: The Evolution of Indie Culture*. New York: Henry Holt and Company, 2009.

Oliver, Mary Beth. "Exploring the Paradox of the Enjoyment of Sad Films." *Human Communication Research* 19, no. 3 (1993): 315–42.

———. "Tender Affective States as Predictors of Entertainment Preference." *Journal of Communication* 58 (2008): 40–61.

Oliver, Mary Beth, and Anne Bartsch. "Appreciation as Audience Response: Exploring Entertainment Gratifications beyond Hedonism." *Human Communication Research* 36 (2010): 53–81.

Ong, Walter J. *Orality and Literacy: The Technologizing of the Word*. New York: Routledge, 1999.

Pearce, W. Barnett, and Karen A. Foss. "The Historical Context of Communication as a Science." In *Human Communication: Theory and Research*, edited by Gordon L. Dahnke and G. W. Clatterbuck, 1–20. Belmont, CA: Wadsworth, 1990.

Pellegrin, Pierre. "The Aristotelian Way." In *A Companion to Ancient Philosophy*, edited by Mary-Louise Gill and Pierre Pellegrin, 235–44. Malden, MA: Wiley-Blackwell, 2006.

Perelman, Chaïm, and Lucie Olbrechts-Tyteca. *The New Rhetoric: A Treatise on Argumentation.* Notre Dame, IN: University of Notre Dame Press, 1969.

Perlmutter, David D. *Blogwars: The New Political Battleground.* New York: Oxford University Press, 2008.

Peters, John Durham. *Courting the Abyss: Free Speech and the Liberal Tradition.* Chicago: University of Chicago Press, 2004.

Pettitt, Thomas. "Before the Gutenberg Parenthesis: Elizabethan-American Compatibilities." Paper presented at "MIT5: Creativity, Ownership, and Collaboration in the Digital Age, Traverse City, MI, April 25, 2007." http://web.mit.edu/comm-forum/legacy/mit5/papers/pettitt_plenary_gutenberg.pdf.

———. "Bracketing the Gutenberg Parenthesis." *Explorations in Media Ecology* 11, no. 2 (2012): 95–114.

Pfister, Damien Smith. "Networked Expertise in the Era of Many-to-Many Communication: On Wikipedia and Invention." *Social Epistemology* 25 (July 2011): 217–31.

Plato. "Gorgias." In *The Rhetorical Tradition: Readings from Classical Times to the Present*, 2nd ed., edited by Patricia Bizzell and Bruce Herzberg, 87–138. New York: Bedford/St. Martin's, 2001.

Postman, Neil. *Amusing Ourselves to Death: Public Discourse in the Age of Show Business.* New York: Penguin, 2006.

Poulakos, John. "From the Depths of Rhetoric: The Emergence of Aesthetics as a Discipline." *Philosophy and Rhetoric* 40, no. 4 (2007): 335–52.

Poulakos, John, and Steve Whitson. "Rhetoric Denuded and Redressed: Figs and Figures." *Quarterly Journal of Speech* 81 (August 1995): 378–85.

Poulakos, Takis. "Isocrates's Use of Narrative in the *Evagoras*: Epideictic Rhetoric and Moral Action." *Quarterly Journal of Speech* 73 (August 1987): 317–28.

Poulakos, Takis, and David Depew, eds. *Isocrates and Civic Education.* Austin: University of Texas Press, 2004.

Prasad, Akhil, and Aditi Agarwala. *Copyright Law Desk Book.* New Delhi, India: Universal Law Publishing, 2009.

Quintilian. *Quintilian: The Orator's Education, Books 3–5.* Translated by Donald A. Russell. Cambridge, MA: Harvard University Press, 2002.

———. *Quintilian: The Orator's Education, Books 6–8.* Translated by Donald A. Russell. Cambridge, MA: Harvard University Press, 2002.

———. *Quintilian: The Orator's Education, Books 9–10*. Translated by Donald A. Russell. Cambridge, MA: Harvard University Press, 2002.

———. *Quintilian: The Orator's Education, Books 11–12*. Translated by Donald A. Russell. Cambridge, MA: Harvard University Press, 2002.

Ramus, Peter. *Arguments in Rhetoric against Quintilian: Translation and Text of Peter Ramus's* Rhetoricae Distinctiones in Quintilianum. Edited by James J. Murphy. Translated by Carole Newlands. Carbondale: Southern Illinois University Press, 2010.

Rancière, Jacques. "The Aesthetic Revolution and Its Outcomes." In *The Sublime*, edited by Simon Morley, 67–69. Cambridge, MA: MIT Press, 2010.

Reich, Steve. "Music as a Gradual Process." In *Audio Culture: Readings in Modern Music*, edited by Christoph Cox and Daniel Warner, 304–6. New York: Continuum, 2004.

Reimer, Bennett. *A Philosophy of Music Education*. 2nd ed. Englewood Cliffs, NJ: Prentice Hall, 1989.

Reynolds, Glenn. *An Army of Davids: How Markets and Technology Empower Ordinary People to Beat Big Media, Big Government and Other Goliaths*. Nashville: Thomas Nelson, 2006.

Reynolds, Simon. *Rip It Up and Start Again: Postpunk 1978–1984*. London: Faber and Faber, 2005.

Rhetorica ad Herennium. In *The Rhetorical Tradition: Readings from Classical Times to the Present*, 2nd ed., edited by Patricia Bizzell and Bruce Herzberg, 243–82. New York: Bedford/St. Martin's, 2001.

Richardson, Riché. "The Bed Intruder—News Video Goes Viral: Antoine Dodson as Internet Celebrity and Commodity." *Technoculture: An Online Journal of Technology in Society* 4 (2014): 1–18.

Rimmer, Matthew. "The Grey Album: Copyright Law and Digital Sampling." *Media International Australia* 114, no. 1 (2005): 40–53.

Rodgers, Tara. *Pink Noises: Women on Electronic Music and Sound*. Durham, NC: Duke University Press, 2010.

Rose, Margaret A. "Post-Modern Pastiche." *British Journal of Aesthetics* 31, no. 1 (1991): 26–38.

Rueckert, William H. *Encounters with Kenneth Burke*. Urbana: University of Illinois Press, 1994.

Rundell, W. M. F. "Cicero and Clodius: The Question of Credibility." *Historia* 28, no. 3 (1979): 301–18.

Sauerberg, Lars Ole. "Preface: The Gutenberg Parenthesis—Print, Book and Cognition." *Orbis Litterarum* 64 (2009): 79–80.

Schaeffer, John D. *Sensus Communis: Vico, Rhetoric, and the Limits of Relativism*. Durham, NC: Duke University Press, 1990.

Schiappa, Edward. "Neo-Sophistic Rhetorical Criticism or the Historical Reconstruction of

Sophistic Doctrines?" *Philosophy and Rhetoric* 23, no. 3 (1990): 192–217.

———. *Protagoras and Logos: A Study in Greek Philosophy and Rhetoric.* Columbia: University of South Carolina Press, 1991.

Seabrook, John. *The Song Machine: Inside the Hit Factory*. New York: Norton, 2015.

Segev, Elad, Asaf Nissenbaum, Nathan Stolero, and Limor Shifman. "Families and Networks of Internet Memes: The Relationship between Cohesiveness, Uniqueness, and Quiddity Concreteness." *Journal of Computer-Mediated Communication* 20, no. 4 (2015): 417–33.

Sellnow, Deanna, and Timothy Sellnow. "The 'Illusion of Life' Rhetorical Perspective: An Integrated Approach to the Study of Music as Communication." *Critical Studies in Media Communication* 18, no. 4 (December 2001): 395–415.

Shapiro, Peter. "Deck Wreckers: The Turntable as Instrument." In *Undercurrents: The Hidden Wiring of Modern Music*, edited by Rob Young, 163–80. New York: Continuum, 2002.

Shifman, Limor. *Memes in Digital Culture.* Cambridge, MA: MIT Press, 2013.

Shiga, John. "Copy-and-Persist: The Logic of Mash-up Culture." *Critical Studies in Media Communication* 24, vol. 2 (June 2007): 93–114.

Sinnreich, Aram. *Mashed Up: Music, Technology, and the Rise of Configurable Culture*. Amherst: University of Massachusetts Press, 2010.

Sonvilla-Weiss, Stefan. "Introduction: Mashups, Remix Practices and the Recombination of Existing Digital Content." In *Mashup Cultures*, edited by Stefan Sonvilla-Weiss, 8–23. New York: Springer Wien, 2010.

Spitzer, Michael. *Metaphor and Musical Thought*. Chicago: University of Chicago Press, 2004.

Stewart, Jesse. "Articulating a Hip-Hop Sampling Aesthetic through Film." In *Sampling Media*, edited by David Laderman and Laurel Westrup, 143–54. New York: Oxford University Press, 2014.

Taylor, Timothy D. *Strange Sounds: Music, Technology and Culture.* New York: Routledge, 2001.

Tester, Keith. *Media, Culture and Morality.* New York: Routledge, 1994.

Theall, Donald. "The Role of Aesthetic Theory in (Mass) Communication Theory." *Quarterly Journal of Speech* 61 (October 1975): 271–78.

Timmerman, David M., and Edward Schiappa. *Classical Greek Rhetorical Theory and the Disciplining of Discourse*. Cambridge: Cambridge University Press, 2010.

Tola, Fernando, and Carmen Dragonetti. "Nagarjuna's Conception of 'Voidness' (Sunyata)." *Journal of Indian Philosophy* 9, no. 3 (1981): 273–82.

Too, Yun Lee. *The Rhetoric of Identity in Isocrates: Text, Power, Pedagogy*. Cambridge: Cambridge University Press, 1995.

Toop, David. "Replicant: On Dub." In *Audio Culture: Readings in Modern Music*, edited by Christoph Cox and Daniel Warner, 355–57. New York: Continuum, 2004.

Toulmin, Stephen. *The Uses of Argument*. Cambridge: Cambridge University Press, 1958.

United States Copyright Office, Library of Congress. *Copyright Law of the United States and Related Laws Contained in Title 17 of the United States Code.* Washington, DC: Government Printing Office, 2012.

Varèse, Edgard, and Chou Wen-chung. "The Liberation of Sound." *Perspectives of New Music* 5, no. 1 (1966): 11–19.

Vivian, Bradford. "Style, Rhetoric, and Postmodern Culture." *Philosophy and Rhetoric* 35, no. 3 (2002): 223–43.

Walker, Jeffrey. *Rhetoric and Poetics in Antiquity.* New York: Oxford University Press, 2000.

Watson, Gay. *A Philosophy of Emptiness.* London: Reaktion Books, 2014.

Watson, Mike. *Can the Left Learn to Meme? Adorno, Video Gaming, and* Stranger Things. Dexter, MI: Zero Books, 2019.

Weber, Steven. *The Success of Open Source*. Cambridge, MA: Harvard University Press, 2004.

Weiskel, Thomas. "The Logic of Terror." In *The Sublime*, edited by Simon Morley, 157–58. Cambridge, MA: MIT Press, 2010.

Welch, Kathleen E. *Electric Rhetoric: Classical Rhetoric, Oralism, and a New Legacy*. Cambridge, MA: MIT Press, 1999.

Wess, Robert. "Representative Anecdotes in General, with Notes toward a Representative Anecdote for Burkean Ecocriticism in Particular." *K. B. Journal* 1, no. 1 (2004). http://www.kbjournal.org/node/54.

Westrup, Laurel. "Thinking through Sampling, Literally." In *Sampling Media*, edited by David Laderman and Laurel Westrup, 228–46. New York: Oxford University Press, 2014.

Whitson, Steve, and John Poulakos. "Nietzsche and the Aesthetics of Rhetoric." *Quarterly Journal of Speech* 79 (May 1993): 131–45.

Wichelns, Herbert. "The Literary Criticism of Oratory." In *Readings in Rhetorical Criticism*, 3rd ed., edited by Carl R. Burgchardt, 3–28. State College, PA: Strata Publishing, 2005.

Williams, Raymond. *The Long Revolution*. Orchard Park, NY: Broadview Press, 2001.

Wilson, Ross. *Theodor Adorno*. New York: Routledge, 2007.

Yoo, Christopher S. "Rethinking Copyright and Personhood." *Faculty Scholarship at Penn Law* 423 (2019): 1039–78.

Zorn, John. "The Game Pieces." In *Audio Culture: Readings in Modern Music*, edited by Christoph Cox and Daniel Warner, 196–200. New York: Continuum, 2004.

Zupančič, Alenka. *Ethics of the Real: Kant, Lacan*. New York: Verso Press, 2000.

INDEX

W

Y